DIGITAL
JOURNALISM

Janet Jones & Lee Salter

DIGITAL JOURNALISM

Janet Jones & Lee Salter

$SAGE

Los Angeles | London | New Delhi
Singapore | Washington DC

SAGE Publications Ltd
1 Oliver's Yard
55 City Road
London EC1Y 1SP

SAGE Publications Inc.
2455 Teller Road
Thousand Oaks, California 91320

SAGE Publications India Pvt Ltd
B 1/I 1 Mohan Cooperative Industrial Area
Mathura Road
New Delhi 110 044

SAGE Publications Asia-Pacific Pte Ltd
33 Pekin Street #02–01
Far East Square
Singapore 048763

Library of Congress Control Number: 2011921544

British Library Cataloguing in Publication data

A catalogue record for this book is available from the British Library

ISBN 978–1–4129–2081–0
ISBN 978–1–4129–2082–7 (pbk)

Typeset by C&M Digitals (P) Ltd, Chennai, India
Printed and bound by CPI Group (UK) Ltd, Croydon, CR0 4YY
Printed on paper from sustainable resources

Contents

Introduction

[It] won't last. It's a flash in the pan.
US newspaper editors worried that the new medium would capture many of their readers by covering news as it happened.

These comments weren't made in reference to the internet, but to television and despite this kind of rhetoric, journalism has remained robust and the news industry resilient in the face of technological, political, cultural and economic change. Nevertheless, there are significant moments in history in which settled conventions of information and communication have been considerably disrupted. Some scholars refer to these as revolutionary moments – information revolutions.

Gutenberg's invention of the printing press in 1450 stands out as moment where the monks' monopoly on reproducing culture through their scribes gave way to moveable type and ultimately a more democratic form of communication. The filters through which information flowed were challenged as was the power of the Church.

Thereafter, with increasing literacy, material and technological development, the printing press underpinned all sorts of radical changes around the world. Throughout Europe, South America, North America, Asia and Africa cheap and effective methods of producing written news facilitated revolutions and rebellions that overthrew numerous imperial regimes. Social movements of women, black people and workers all utilised printing technologies and journalistic practices to challenge the social and political orders throughout the nineteenth and twentieth centuries.

Without Gutenberg's press, journalism would not have developed in the way it did, and without journalism the medieval social and political order may not have faced such a vociferous challenge.

In contrast to the press, in the case of the emergence of radio and television technologies, the state played a much more pro-active role, taking control of the means of distribution and regulating production very carefully. Journalists and press barons, embedded in their traditions of work and profit making, were initially sceptical of these new media and much of the early rhetoric surrounding these new innovations was to disparage them. For instance, of TV news, *Time Magazine* writers opined that television 'programs have added little to the technique of reporting, have often been no better than radio newscasts – and sometimes not as good'

(*Time Magazine*, 1952). Never far away from the naysayers are the doom-mongers, who prophesise the destructive potential of change. Opposed to them are the optimists, for whom the same destructive potential is to be welcomed as renewal.

With every new distribution medium, be it the telegraph, radio, television or now the internet and mobile phones, there are always those who say that things will never be the same again; but, the change is rarely quite as radical as pundits first prophesise. The key objective for journalists and news executives is to understand and adapt to technological change. However, as in the early days of television, so too during the first decades of digital journalism, the potential of new technology was rarely understood.

Today, some believe that despite its many advantages, digital technologies are being used more as tools for keeping people at a distance than truly engaging them by bringing ideas and people together. Journalism as it develops digitally might be seen as a microcosm of these concerns. The pressure to change is strong, but with journalism as well as other facets of social life, there are equal and opposite forces attempting to re-establish old norms, power structures and processes. Look a little deeper and you can see that, as with Gutenberg's press, the forces that seek to control and re-establish the status quo often work to mitigate the radical potential of new technologies. The reality is perhaps somewhere between a utopian vision of a revitalised society and the way things used to be.

The problem is that it's never easy to tell how profound that change will be or even what direction it might take. In hindsight this new digital generation of journalistic media products might be credited with breaking down important cultural barriers and hierarchies of information and profoundly changing institutions. Or it might seem in 20 years time that not much has really changed. We may still be getting our news from the four or five dominant corporations with Rupert Murdoch's media empire even more prevalent than it is today. Indeed, a number of scholars have argued that new media technologies are being adopted in such a way as to increase rather than dilute corporate domination. What are we to make of observations that rather than democratisation, 'Web 2.0' offers merely 'superficial observations of the world around us rather than deep analysis, shrill opinion rather than considered judgment' and that, 'the information business is being transformed by the internet into the sheer noise of one hundred million bloggers all simultaneously talking about themselves' (*The Australian*, 2007). Does this reflect the debasement of journalism, or ought we to regard such observations as merely reflecting the conservative tendencies of vested interests? The naysayers would argue that we've simply added two new media to our reception repertoire – our computers and mobile phones with the filters through which news information flows barely changing.

The democratic potential of digital journalism is often seen as a threat to the integrity of journalism, but at the same time cannot be rejected outright.

Time Magazine proudly announced in 2006 that we all deserved the honour of 'person of the year' as we all were part of a new 'Web 2.0' society characterised by openness and sharing – 'in 2006, the World Wide Web became a tool for bringing together the small contributions of millions of people and making them matter'. The same article strikes a more Jeremiah tone in its closing paragraphs asking whether it isn't possibly 'a mistake to romanticise all this any more than is strictly necessary. Web 2.0 harnesses the stupidity of crowds as well as its wisdom.' (*Time Magazine*, 2006).

Despite the inevitable fallibility of crystal ball gazing, we take as our starting point the idea that there have been some important shifts around journalism scholarship over the past few years. We contend that although affordances enabled through digital media do not create cultural change in isolation, it is useful to reflect on how the rapid expansion of digital technologies has challenged the traditional conceptual lens through which we study the subject. Hence, to make sense of ongoing technological changes and their relation to political, legal and economic structures underpinning journalism, there needs to be a considerable amount of theoretical renewal in the way news culture is talked about.

This book gives an overview of the issues and debates facing journalism as the industry struggles to cope with the implications of new technologies. In so doing it looks at the changing conceptualisation of journalism as a particular practice. Journalism, as with any practice is situated in a historical tradition (or set of traditions), and by understanding some of the previously conceived threats to journalism, we begin to realise the resilience of the practice of journalism and its ability to change with the times.

The practice of journalism does not exist in isolation. Rather it takes place in symbiotic relation to political, legal, economic and technological structures. Just as journalism changes, responding to its environment, so too do the structures within which it is situated. To understand what is happening to journalism it is important to understand this structural context. For example, although the online environment does follow the contours of national borders, it is less constrained by them than television or newspapers. This means that the nationally based legal and regulatory regimes to which television and newspapers have been structured are challenged by the online environment. However, law is active – it responds and reacts to changing circumstances. So, whilst online journalists may perceive themselves as being relatively free from interference, governments around the world are continually making new laws governing the online environment.

In Chapter 1 we set the scene for the investigation, by showing some of the concerns journalists have about the online environment and the claims people make to be 'doing journalism'. We show how the failure of news industries to respond to the internet at an early stage reflects broader historical trends in news organisations – despite there having always been an intimate connection between new technologies and journalism, each new technology is initially conceived as a threat and is thus initially ignored or even ridiculed. A number of commentators refuse to accept that many of the online and digital practices constitute journalism. We answer this in the rest of the book by considering new forms of journalistic practice, but in Chapter 1 we highlight a crucial factor: that ever since the first journalists, there has never been a single journalistic practice. In this sense the digital environment does facilitate completely new forms of journalism, but many of these have roots in 'old media' practices.

In Chapter 2 we begin to consider one of the key issues for journalism, and one of the most important 'disruptions' to the modern news industry: the business or 'political economy' of journalism. Historically political economy has constrained and challenged journalism as investors seek to use journalism to make money. The fact that there had been 'spectrum scarcity' in traditional media means that not everyone could have a newspaper, radio or television station. Consequently the ownership of these projects was restricted to a small number of individuals and giant corporations. The internet promised to end this by enabling a seemingly limitless number of people to have their say. However, we show in Chapter 2 that such promise is restricted by the economics of online space, with evidence pointing to a continuation of corporate dominance of online journalism.

In Chapter 3 we go into more detail on the experiments with 'business models' online. Here we outline the efforts large corporate news producers are making in their attempts to revive the 'industry'. We also consider the ideas of more innovative thinkers, 'digital natives', who are working to develop completely new modes of journalism that either do not require funding or require completely different funding models.

In Chapter 4 we consider some of the key issues of truth and trust in online journalism. Whilst many of the criticisms of the online environment have pointed to instances of rumour and outright lies circulating without impediment, here we try to contextualise this criticism by noting criticisms of the performance of 'traditional media'. We demonstrate that whilst it is true that there is plenty of 'bad information' online, there are also many more easily accessible mechanisms to evaluate information online than there have been in other media.

Chapter 5 draws on the issues raised in Chapter 4, applying them to the way the BBC, a traditionally trustworthy brand, has moved to reinvent its journalism in the digital arena. We see how the BBC has always struggled to make the move to a more interactive and engaging online environment in fear of losing its credibility and authority. Further to this, the lack of spectrum scarcity online has been argued by some commentators to invalidate the very concept of public service on which the BBC was founded.

Chapter 6 looks at challenges to the professional identity of journalists as the division between spheres of journalistic production and consumption became less defined and we investigate new alignments of productive power and distributive capacity suggesting ways professionals and amateurs might work together on local news to foster an 'enhanced localness'. We ask if, when old and new understandings of what journalism is work side-by-side, a complementary news ecology might emerge allowing digital journalism to flourish on both a civic and commercial basis.

In Chapter 7 we look at the increasing tendency of news consumers to disappear down their cultural boltholes (see Leadbetter, 2009). The moral panics associated with news customisation and the rise of factual-entertainment within the news diet of citizens has led to much hand wringing about the future of the public sphere and we consider some of the implications of individuation of news and point to the possibility of democratic disruption as individualised news consumers replace citizens.

Chapter 8 looks at what happens when news goes mobile, and how this new method of news consumption is changing people's relationship with the news they encounter on the move. It focuses on the theoretical aspects of remediation, and on the ways in which new modes of content delivery are changing the relations between journalists, news and audiences. In addition this chapter looks at how the dramatic rise in mobile phone use has the potential to disrupt the political process by playing an important role in the maturation of democracies.

In Chapter 9 we turn to an extended chapter that considers the legal framing of journalism. All too often the online and digital environments seem to be realms of absolute freedom, apart from the state and political authorities. However, this is far from the case. We see in this chapter how existing laws and policies still govern online environment and the practice of journalism, raising some very interesting contradictions. We also consider how novel issues of internationalism (or globalisation) and anonymity have resulted in novel legal measures to constrain online journalism.

Journalism as a Practice

Everyone is a witness, everyone is a journalist (Indymedia)

The suggestion that the internet offers to ordinary people wishing to write, comment and report has led to a plethora of responses. The idea that everyone is a journalist has led some to bemoan the 'end of journalism', whilst others have celebrated it.

The array of new forms of digital news production has caused consternation in some circles. In an article for the *Press Gazette* in 2006 Linda Jones argued that bloggers should not be considered journalists, for they are simply not subject to the same processes and pressures as 'real' journalists. Bloggers are not pressured by sub-editors, editors and lawyers at their place of work; they are not trained to consider content that might be libellous or contemptuous; they do not consider the value of their writings to audiences; and do not consider grammatical and stylistic issues. In other words, Jones implies that journalists are defined as such through their institutional context, which bloggers in particular lack (Jones, 2006).

On the other hand, during an address to the Heyman Centre for the Humanities at Columbia University, John Pilger noted that 'It is said the internet is an alternative; and what is wonderful about the rebellious spirits on the World Wide Web is that they often report as journalists should.' Similarly, in an article for the *Washington Post*, Jay Rosen emphasised 'how disruptive web technology is to traditional journalism'. He explains how the internet has 'busted open' the 'system of gates and gatekeepers' by allowing sources communicate direct to the public and by facilitating collaborative journalism, resulting in a 'new balance of power between producers and consumers'.

We cannot seriously consider the possibilities of online journalism, or evaluate it, without considering first what journalism is. The question of whether blogging 'is' journalism really depends on what one means by journalism and what sort of blog one refers to. According to *Technorati* in May 2010 of the five most popular blogs, four were musings on gadgets and technology. Indeed, many bloggers dedicate their time to releasing lists of links to everything from pirated computer software to pornography sites. So, some blogs are self-consciously journalistic, but others are not. Consequently such blanket assertions as 'bloggers are...' are as unhelpful as those that tell us 'journalists are...'.

Journalism and Old New Technologies

It was perhaps inevitable that journalists would construe the early internet as a threat. As early as 1995 *The New York Times* referred to the 'lure and addiction of life on line' (18 March 1995). *The Globe and Mail* reported that 'a growing number of on-line users have become junkies' (15 October 1995). The drug metaphor would continue over the next year, with *USA Today* reporting that 'Obsessive internet users have a true addiction' (1 July 1996), and then pass across the Atlantic to *The Sunday Times* which informed us that the 'internet traps surfers in addictive Web' (9 June 1996) and the *Daily Mail* explaining the specific problem of a '"Cocaine-like rush" for users locked in a fantasy world' (4 January 1996).

More specifically as relates to journalism, print journalists muddled the medium with an institution or even the practice of journalism. For instance the *Toronto Star* contrasted the internet with more familiar media. In contrast to the internet, 'Conventional news media – newspapers, TV, radio – come equipped with editors whose job it is to cast a skeptical eye on stories' ('A media virus from internet', 13 May 1995). The *Denver Post* reiterated the theme a couple of years later: 'mainstream journalists are stuck with the facts, no matter how much they may spin them. But the internet ... operates under no such restrictions and seems rather proud of it' ('Truth's values plummet on "Net",' 2 November 1997).

So whereas other media are truthful, the internet is anthropomorphised into a liar. At the same time, however, it is not just the factual nature of other media that gives them an advantage, but also their communicative capacities. Indeed an analysis in *Media Guardian* informed us that 'Newspapers offer a forum for debate and analysis which cannot be provided either by new computer services or by TV and radio. As well as breaking scoops, papers can explain the whys, whats and wherefores in a way other superficial media cannot' ('The online age and us', 24 April 1995). *The Sunday Times* took a similar position, explaining to its readers, 'The fact that consumers can now access an immense variety of unfiltered news sources raises issues of trust and credibility. Most newspapers and broadcasters are anchored in both history and accountability, and a great many websites have neither' ('Screening out the lies', 23 January 2000).

More recently, *The Australian* complained:

all were going to be democratised by Web 2.0. But democratisation, despite its lofty idealisation, is undermining truth, souring civic discourse and belittling expertise, experience and talent. It is threatening the future of our cultural institutions.... [Web 2.0 is] the great seduction...[peddling] the promise of bringing more truth to more people: more depth of information, more global perspective, more unbiased opinion from dispassionate observers. But this is all a smokescreen... [Instead, all] the Web 2.0 revolution is really delivering is superficial observations of the world around us rather than deep analysis, shrill opinion rather than considered judgment. The information business is being transformed by the internet into the sheer noise of one hundred million bloggers all simultaneously talking about themselves. ('Disentangle it now, this web of deceit', *The Australian*, 4 August 2007)

A year later *The Independent* railed against the BBC's use of Twitter in its reporting of the Mumbai massacre. The commentary informed us that 'whereas in the old days only professional journalists (weathered men with Press Cards tucked into their hat bands) would have been able to contribute to that news feed, now it appeared that anybody with a Twitter subscription could have a crack', adding, 'Twittering is not the way to provide news' (2 December 2008). Of course today *The Independent*'s website utilises many of the technologies seen to debase journalism, including Twitter.

We see here a number of concerns about digital journalism based on varieties of technological determinism. This is to say that much of the discourse abstracts technologies from their use and suggests determinate, usually deleterious effects on journalism.

In fact, journalists and news organisations have a tradition of scepticism towards new technologies, yet this scepticism masks the intimate relations journalists and news organisations have with the technologies they use as well as the way in which uses are developed.

In the first instance, from the telegraph to the satellite, journalists have always utilised technologies in news gathering. Postal systems, phone networks, vox pops, and 'wire' services have uncontentiously helped journalists collect information.

For example, the method of writing news for newspapers takes the form of the inverted pyramid, which Stuart Allan (2004) shows emerged from an interaction with technology. He suggests that the use of the telegraph, especially by the Associated Press (AP) led to a training system in which the 'inverted pyramid' was taught because 'unreliable telegraph lines made it necessary to compress the most significant facts' into the lead paragraph. There was also an economic dimension to the conventionalisation of newspaper discourses. The expense of using the telegraph also meant that 'Each word of a news account had to be justified in terms of cost', leading to a more efficient, straightforward use of language (Allan, 2004: 16–18). Chapman (2005: 93) adds that the use of the telephone had the impact of concretising the division between field journalists who 'became entirely responsible for the gathering and initial drafting of news' and desk journalists who 'stayed in the office and fine-tuned this output to the house style'.

In order to better understand the capacity journalism has for adaptation to new technologies, and to recognise the continual need to adapt, we need this historical perspective. This enables us to see that, against technological determinism, the approaches of the social shaping of technology in fact demonstrate that human influence is much greater than understood by technological determinists and that possible uses are far more flexible than might be thought. Indeed, a technology has no impact outside the context of its institutionalised forms of use (Salter, 2004). For example, 'the internet' should not be compared with newspapers at all – the proper comparator would be paper, of which the newspaper is an institutionalised form of use. Uses become conventionalised in practices, such as journalism. Indeed, paper may be used for money, pornography or newspapers. Television may be used for closed circuit television, shopping or comedy sketch shows. None of these uses are inherent in the medium and they are certainly not necessarily exclusive.

Television as New Media

New technologies only prescribe uses in a very minimal sense. Television news, for example, was not preformed for news. Rather, its use for journalism was first constrained by pre-existing conventions for other media, alongside entrenched interests that profited from those conventionalised forms of use. Specific television news conventions – initially borrowed from radio – were developed over a number of years, and continue to develop today, as do the technologies used.

The initial confusion over how to do television news in the UK is described by BBC journalist Andrew Marr:

> The BBC's first answer was to ignore the pictures almost entirely, in the cause of pure news. The newsreels were still being brought in, often out of date and lacking real sound... By the early 1950s the BBC had its own newsreel department... But [the newsreels] were really short feature films... For the BBC News people, who had grown up in the culture of words, this was fine. Moving pictures could never be serious. They conceded that news bulletins should be aired on television too. But how to marry the raw visual power of film with the sacred duty of news reporting? No one could figure that out. (Marr, 2004: 270)

Part of the problem, according to Marr, was that the audio and visual provisions at the time were located in different departments (it is worth remembering that the introduction of sound into film at the time was by no means natural. Technologies for playing sound to match images were available long before they were widely used). Consequently, a compromise was reached wherein 'radio would provide the words, TV the pictures'. Marr describes the early television news service thus:

> The news was ... dealt with in words alone, with carefully printed captions, like paragraph headings in a newspaper, held up in front of the camera while an unseen announcer read the appropriate item of news. There then might be a series of still pictures or ... hand drawn maps. Sometimes a hand would appear from off screen ... helpfully pointing to something. (Marr, 2004: 270–1)

In addition to the internal wrangling between departments within the BBC, Stuart Allan has noted the impact of institutional constraints on the early conventions of television news. He explains that the:

> ten minutes of news was read by an off-screen voice in an 'impersonal, sober and quiet manner', the identity of the [always male] newsreader being kept secret to preserve the institutional authority of the BBC. (Allan, 2004: 36)

Things fared little better in the US. The 28 January 1952 edition of *Time Magazine* reported the perceived debacle of television broadcasting there:

> In the first years of television, US newspaper editors worried that the new medium would capture many of their readers by covering news as it happened. So far, the worries have been groundless; TV news programs have added little to the technique of reporting, have often been no better than radio newscasts – and sometimes not as good.

It then went on to report on a new innovation in television news reporting at NBC, 'an ambitious two-hour global news roundup' called *Today*, recounting two significant incidents:

> the ranging TV eye fixed on Admiral William M. Fechteler, Chief of Naval Operations, on the steps of the Pentagon on his way to work. 'Can you give us a pronouncement on the state of the Navy?' asked NBC's reporter. 'Well, I don't know,' said Admiral Fechteler. 'When I left it yesterday, it was in great shape.' 'Thank you, Admiral Fechteler,' cried the reporter triumphantly. Said critic Crosby: 'The fact is Admiral Fechteler hadn't opened his mail yet.'

Communicator Garroway went on with his program: 'Hello, Ed Haaker in Frankfurt. Tell me the news in your part of the world.' Replied Haaker: 'The big news is the weather. We had our first big storm of the year. We're really chilly.' Said Garroway: 'You're not alone. Goodbye, Ed.' (*Time Magazine*, 28 January, 1952).

We can see then, that in each case, there were no pre-existing conventions for using these new media, and a period of adjustment emerged. Debates raged about whether it was even possible to 'do' news on television, and even whether television itself would last – Andrew Marr cites a BBC executive opining that 'Television won't last. It's a flash in the pan'! (Marr, 2004: 268). Once it was recognised that television would not go away, newspaper people expressed anxiety over the future of newspaper publishing – would newspapers survive the television age? Similarly, radio people questioned whether there was a future for radio.

Binds and Opportunities

Despite the initial scepticism towards television, it would appear very strange today to question its value to journalists. The attempt to shoehorn the practices of newspaper journalism into television seem misguided now that we regard television as a form of journalism in its own right. The same is proving to be the case with the internet and associated technologies today as new forms of journalism and new journalistic conventions are being established.

Indeed, despite the misgivings outlined above, we see that there have always been more sober voices within the industry. Some commentators recognised early on that the core elements of the practice of journalism are maintained despite the medium. *Editor and Publisher* reported on the head of Associated Press' take on the impact of the internet on journalism: Lou Boccardi was reported as suggesting, 'Whether it appears on a printed page, or a series of pixels on a computer screen, journalism must be accurate, objective and fair ... As we look excitedly at the interactive world and its promise, with its changing tools of communication, it is important to remember that the principles of the news piece do not change' ('AP chief: Beware of yellow journalism in cyberspace' *Editor and Publisher Magazine*, 11 February 1995.). Perhaps Boccardi overstates the continuity, for the principles of a news piece surely do change, but the principles behind good journalism do not.

Indeed, concerns over the veracity and quality of information on the internet may go some way to explaining the conservatism of early internet news ventures. When the big news corporations moved onto the internet, they did much the same as the newspapers companies that first went on to television – they simply transferred the data to the new medium, in the main without considering the potential of the internet.

For example, in September 1994, *The Times* trumpeted its new 'internet computer network', wherein 'From today, readers in any country will be able to call up articles from these pages on their personal computers, using a modem. They will also be able to communicate their ideas and questions directly to our specialist media writers and to other readers, using the same basic tools'. *The Times* network would offer a 'daily summary of the main items in *The Times*, other specialist content and, eventually, an archive'. It would provide access to databases in academic institutions, associations and corporations 'on every continent', and access to a variety of other sites from the CIA World Factbook to humorous and entertainment sites ('Welcome to *The Times* internet computer network', 21 September 1994). Almost a year later, the parent company of *The Times*, News Corporation, aimed to launch a 'global online newspaper' that would 'draw on all the News Corporation titles worldwide' (*The Times*, 3 June 1995). Similarly the 1996 launch of *The Sunday Times* boasted the transferral of the newspaper online, though by now it had added a frequently updated 'rolling news' service as well as games, classified advertising, television guide and weather (*The Sunday Times*, 7 January 1996).

Tellingly, by 1996, *The Times* boasted that '98 per cent of the text which appears in the printed edition can now be accessed online. Unlike other electronic newspapers, which edit their stories before they appear, the internet editions are exactly the same as the published versions' ('Internet *Times* goes from strength to strength', *The Times*, 3 April 1996). This is to say that *The Times* made a virtue of shovelware – the reproduction of offline material online. There was no real attempt to consider the development of specifically online journalism.

The main concern of many news executives was merely how to make money from what was perceived as just a new platform of delivery. Such an approach was common across the globe. *USA Today* explained that its online service would offer access to the worldwide web, bulletin boards and email. It would draw on its newspaper content – though it 'would not be a clone' – but it would cost $14.95 monthly for three hours online; additional hours were $3.95 each ('*USA Today* nabs place in cyberspace', *USA Today*, 22 March 1995). The *Financial Times* summarised the limited scope of early business models thus, 'Several business models have emerged as publishers attempt to tap into this potentially important new market. These range from offering "teasers" to on-line readers in the hopes of persuading them to subscribe to magazines and newsletters, to experiments with electronic distribution of book manuscripts' (4 October 1994: 5).

It must be borne in mind that the limited scope of early forays into 'online journalism' reflected the context in which it was situated. At the time, the 'internet' actually consisted of discrete networks, such as Compuserve and AOL, which controlled access to other networks. It was also the case that these restricted networks provided the infrastructure for online presence, so newspapers had to work within that infrastructure. Business models attempted to use the online newspaper to connect people to an isolated and controlled computer network rather than encourage them to embrace a borderless, global, hyperlinked internet.

However, as the internet developed, the tide turned against shovelware. By 1999 *The Independent* had recognised the potential of online journalism was being stymied by conservative business and journalistic models. In November 1999, it reported its launch of 'a completely new website that broke with the conventions of online newspapers'. It went on to explain its approach to online journalism:

> Indeed, we went out of our way to ensure that it looked nothing like a newspaper. This is a website with no deadlines, constantly refreshed (although we do sleep between 1am and 7am) and organised into a series of channels, with the latest DHTML (dynamic hypertext mark-up language), making navigation as easy as it gets....

> There is no point in taking every item from the newspaper each night and replicating it on the Web. It's been tried and has failed (although some organisations persist with this outdated strategy). If you put every word on the Web, there is no incentive for people to buy the titles. What's more, many of the key features and much of the unique appeal of a broadsheet do not necessarily translate to the Web. Internet users want bites of information; some will stay and read in greater depth, but many will be off to the next site. ('Introducing *The Independent* Online', 9 November 1999)

Finally, news organisations had understood that the internet was a different medium and would require a different set of resources, different methods, new conventions and new relations. But what of this promise? How radical a change could the internet bring about? Could it be the case, as so many pundits speculated, that an 'information revolution' would transform people's relation to information? Would journalists be necessary anymore? Could the grip of the corporate giants over the mediascape be loosened?

But is it Journalism?

Understanding the fate of journalism in an ever changing technological environment necessitates consideration of what we mean when we refer to 'journalism'. Allan (2006) considers journalism to consist of reasonably stable sets of conventions, citing blogging as one form of online activity that has settled on a set of conventions that constitute journalism, but the fundamental principles of the practice of journalism may or may not be adhered to in blogging. The point, however, is that journalism is not associated with a particular technology, but new technologies tend to be thought of as threats to this practice.

The question of what journalism is is important not just with regard to academic interest – it is also a crucial practical question. For example, as more and more ordinary people can lay claim to the title of 'journalist', as we shall see, the question of who is recognised as a journalist, and therefore entitled to journalistic privilege, becomes increasingly pertinent.

Attempts to define journalism run into difficulties when they are too general. For example, Singer (2003: 144) refers to a journalist as a 'person who gathers (reports) and processes (writes) accurate and important information so it can be disseminated to a wider audience.' Surely such a broad description would include publicists, stock market analysts and gospel writers? But then can a more limited description explain the full range of journalistic practices?

Andrew Marr's (2004: 9) history of journalism marks Daniel Defoe, in the early eighteenth century, as a significant character in the history of journalism for Marr claims he was one of the first journalists who 'believed in going and seeing with his own eyes. He wanted to witness with his own ears... [he] travelled and wrote down and interviewed'. But Marr refers to Defoe as a reporter – that is as a particular type of journalist. Such an understanding of the role of reporters continues to be the case today. David Randall, in his significantly titled *The Universal Journalist* argues that:

> The heroes of journalism are reporters. What they do is find things out. They go in first, amid the chaos of now, battering at closed doors, sometimes taking risks, and capture the beginnings of the truth. And if they do not do that, who will? Editors? Commentators? There is only one alternative to reporters: accepting the authorized version. (Randall, 2000: 1)

There is, then, an argument that reporters perform a particular task within journalism, on which other journalistic forms depend. But if these descriptions define reporters, what are journalists?

Karen Sanders (2003: 9) makes the distinction between literature and journalism, arguing that the latter is distinctive because it 'has an exterior reference, a reference to the world of events about which it provides information to others'. However, it is not just this 'reference to the world of events' that defines journalism, because historians, political writers and sociologists write with such reference points.

For Michael Schudson (2001: 159) there is a presentational or stylistic element that distinguishes journalism – it is a particular way of presenting information; it is not 'only a... style of prose but the self conscious articulation of rules with moral force that direct how that prose shall be written and provide a standard of condemnation when the writing does not measure up.'

We can perhaps draw these insights together with G. Stuart Adam's (1993) attempts to spell out a coherent definition of the practice of journalism. He suggests that:

A preliminary definition might go like this: Journalism is an invention or a form of expression used to report and comment in the public media on the events and ideas of the here and now. There are at least five elements in such a definition: (1) a form of expression that is an invention; (2) reports of ideas and events; (3) comments on them; (4) the public circulation of them; and (5) the here and now. (Adam, 1993: 11)

For Adam journalism is a cultural practice that is driven by what he refers to as the 'Journalistic Imagination' which is 'the primary method of framing experience and forming the public consciousness of the here and now. Its principles are immanent, more or less, in every journalist and in every journalistic institution' (Adam, 1993: 45).

What Adam adds to the mix here is the concept of the public. The journalist interfaces with the public, and it is for this reason that she must ensure that she follows proven principles of journalism. So, journalism is not just a style of writing but a mode of address that refers to the citizens that make up a public.

In *The Elements of Journalism*, Bill Kovach and Tom Rosenstiel argue that the practice of journalism aims to provide 'independent, reliable, accurate and comprehensive information that citizens require to be free' (Kovach and Rosenstiel, 2003: 11). To do this they propose concrete commitments of journalists to the truth, to citizens, to verification, to independence from those they cover, to monitor power, to provide a forum for public criticism, to be interesting and relevant, to be comprehensive and proportional and to exercise their personal conscience (Kovach and Rosenstiel, 2003: 13). Elsewhere Kovach (2005) adds that 'Journalism does more than keep us informed – journalism enables us as citizens to have our voices heard in the chambers of power and allows us to monitor and moderate the sources of power that shape our lives'.

The journalist John Lloyd (2004) has argued at length that such failings reflect a deep problem with the media, in which journalistic standards have dropped significantly. According to Lloyd the need to dispassionately report facts has been replaced by journalists 'acting as an opposition' because the political parties had become too close to each other. As a consequence of this 'The division between news and comment has tended to erode and the habit of comment has become general', and newspapers have come to privilege 'reportage which is suffused with moral or other judgements' (Lloyd, 2004: 16). We can see then, that many of the charges levelled at internet-based journalism are not restricted to journalism that takes place via a particular medium. Rather they are perceived problems with the practice of journalism as such.

However, the criticisms of Lloyd and others tend to be based on a liberal conception of journalistic professionalism. Against this, a number of critical theorists have argued that 'professional' journalism plays an ideological role, by socially constructing the world in accord with a hegemonic worldview. The work of Stuart Hall et al. (1978)

and of the Glasgow Media Group (1976) was pioneering in demonstrating that, as the Glasgow Group put it, 'the news is not a neutral product. For [it] is a cultural artefact; it is a sequence of socially manufactured messages, which carry many of the culturally dominant assumptions of our society'. This occurs, according to Hall and colleagues, because of a 'systematically structured over-accessing by the media of those in powerful and privileged institutional positions. The media thus tend, faithfully and impartially, to reproduce symbolically the existing structure of power in society's institutional order' (Hall et al. 1978: 58).

The liberal denial of the 'bias of neutrality' stems from a particular self-understanding of journalists, described by Mark Deuze (2005a) as the 'occupational ideology of journalism' or what Aldridge and Evetts (2003: 547) refer to as a 'powerful occupational mythology'. This is to say that the self-understanding of journalists doesn't necessary tell the whole story. Against this dominant, liberal form of journalism there has for centuries been a tradition of radical journalism. James Curran (2003) has conducted one of the most important scholarly enquiries documenting this tradition. This tradition of journalism has often taken the side of the weak but has also tended to adopt a colloquial, ironic and irreverent tone. The appeal of the radical press' tone can be seen in its adoption by today's tabloid newspapers. It was not, however, just the tone of the radical press that was different. So too was its subject matter and its form of organisation – to this day radical media projects are organised on a non-commercial basis, working relations are non-hierarchical and the separation between reader and writer is reduced.

This ethic of commitment to citizens has been influential in the US, where the 'public journalism' movement started. One of the key advocates of public journalism, Jay Rosen (1999) explains that journalism is a practice that is inherently linked to democracy and the public sphere, and is framed by standards and ethics of production. For Rosen, the journalist should have a deep connection to her public, to citizens. In many public journalism projects the journalist would write with citizens in focus groups, which meant that journalism took place as a collective or collaborative effort.

This focus on the journalists' loyalty to citizens leads us to consider advocacy or campaigning journalism. This form of journalism is tied to investigative journalism, and requires a much more active, adversarial journalism than simply reporting the 'facts as they are'. Campaigning journalists, such as the late Paul Foot, take sides on issues, selecting stories and writing them from a particular perspective. For instance, the British journalist Martin Bell called for a 'journalism of attachment' that takes the side of the weak. Such an approach does not mean that one need abandon journalistic principles. On the contrary, the argument of campaigning journalists is that they cover those too weak to attract attention from the routine journalists.

Table 1.1 Shared journalistic principles across states

Accuracy
Protection of sources
Opposition to discrimination on the basis of race, religion or sex
Independence
Fairness and the separation of fact and value
The commitment to the public/citizenry

Pilger (2004) cites the American journalist T.D. Allman to explain how campaigning journalism corrects the hidden biases of so called 'objective' reporting of the facts: 'Genuinely objective journalism... not only gets the facts right, it gets the meaning of events right'. As such the campaigning journalist's role consists in 'rescuing "objectivity" from its common abuse as a cover for official lies' (Pilger, 2005: xiv). So, the campaigning journalist does not abandon objectivity but contests the objectivity of other journalists. As the US columnist and founder of the Institute for Public Accuracy, Norman Solomon (2006) explains in response to an Associate Press item that 'objectively' reported that 'Poor nutrition contributes to the deaths of some 5.6 million children every year':

> We're encouraged to see high-quality journalism as dispassionate, so that professionals do their jobs without advocating. But passive acceptance of murderous priorities in our midst is a form of de facto advocacy.

As the philosopher Herbert Marcuse put it 40 years before:

> if a newscaster reports the torture and murder of civil rights workers in the same unemotional tone he uses to describes the stock-market or the weather... then such objectivity is spurious – more, it offends against humanity and truth by... refraining from accusation where accusation is in the facts themselves. (Marcuse, 1969: 98)

A number of scholars have considered the centrality of cultural context on the development of particular norms of journalism within specific states, such as the objectivity norm that emerges in US newspapers (Schiller, 1981; Schudson, 2001). In contrast to the US experience, in the UK the objectivity norm was not led by newspaper journalists, but by television journalists.

Outside the UK and US, Hallin and Papathanassopoulos (2002) point out that today journalists in southern Europe and Latin America have maintained their traditions of advocacy. They suggest that 'in contrast with the Anglo-American model of professional neutrality, journalism in southern Europe and Latin America tends to emphasize commentary from a distinct political perspective' (Hallin and

Papathanassopoulos, 2002: 177), whilst publicly espousing the ideals of neutral professionalism. In Italy the press did not break its ties to political parties until the mid-1990s, a change which television has yet to go through. Jean Chalaby (1996) has made a similar argument that 'objective' journalism is an Anglo-American invention. She notes that the particular practices of modern journalism, such as interviewing and reporting facts, were developed in the US, and contrasted with the opinionated, commentary-based journalism of Europe. However, she also suggests that these 'Anglo-American' journalistic norms are being adopted around the world.

We see from the codes of conduct and codes of ethics of journalistic associations and media organisations around the world that the Anglo-American mode is becoming dominant. The Qatari television news station Al Jazeera's Code of Ethics demands that journalists, 'Adhere to the journalistic values of honesty, courage, fairness, balance, independence, credibility and diversity giving no priority to commercial or political considerations over professional ones'. They also aim to 'present diverse points of view and opinions without bias or partiality' and to 'distinguish between news material, opinion and analysis to avoid the pitfalls of speculation and propaganda'.

Likewise, a survey of codes of conduct from states as diverse as India, Malaysia, Britain, Qatar, Russia and Indonesia shows clear similarities in the understanding of the behaviour of journalists. All such codes recognise the principles outlined in Table 1.1 (see page 12).

There are of course many cases where the Anglo-American model of journalism is not adhered to in the UK and US, and there are a number of divergences in the guidelines that reflect national particularities. In Malaysia, for example, besides the usual clauses on neutrality and truth, the Cannons of Journalism prepared by the Malaysian Press Institute incorporates adherence to the principles of Rukunegara (the basis of the Malaysian state), which includes contributing to nation-building and upholding the standards of 'social morality'. The Press Council of India's extensive Norms of Journalistic Conduct stresses that journalists 'exercise due restraint and caution in presenting any news, comment or information which is likely to jeopardise, endanger or harm the paramount interests of the state and society'. In Indonesia, the Alliance of Independent Journalists' Code of Ethics stipulates that 'A journalist does not present news, which graphically portrays indecency, cruelty, physical or sexual violence'.

Beyond Definition?

It seems, then, that commentators who bemoan innovations in technology as being disruptive to journalism would not be able to point to a single shared definition of what journalism actually is. There are indeed many forms of journalism that change across time, technology, culture and space. Although there certainly are shared principles of journalism, or of journalistic ideology, it is normal for there to be a diverse range of specific practices. Indeed, we are faced with a problem in terms of how we can evaluate digital journalism when a single evaluative mechanism for journalism of any kind is missing. This problem is compounded in an internet environment that transcends national journalistic cultures.

In this book we show how digital technologies expand the range of possibilities afforded to journalists. Blogging, Twittering, Facebooking, Googling and the full range of communicative techniques are merely tools of journalism. They are part of the toolkit. It may seem strange that the range of voices, the amount of information and the methods of communication available should be regarded as problems for journalists, but they are seen this way only when they are not understood, only when they are seen as obstacles rather than aids. If journalists piece stories together out of bits of information, what better tools are there than ones whose very nature is in the processing and distribution of bits!

Journalists' use of technologies for news gathering has historically strengthened journalistic practice. Rather than ridicule or ignore new technological innovations journalists must face them and consider not just current common uses but also how to use them to best develop journalistic practices. In the next chapter we will consider some of the key issues in online journalism.

A Political Economy of Online Journalism

In capitalism the abstract liberal notion of 'equal competition' is fundamentally constrained by the concrete realities of capital accumulation and the accompanying norms of social stratification, which lead to major inequalities in the distribution of economic resources, educational and political power among the population of any and every capitalist society no matter how advanced and civilised it has become. (McNair, 1998: 22)

Structuring Journalism

In the previous chapter we saw that the relation of journalism to media technologies is a complex one. In the first instance, 'journalism' is not a single thing. There are types and forms of journalism – perhaps we can call them 'traditions' – that differ within a country, between countries and between media. That said, there are principles that all traditions claim to share, most particularly a commitment to tell the truth and to assist the public.

We also saw how mainstream journalism has dealt with new technologies historically, and that it is quite conservative in the face of new media technologies. In one sense, journalists are cautious rather than sceptical. Prior to the internet journalists and media organisations had, over many years, developed conventions for reporting in newspapers, on radio and television. It is perhaps understandable that they did not want to jump aboard a new technology without caution.

There are, however, other significant constraints on the journalistic uses of new technologies, many of which go unnoticed in the day-to-day experiences of journalists and readers. We shall refer to these constraints as the political economy of journalism. Journalism as a practice cannot realistically be separated from the organisations in which it is institutionalised. In turn, those organisations cannot be separated from the social structures in which they are situated – in much of the world today, these structures are usually partially democratic, and partially capitalist. In this chapter we will consider some of the institutional constraints that journalists face in their work. We will then consider the degree to which these constraints are lessened in the digital environment.

A Political Economy of Journalism

Perhaps a majority of journalists would subscribe to what is referred to as the 'liberal pluralist' view (see Allan, 2004 and McNair, 1998) or 'competitive paradigm' (see McNair, 1998) of journalism. The ideas of liberal pluralism developed at the same time as journalism developed as a profession. Indeed, during the struggle to free the press from government control in the eighteenth and nineteenth centuries, journalists and pamphleteers like Tom Paine drew heavily on liberal political theory to argue against suppression and censorship (for a worthy account of the liberal democratic underpinnings of the modern media, see Keane, 1991).

For liberal pluralists the main source of control over the work of journalists and the main threat to their work is the government of the day. They seek protection in the form of economic freedom from the state. However this orientation gives liberal pluralism a blind spot to other forms of control.

Most significantly, liberal pluralists are charged with ignoring systemic constraints that stem from economics, or the 'political economy'. John McManus (1994) has explained the political economy of journalism at three levels: the macro, meso and micro. The macro level refers to the dynamics of corporate actions, including ownership, profit-making and the relations between corporate interests. At the macro level, news organisations and outlets (such as newspaper and television programmes and stations) are regarded as nothing more than commodities to be bought or sold in the interests of profit. They are seen only as stocks and shares with prices that rise and fall in accord with stock market movements. At the meso level McManus regards the internal relations of a news organisation – especially issues of resourcing and management. At the micro level McManus refers to the responses of journalists to market demand for stories by consumers trained in making particular types of market decisions.

At the macro level can be seen a historical barrier to 'market entry' and an explanation as to why corporate interests dominate news production. A national newspaper such as *The New York Times* (daily circulation: 1,100,000) costs around £500,000,000 per year to produce and distribute, whereas a local freesheet, such as *East End Life* in London (weekly circulation: 75,000) costs around £1,000,000 per year. Television stations are also very expensive, especially in terms of the costs for carrying channels. Carriage charges (the cost to use a platform to broadcast a channel) vary between platforms (cable, digital terrestrial and satellite) and within platforms, currently from £300,000 to tens of millions for a channel on the Sky Digital platform and upwards of £2,000,000 for a digital terrestrial channel. Thus there are significant barriers to entering the news market, which means that only organisations with significant capital, or which can convince corporate investors of a good (i.e. profitable) business plan are able to enter the marketplace of ideas.

At the macro level the market is infected with inequitable power relations that enable some to benefit more than others. One of the most important limits on the market is that profit rather than need drives it. Scholars have argued that the 'market' has a tendency to prioritise trivial stories (Franklin, 1997), to monopoly power (Herman and McChesney, 1997), and to move journalism away from observation and investigation and towards churnalism, the recycling of press releases and campaign notes wherein the copy is provided by public relations companies for free and the journalist merely edits it (Davies, 2008).

As a basic economic rule, the income generated by a story (made up of short term sales increase and long term prestige) will be weighed against the cost of producing it. These are decisions made at the meso level, which filter down to restrict decisions made at the micro level. Thus economic decisions made at the meso level rather than raw consumer demand can help explain the news landscape. Celebrity and human-interest stories may indeed be popular, but the motivation for their production is that they are cheap and profitable.

Quality journalism costs. For example, Zachary M. Seward (2009) of Nieman Journalism Lab reported that an editor of *The New York Times* magazine estimated the cost of one particularly in-depth and lengthy investigative piece to have been around $400,000. Seward reports that *The New York Times'* Baghdad bureau costs $3 million a year, and *The Washington Post's* one costs $1 million. The *Miami Herald's* investigation into the 2000 US presidential election results in Florida alone cost $850,000. This highlights a key challenge to some forms of online journalism – the need to attract resources. The unequal access to resources online constitutes a 'digital divide'.

Scholars and journalists alike have expressed concern over the impact of political economy on what Kovach and Rosenstiel highlight as the democratic role of journalism. Such arguments about the 'health' of democracy can be usefully illustrated with the analogous case of the pharmaceutical industry. One might expect the pharmaceutical industry to respond primarily to the human need to prevent and cure diseases and to stay alive. However, human need is not the primarily interest of the pharmaceutical industry. Rather, as capitalist enterprises, they are required by law to prioritise profit above all else. This has a range of consequences.

First, the medicines most likely to be developed are those that can be produced at a high level of profitability (the focus on, say, celebrity stories). Second, the desire for profitable (and perhaps unnecessary) drugs will be created through marketing and public relations (Moynihan and Henry, 2006; Moynihan et al., 2002). Third, those drugs that are proven to be profitable will be reproduced at the expense of new drugs (Moynihan et al., 2002), akin to churnalism. Consequently, The International Policy Network reports that whilst 90% of the world is at risk from infectious diseases only 10% of the world's total research and pharmaceutical resources is spent on them' (Stevens, 2004).

Thus Kovach and Rosenstiel's (2001: 17) suggestion that 'the primary purpose of journalism is to provide citizens with the information they need to be free and self-governing' faces a problem when we consider the micro level. The problem, says journalist and media critic Robert McChesney, is that when we see bad journalism, we must remember that it very often stems 'not from morally bankrupt or untalented journalists, but from a structure that makes such journalism the rational result of its operations' (McChesney, 2002). As Brian McNair put it, critics often 'overestimate the degree to which journalists are free agents … the journalist is a cog in a wheel over whose speed and direction he or she may have little or no control' (McNair, 1998: 62).

Ownership and Control

At the macro level, owners of media corporations have always tended to have two objectives: to make money and to influence policy. In *Power Without Responsibility* James Curran and Jean Seaton document the way that in the first half of the twentieth century, press barons 'maintained their personal domination with extreme ruthlessness' (Curran and Seaton, 2003: 41, Chapter 5). Daniel Chomsky has documented a similar level of proprietorial control at *The New York Times* during the same period (Chomsky, 1999).

Such control is less common today, though still occurs. Some media outlets are still owned by individuals with an interest in using them to further political aims. For example, Rupert Murdoch owns News Corporation which in turn owns many dozens of television and radio stations, film production companies, newspapers and magazines around the world, including the UK's biggest selling newspaper, *The Sun*, Fox News in the US and *The Australian*. It is well known that Murdoch ensures that his media empire reflects his right-wing political views and supports specific policies that he favours. In 2001, a former *Times* journalist reported in the *Evening Standard* that Murdoch's control at *The Times* was such that, 'journalists are censored by executives frightened of offending their proprietor', and that editors were 'living in "terror" of irritating Mr Murdoch' (Kiley, 2001). Other editors have echoed such claims about Murdoch's desire to control his publications (see Allan, 2004: 10–12), which played no small part in the Bancroft family's reluctance to sell *The Wall Street Journal* to Murdoch in 2007 without a guarantee that he would ensure editorial autonomy. Other media moguls, such as Silvio Berlusconi in Italy, are known to use their media empires very directly for political ends.

In some media firms the identified owner, such as the Ochs-Sulzberger family at *The New York Times*, share ownership with financial institutions but retain voting rights (in the form of important 'Class B' voting shares). Other firms, such as Time Warner are owned mainly by financial institutions – in this case it is 73% owned by US Trust Co, Capital Research, Axa, Barclays Bank, Citygroup bank, Wellington Management Company, State Street Corporation, Dodge Street and Cox, and other corporate investment groups. Whereas individual proprietors like Murdoch may demand particular political stances in his publications, such institutional investors are driven by one demand – make money.

Making Money

The ability to make money from journalism of course depends on generating income. For news operations this usually comes from customers purchasing access or from advertisers purchasing access to customers. Although liberal pluralists tell us that journalism funding comes from customers making choices in the marketplace, research shows that in fact advertising is the most significant element of funding newspapers and television news.

As early as the 1960s media theorist Marshall McLuhan informed us that, 'our press is in the main a free entertainment service paid for by advertisers who want to buy readers' (McLuhan, 1994: 208). More recently the UK's National Union of Journalists (NUJ) reports that advertising 'accounts for over 80% of total newspaper revenue' (NUJ, 2007), though this figure does vary by type of newspaper. Andrea Mangani reports similar ratios in France, Germany, Netherlands and Spain – in all of these countries except France, more revenue was generated from advertising than newspaper sales (Mangani, 2007).

The consequence of this is, as Robert L. Craig (2004) suggests, that media are 'structurally dependent' on advertising, so much so that advertising acts as a form of indirect social control on context, effectively censoring 'viewpoints they don't like'. We refer to this as a structural influence of advertising insofar as advertising has traditionally supported the establishment and sustenance of newspapers and television shows. Thus, whilst advertisers may not normally have influence on particular stories, they do influence which publications can be sustained. This influence is perhaps misunderstood by journalists like Nick Davies (2008), who refute the impact of advertising on journalism.

Nevertheless there is also evidence of direct influence. Ben Bagdikian confirms that in the US advertisers have traditionally exercised considerable influence over media content, and 'censoring of information offensive to advertisers continues. News that might damage an advertiser generally must pass a higher threshold of drama and documentation than other kinds of news' (Bagdikian, 2000: 164).

Indeed, from the advertiser's perspective we hear the same story, in this instance creating a disincentive to broadcast news at all. The creative director of an advertising agency wrote in the advertising journal *Strategy*, 'editors know a good scandle [sic] or disaster sells papers. Trouble is, they do not sell image ads, in which rose-colored glasses make companies and products look their best ... What is a company to do but find a nice, safe 30-second tv spot next to a sitcom or the Jays' broadcast?' ('iNewspaper: the medium of the message', *Strategy*, 2 November 1992).

In many respects the internet has contributed to a crisis of profitability in journalism. As Rupert Murdoch (2009) put it, 'the old model (of publishing) was founded on quasi-monopolies such as classified advertising – which has been decimated by new and cheaper competitors such as Craigslist, Monster.com, CareerBuilder.com, and so on'. Thus newspapers and television stations have reported significant declines in advertising revenue due to the extra advertising space online. In economic terms, the increase in the supply of advertising space has caused prices to fall. Eckman and Lindof have noted that, 'Newspapers now try to cope with declining circulation rates and shrinking profit margins by developing content and promotional strategies in the "grey area" between news and marketing', creating advertorials. They go on to explain that, 'With advertorials, not only do advertisers get an advertisement that mimics a credible news story, but often the advertiser has the opportunity to control the entire environment within which the message is embedded' (Eckman and Lindof, 2003: 65). We will discuss the details of the impact of online advertising in the next chapter.

Television news has an even more difficult time attracting advertising. It is expensive to produce, generally unprofitable and competes with other more profitable programming. Keith Brown of the Federal Communication Commission and Roberto Cavazos' (2003) study of advertising on US television found that in the US, sitcoms and similar programmes attracted a greater amount of more expensive advertising than news programmes. They also found that broadcast networks actually forgo advertising-unfriendly programme content, but that subscription channels are more likely to screen advertising-unfriendly content.

The situation is similar in the UK. For example, asked about the challenges of providing quality news programmes on the UK's Channel 4 at a House of Commons Select Committee hearing in April 2005, the Chair of Channel 4, Luke Johnson explained that, 'All forms of news will lose money but Channel 4 News certainly loses money'. The Managing Director at the time, David Scott, informed the Committee that, 'Channel 4 News costs about £20 million a year and has very little advertising revenue attached to it'. Consequently, there is motivation not to run news programmes. Scott went on to say, 'Certainly if we did not have that news programme in that slot we could put a programme in it which would probably cost substantially less and generate an audience several times the size'.

Cutting Costs, Cutting News

Perhaps the internet is to blame for the supposed 'crisis of profitability' hitting news around the globe, or perhaps it is being used as an excuse to make cuts. Indeed the economic difficulties faced by traditional news platforms started long before the internet arrived, spurred on by digitalization more generally. Either way it is clear that in many 'rich' nations, investment in many areas of news is being cut as profits rates appear to be declining.

The normal response of capitalist enterprise to declining profits is to merge and cut, which analysts argue results in a narrowing of the news net as material is copied, reproduced and shared across outlets. In the UK for example, five conglomerates account for 73% of newspaper circulation (NUJ, 2007).

This pattern of concentration is repeated across the world. In reference to Europe, the International Federation of Journalists (IFJ) reports that, 'media concentration has been on the rise in all parts of Europe. It is reaching new levels of concern particularly in relationship to the domination of a number of markets by transnational companies'. The IFJ points to increasing cross-media ownership, vertical integration, and internationalization as significant problems: German and Swiss companies 'own 80 percent of Czech newspapers and magazines', and foreign capital 'also dominates print media in Bulgaria, Hungary, Poland, and the Baltic states' (IFJ, 2005). The situation has for a long time been the same in the US. As Ben Bagdikian wrote in 2000, 'For the first time in US history, the country's most widespread news, commentary, and daily entertainment are controlled by six firms that are among the world's largest corporations, two of them foreign' (Bagdikian, 2000: xiii).

The business side of journalism seems here to conflict with the supposed democratic role of journalism. According to the NUJ:

> There is little doubt that the pursuit of higher profit margins has been elevated by newspaper publishers to a dogma above standards in journalism, the welfare of their staff and the public interest of their readers.

As a consequence of this:

> The direct relationship between cost-cutting including loss of jobs and poor pay and conditions and the reduction in editorial standards and loss of quality is now self-evident. (NUJ, 2007)

Indeed, the motivation to cut back on news and current affairs programming is intensifying. Consequently, commercial channels have dropped much of their public service programming, including current affairs, to such a degree that recent reports have stated that, 'commercial television has effectively vacated political and economic current affairs, which is now covered almost exclusively by the BBC' (Barnett and Seymour, 1999), and that generally peak time current affairs programming declined by 35% between 1993 and 2004 (Jury, 2005).

A Political Economy of Online Journalism

What, then, is to be made of this supposed crisis of news or crisis of journalism, with advertisers evidently fleeing news sponsorship, audiences apparently abandoning news, profit rates declining and cuts damaging the capacity to produce news? For all the blame that news executives lay at the feet of the internet, there is certainly a strong argument that it was their own reluctance to respond to the potential of the internet for improving and enhancing news production that caused the problems for journalism. As Jeff Jarvis (2009b), a well known US journalism academic and prolific blogger, put it in an open letter to the Newspaper Association of America:

> You've had 20 years since the start of the web, 15 years since the creation of the commercial browser and craigslist, a decade since the birth of blogs and Google to understand the changes in the media economy and the new behaviors of the next generation of – as you call them, Mr. Murdoch – net natives. You've had all that time to reinvent your products, services, and organizations for this new world, to take advantage of new opportunities and efficiencies, to retrain not only your staff but your readers and advertisers, to use the power of your megaphones while you still had it to build what would come next. But you didn't. You blew it. And now you're angry.

Essentially the news industry became complacent, depending on business models and revenue sources that were regarded as inexhaustible. Its attitude has been to defend its cosy set up at all costs, as can be seen in statements by News Corporation chief Rupert Murdoch (*The Guardian*, 2009) and the head of Associated Press (*The New York Times*, 2009a) calling for the aggressive protection of intellectual property rights and existing revenue streams. Jarvis' point is that such an attitude has been suicidal. However, Murdoch and the Associated Press represent significant and powerful interests, which have been served through decades of privatization and commodification of information. The battle between them and the new generation of news producers has historical precedence.

The argument of the commercial news industry is based on a particular understanding of news, media and information as exchangeable commodities. This understanding is shared by most capitalist states, led by the US. For example, when in the 1970s governments from poor countries and their supporters in the rich world suggested a New World Information and Communication Order (NWICO), which would effectively understand information and communication as public goods, it was met with the US government's urge to 'recast information into a general foundation for profit-seeking market expansion'. As in the 1970s the US became 'increasingly cognizant of the need to combat stagnation', it sought to defeat the NWICO movement, succeeded in so doing, and thus secured an international basis for information to take the commodity form. Accordingly, the state managed to open 'a vast new field to capital, to advance and enlarge markets for new information technology hardware, software and services, and to develop and extend networked business processes' (Schiller, 2007: 38–41). Thus was created the 'information economy' within which online journalism is situated. We will consider the legal implications of this in Chapter 9.

For now we can reflect on how the outcome of the battle in the 1970s can help explain the online news landscape today and consider how much change there has been. Elisia Cohen (Cohen, 2002: 544) has applied McManus' (1994) analysis to online journalism. She concludes that:

> the internet itself does little to alter the macro- and micro-level constraints on journalists presented by media firms and their desired audiences. Put simply, media firms largely control what is seen and left unseen on Web sites ... The influence of media conglomerates on news production functions in much the same way as in traditional media, if not more so ... Clearly, news firms and journalists, in turn, draw advertisers and investors to support online journalism efforts. Microlevel market pressures also are not eliminated from these journalistic endeavors on the internet, where audience patterns and rationales for news consumption choices appear less certain than with older media.

Such continuity is confirmed by the research of political economist Robert McChesney who extended his analysis of print and broadcast media to online media, asking whether the latter presents a challenge to the dominance of the corporate behemoths. McChesney (2002) concludes with a categorical 'no', offering a number of reasons to explain why 'the internet won't sink the media giants'.

First he argues that the large media corporations are willing to take losses on the internet. Disney or Time Warner or Viacom can afford to lose hundreds of millions annually on new media projects 'if it means their core activities worth tens of billions of dollars are protected down the road'. He argues that as with any other investment, 'losses appear to be the key to the future', especially when those losses protect much bigger multi-billion dollar investments. Perhaps most importantly, when the economic situation deteriorates, as it did in the first years of the twenty-first century when the 'internet bubble' burst and then again from 2008, the largest corporations have the resources to ride out the bad times.

Secondly, large media corporations have existing digital programming from their other ventures that they can transfer to new media at a minimal cost. 'Shovelware' is a very clear example of this strategy. Moreover, multimedia news has seen an escalation of multi-platform reproduction, thereby reducing the unit cost.

Thirdly, McChesney points to the strategy of cross media promotion, whereby a corporation might promote a product through a variety of media holdings, from promotions in newspapers to the web addresses advertised within television programmes. Again, the bigger the firm the easier and cheaper it is to publicise and market products. We might add that bigger firms have greater advertising and marketing budgets to boot. This presence extends to the deals made by media corporations with software and web portal companies. It can also be seen in the vertical integration of media corporations (as content producers and distributors), internet service providers (ISPs), and software and hardware manufacturers, which has enabled them to steer web users to certain content and certain types of 'interaction'. It is the non-commercial versions of these relations that Murdoch et al. are railing against.

Fourthly, he notes that much of the venture capital for internet content start-up companies comes from established media firms. By the time McChesney was writing General Electric, for example, had invested over $2 billion in more than 20 internet companies, in addition to NBC's (owned by General Electric) own web activities. In addition to their own holdings and investments in new ventures, the biggest corporations can simply buy out potential competitors and other successful ventures. For instance, in 2005 News Corporation paid half a billion dollars for MySpace; in 2009 the investment company Anschutz used its subsidiaries, specifically Examiner.com, to purchase user-generated news site, NewPublic; in 2007 Microsoft paid a quarter of a billion dollars for only a 1.6% stake in Facebook; in 2006 Google paid more than one and a half billion dollars for YouTube; and in 2007 Microsoft and GE-owned news company MSNBC paid an undisclosed sum for the citizen journalism site Newsvine.

Finally, because of the size of and traffic to the websites of the media giants, they stand to attract the lion's share of advertising and other revenue. Whereas an internet start-up may take years to develop a significant audience, the big corporations can use their power to make a much more rapid impact, and to generate (direct and indirect) revenue much more quickly. As Thurman informs us, advertising still has a strong influence on audience construction for online journalism. Advertisers still desire a national audience, even to the point at which news websites may hide geographical distribution of readership (Thurman, 2007).

But Good Journalism Costs Money

Clay Shirky, an expert in economics and culture, suggested that large corporations are no longer needed to organise journalism. With the costs of communication falling he believed it possible to coordinate the output of a group from outside the walls of an institution. Traditional organizations, he argued, are inherently exclusionary and an unnecessary professional class is manufactured as a by-product of this exclusion.

Using the web photo-sharing site Flickr as a case study, he cited examples of how the internet can be used to coordinate groups without recourse to institutional rules. Flickr's commercial model is based on the public's donations of photos.

> If (Flickr) were an institution it would have to turn these donators into paid, professional photographers, essentially creating a professional class of photographers who are assigned a goal. When you build cooperation into the infrastructure, which is the Flickr answer, you can leave people where they are and take the problem to the people rather then fill an organisation with professionals. In this way, you get the same outcome without the institutional difficulties. You lose the institutional imperative and lose the right to shape other people's work but you also lose the direct costs. (Shirky, 2005)

The underlying principle governing new social structures such as Flickr is that corporations no longer 'plan' work for employees, instead they 'coordinate' activities and contributions from prod-users.

Yet what Shirky does not address here is the issue of resourcing. Whilst in a sense, his notion of prod-users is libratory, in another sense it may introduce further social exclusion, another digital divide, as those who have the finances, education, expertise and time to contribute free labour do so, leaving those without those resources excluded.

Indeed, critical political economists make important points about these relations. Good journalism, as good democracy, takes time and resources. As we we've seen above, a strong investigative piece can cost tens of thousands of pounds. Although critical political economists argue that many news organisations have surpassed the function of attracting investment to support journalism, and tend instead to use journalism to support investor profits, it remains true that journalists need resources, even as more and more technologies become more readily available.

Journalists and analysts alike have asked questions of the impact of new technologies on the working routines of journalism. Given the range of pressures under which journalists labour, it is perhaps unsurprising that journalists have tended to be wary of the introduction of new technologies whilst managers have often been enthusiastic.

New media technologies tend to stimulate new hopes as well as new fears as outlined in the previous chapter. It is true that the internet and other digital technologies have enormous potential being exploited to improve journalism. In contrast to the costs of production of broadcast and newspaper news, the simplest website can be set up and run with little financial cost. The internet also lends itself to less complex and less bulky forms of organisation than other media forms, for it is built as a distributed network, which means that it is designed so that the 'load' can be distributed over many sites.

With cheaper, more responsive, time and labour-saving technologies, the amount of time and resources journalists can dedicate to a story may increase dramatically.

However, media control is not solely a function of the technologies used. Rather, it is also a result of the economic forces explained above. Accordingly, the potential of the online environment is not always regarded in terms of how to improve journalism, but rather, from the management point of view, how to increase revenue and decrease costs. From this perspective, the internet has all too often been regarded as an economic opportunity more than an opportunity to change and improve journalistic practices. Indeed, some of the research on digital newsrooms has indicated that new technologies have had a deleterious effect on journalistic quality.

On this account, when new technologies of production are deployed in media organisations, the general trend is for their deployment to be controlled by managers with the intention of increasing 'efficiency' and cutting costs (Braverman, 1974; Hardt, 1990; Bromley, 1996, 1997; Cottle, 1999). Rather than allowing, say, journalists to do more journalism or engage the public more effectively, the tendency has been for the deployment of new technology to be dependent on cuts in funding. This has meant new technologies often result in journalists being made redundant, re-skilled and spending time that might otherwise be spent engaging the public carrying out technical tasks such as editing. This means that time 'in the field' is reduced as journalists have to undertake tasks on a rota.

As Simon Cottle explains in his study of the deployment of new technologies at the BBC:

> new technologies, multimedia news production and associated practices of multi-skilling at this [Bristol] BBC newscentre have, despite corporate and management claims to the contrary, contributed to the production of more standardised news treatments and formats, and led to more superficial journalist involvement with selected news stories and their sources. (Cottle, 1999: 38).

Ultimately, Cottle's research shows that the '"radical" promise of new digital technologies is not borne out' and when their deployment, even in non-commercial media organisations such as the BBC, is motivated by the desire to cut costs and reduce the number of paid workers, it is 'unlikely to encourage "radical new directions in programme making"' (Cottle, 1999: 38). Because of managerial control over the deployment of digital technologies as a means to increase the workload and decrease costs, Cottle found that, amongst journalists:

> [t]here was no consideration ... of how palmcorders or videophones, for example, could provide the means for increased audience news access or even opportunities for limited editorial control, or how e-mail could facilitate audience feedback and/or enhanced source interventions, or how the internet could be harnessed to locate and expand the range of regular news sources. (Cottle, 1999: 40)

Similar findings have occurred in research conducted elsewhere in the UK (Ursell, 2003), as elsewhere – in Spain (Avilés et al., 2004), Catalonia (Domingo, 2006,

2008), and the US (Dupagne and Garrison, 2006). Boczkowski and de Santos (2007) have shown how these changing technical practices have actually resulted not in greater diversity but in greater homogenisation in Argentinean newsrooms.

When we consider this concern with resourcing, we can make more sense of the conservatism of early forays into online journalism – such as the use of shovelware. It takes enormous resources to adapt newsrooms to new media environments, so unless adaptation is likely to generate extra revenue, it is likely that adaptation will only be undertaken if it can be part of cost cutting exercises. Indeed, for many media executives in the early days of the public internet, the priority was to protect existing sources of revenue – their approach to new media was defensive. Further to this, journalists, editors and executives may simply not know what to do with new media technologies, may not have any idea how to use them.

Researchers elsewhere have given a slightly different view, arguing that with adaptation comes increased journalistic control and the negotiation of autonomy. Hemmingway (2008), for example, argues from her research that journalists felt there was more creative autonomy and innovation with new technologies. In contrast to Cottle's study, Roger Dickinson and Hugo Bigi's (2009) study of Swiss video journalists found that they felt greater creative and journalistic autonomy. They reported that having trained as individual video journalists skilled in a range of journalistic and technical roles, they felt a good sense of motivation and of being much more in touch with the news, compared to a traditional news crew. As Hemmingway found also, the Swiss video journalists felt that they experienced greater creative autonomy and were able to challenge conventions.

Wallace's (2009) research confirms the findings of both researchers who have found problems, and those who have found benefits of the deployment of digital technologies for news work. She argues that her research 'suggests that the impact of new technology on quality of journalism is affected by a complex relationship of professional and commercial imperatives'. Rather than new technologies having a deterministic effect on the quality of journalism, Wallace argues:

> The variability of perceptions of 'quality' journalism is underlined, particularly between journalists and other newsworkers, and their managers. These can be exacerbated by differing management strategies to introduce change, leading to varying degrees of resistance or openness to novel working practices and the possibility of innovative storytelling. Nevertheless, it is argued that new technology can have either detrimental or beneficial influence on journalism standards, dependent on applications. (2009: 698–9)

So as Deuze (2007: 153) proposes, 'technology is not an independent factor influencing journalistic work from outside'. As Henrik Örnebring (2009: 2) points out, 'journalistic concerns over a declining commitment to professionalism must also be put in a wider context', taking into consideration broader socio-economic processes such as the 'deregulation of labour markets, proliferation of short-term contracts and other forms of flexible employment (and the related trend of outsourcing), technologisation of the workplace, concerns over deskilling of parts of the workforce, etc.'

Again, though, we see the role of economics in managing the availability and use of new technologies. Indeed the *Columbia Journalism Review*'s (2010) analysis of online and paper versions of magazines seems to confirm the ongoing significance of economic imperatives. Having discovered that online versions of paper magazines have much poorer editorial standards, the researchers state:

> in the online world, speed is the name of the game. Web sites are interested in maximizing traffic on the theory that that's the way to attract advertisers, and quantity often trumps quality when it comes to that. Thus, given the prevailing business model (advertising is still king), the question arises: Is online content, with its rapid turnaround requirements, held to the same standards as its print equivalents? Survey says no.

However, on Shirky's analysis, perhaps the internet and related technologies can allow journalism to flourish outside of the giant media corporations. A number of the examples of online journalism outlined in this book do precisely that.

Certain forms of use (Salter, 2004, 2011) of internet technologies may enable journalism outside of commercial operations and perhaps escape the constraints of political economy. For example, rather than assuming that investigative journalism is no longer possible because of economic constraints, a number of journalists look to deploy technologies to assist in investigative projects.

Citizens as News Workers?

One of the key projects to use internet technologies to facilitate citizen journalism in commercial organisations was developed in 2006 by Gannett, one of the US's biggest newspaper publishers. In a restructuring reminiscent of the BBC restructuring that Cottle researched, Gannett turned its 'newsrooms' into 'information centres', and the most important part of this restructuring was the introduction of crowdsourcing news production. Crowdsourcing essentially enables an editor or journalist to utilise internet technologies to draw upon information held by or produced by citizens. Readers and viewers are asked by the news organisation to submit or find out information related to a story (Howe, 2006).

This form of journalism did not begin with the internet. Alternative media (Atton, 2001) has a long history of public involvement and collaboration, though perhaps the best example of such innovation can be found in Jay Rosen's 'public journalism' project, wherein a professional journalist would work with groups of citizens in workshops to pursue a story (Rosen, 1999). However, internet technologies have been employed to advance this approach, enabling a far wider range of participation and ever more innovative techniques of collecting and displaying information.

Whilst the corporate sector has seen Associated Press, *The Telegraph*, CNN, *The New York Times* and *The Guardian* employ crowdsourcing to investigate stories, there is also a large number of independent projects, the economics of which will be explained in the next chapter. Such projects include NowPublic, Rosen's NewAssignment.net, and Paul Bradshaw's Help Me Investigate.

Help Me Investigate is probably the closest to a crowdsourced investigative initiative there is. Bradshaw had seen how projects in the US, such as Gannett's, had worked, and noted the inadequacies of traditional investigative journalism – largely that the resources available to an individual journalist meant that data collection on a story may be incomplete. He saw how bloggers had responded to one story in particular, providing masses of additional information, and sought to set up a system in which this sort of news gathering could be formalised. Importantly, Help Me Investigate is largely a news gathering project, in which journalists work alongside citizens. As Bradshaw (*Bad Idea Magazine*, 2010) puts it:

> Help Me Investigate isn't necessarily intended to be a replacement (for traditional investigative journalism). It's so that journalists who have a lead that they don't have the time to explore or they don't think is strong enough to justify spending time on, they could put that on the site, and others who might be passionate about it, or who might owe that journalist something from other investigations, they might do a bit of digging and help them out.

In this sense, the hostility many professional journalists direct towards crowdsourcing and citizen journalism more generally is somewhat misplaced. As Michele McLellan (2009) of the Knight Digital Media Centre suggests, 'citizen journalists cannot replace professionals. But professionals and amateurs can form powerful partnerships to create important journalism. I often hear journalists refer to a widespread belief that citizens can replace professionals in producing journalism'. However, for McLellan, this belief is misplaced. She argues that there are few if any advocates of 'citizen journalists' replacing professional journalists. Rather she, like Rosen and Bradshaw, advocates supplementing and improving professional journalism by virtue of a deeper engagement with citizens.

A number of crowdsourcing projects have tried to retain the journalist–citizen relation, though other projects have rejected professional journalism as a matter of principle. For example the worldwide activist news site, Indymedia (see Chapter 4), has positioned itself against the corporate media and abhors many of the traits associated with corporate media, deciding instead that an open access platform would prevent the forms of organisational and ideological control that constrain corporate media reporting protest and social justice.

There certainly are good arguments for various forms of crowdsourcing and participatory journalism, but the concerns of many journalists, amplified by their associations, remain. It is true that crowdsourcing and user-generated content

(UGC) can contribute to richer journalism, but it is also true that such material is usually exploited by corporate media in the context of economic calculations – it is often seen as cheap or free content for which the contributors need not be remunerated. From the perspective of critics, a customer at a restaurant is not expected to provide the ingredients for her meal, so why should a reader of a website be expected to provide content?

Indeed, research by Vujnovic et al. (2010) on participation in corporate news organisations across ten different democracies has shown that regardless of actual profit generation, user engagement and participatory journalism is seen primarily in economic terms; audiences participate as 'economic labourers'. The economic terms identified by Vujnovic and her colleagues (2010: 289) consist in 'branding, particularly as a means of generating newspaper consumer loyalty', 'building traffic, involving strategies to boost the usage numbers', 'keeping up with or beating the competition' and in some markets, as part of 'cost-cutting rationales'. Perhaps disturbingly, Vujnovic et al. also considered that economic explanations for participation were accompanied by ideological explanations. They suggest that among some journalists there is a genuine democratic concern to improve engagement with audiences but that this engagement lacked substance, resulting in 'a sense of engagement, democratic activity and contribution ... without real democratic action' (2010: 295).

Whilst for well-meaning commentators like McLellan and Bradshaw participation is merely supplementary, it stands to economic logic that the appeal of free 'informational' labour, producing free and low-cost content will be welcomed by executives in terms of its contribution to cost-cutting. Nevertheless, these forms of participation are unlikely to go away. As we will see in the next chapter, business models are beginning to take account of them.

The Perseverance of Inequality?

Whilst the plethora of online journalism projects, from independent blogs to crowdsourcing, from citizen journalism sites to Indymedias are important innovations, and although they likely improve the democratic flow of information, there are still constraints upon them.

It is clear that better-resourced journalism has the potential to be better journalism, again reflecting the digital divide. Money may allow a journalist to pursue a story rigorously and over a long period of time, perhaps even years. Participatory projects represent an important addition to this, but few of those have become part of the staple news diet for citizens. Thus in terms of professionalism and sustainability, participatory projects may be marginalised by their better-resourced corporate cousins.

However, there is another factor to consider in analysing the political economy of online journalism: distribution. One of the main forms of distribution of news online is via search engines. We have explained above how 'the market' can work to marginalise the resource poor, but the promise of the internet was that this would be a thing of the past as spectrum scarcity and distribution costs are abolished online. However, portals and search engines have developed in a way that tends to increase the presence of corporate news sites. Problematically, news and journalism from corporate sources is prioritised on portals.

Such portals are often promoted by internet service providers (companies that provide access to the internet – usually the broadband company one subscribes to) and software and hardware manufacturers, which impose the home page that the users' web browser points to by default. Dahlberg (2005: 163) reports that the home page is changed by fewer than half of those who sign up to an ISP. The range of content that users have access to through the home page will be specially selected, as will the search engines they can use, and the categories of website that they 'recommend'. These two latter are often done in conjunction with search engine companies through sponsorship or commercial use deals.

The importance of the role of portals as access points can be seen in the fact that in 2009 they accounted for 13% of traffic heading to news and media websites. As Heather Dougherty put it, a 'major source [of traffic to news websites] is the front pages of portals such as Yahoo! and MSN, including the personalised versions like My Yahoo and My MSN' (Hitwise, 2009a).

Search engines are most people's primary form of navigation around the web and produce 22% of traffic to news and media websites (Hitwise, 2009a). It might be considered that search engines are technically neutral tools in relation to content, which is the image that search engine companies would like to create. However, this is not the case. There are many ways of manipulating search engines, and there are many companies that specialise in assisting in this process.

Search engines today use a variety of methods to look for websites, including counting the number of links to and from a website, the popularity (not just quality or relevance) of the sites that these links come from, and a 'location matrix', which refers to the URL of the website. This latter means that a site with its own domain name, and those with fewer subdomains come higher in the search results, which means that a website is less likely to be found if it is stored on a free host such as an ISP or Geocities (for example, www.bbc.co.uk would rank higher than www.geocities.com/athens/users/2342/index.html). The outcome of this is that the media giants continue to dominate.

A prime example of the difficulties in searching the internet can be seen in Google, which, as of April 2009, accounted for 73% of searches on the internet. To order and filter its search, Google uses PageRank, which interprets searches so that the more 'popular' and 'important' a web page is, as long as its text includes one's search terms, the higher its ranking. The PageRank algorithm takes the search terms inputted, say 'Iraq war', finds pages with these terms, assesses the location matrix and the number and 'importance' (which is not publicly defined) of links to that page from other websites, and then delivers the results in accord with these factors. The result of this is that those websites with greater market power are more likely to be viewed. In this case, even Google has a tendency to consolidate existing inequalities between information sources. So, for example, the big corporations dominate a search for 'news' on Google UK (September 2010) – in order, the BBC, Sky News, *The Telegraph*, CNN, *The Independent*, *Daily Mail*, Google News, *The Sun* and Wikipedia make up the first nine results of a search. Thereafter, news and corporate news sites make up the next four pages of results, with the University and College Union's news page being the first 'alternative' site on the sixth page and Pink News as the first alternative news source as position 65. Indymedia does not appear at all within the first 20 pages.

The offline analogue of this is the existence of a variety of newspapers and magazines that are unavailable in newsagents, wherein newsagents are predisposed to stock and display more popular and profitable 'lifestyle' magazines. Similarly, serious journalistic output on television is often relegated to late night or early morning slots because of the greater profitability of other programming, resulting in Barnett and Seymour's and Jury's research findings noted above.

Crucially for news and journalism, many of the search engines, such as Yahoo, Google and MSN, offer their own news services, with either original content or by aggregating content from elsewhere. Market power can be clearly illustrated here, wherein between 67% and 85% of traffic to those news services comes from the companies' own sites (Hitwise, 2008).

In addition to these internal relations it should also be noted that searches are of course influenced by the political and cultural context of those inputting terms. For example, the search terms employed reflect choices that are influenced by broader processes of public communication, in particular those adopted by corporate media. For example, someone searching for information about the war in Iraq would find very different content searching for 'invasion', 'resistance' or 'war crimes' than someone searching for 'operation Iraqi freedom', 'terrorists' or 'liberation of Iraq'.

In addition, although there are plenty of websites available, whether people want to read them is a different matter. Hitwise's (2009b) analysis of Google News UK shows that 68% of its traffic is generated by searches for 'celebrity' (24%), 'sport' (18%), 'film and television' (15%) and 'music' (11%). Traffic from 'UK news' and 'world news' accounted for just 5.6% of overall visits.

Although the search and portal companies remain powerful, in March 2010 Hitwise (2010) reported that the social networking site Facebook had become the 'largest news reader', sending even more traffic to news and media websites than Google News did. Both Google News and Facebook are in many respects alternative distributive mechanisms. In particular no one can tell a Facebook user which news articles to post, which sources to use and so on. However, according to Hitwise, the top ten websites visited from Facebook and Google News were all mainstream corporate news sites, with the exception of *The Huffington Post*. *The Wall Street Journal* got 10.37% of its US traffic from Google News, and *The New York Times* received 5.21% of its traffic from Google News. Fox News received 5.5% of its traffic from Facebook and CNN received 5.9% from it (Hitwise, 2010). Thus the activities of users of social media also contribute to the perseverance of the media giants.

Dahlberg (2005) has argued that this dominance has resulted in the corporate colonisation of 'online attention' and has also marginalised 'critical communications'. He argues that the battle for online attention means that '[a]lthough it is relatively straightforward (for those with the resources) to get views published on the internet, having them noticed is another matter' (Dahlberg, 2005: 163). Others have considered the impact of economic colonisation on internet technologies more generally (Salter, 2004, 2005, 2011).

Because of these processes, McChesney (2002) reported that as early as 1998 more than three-quarters of the 31 most visited news and entertainment websites were affiliated with large media firms, and most of the rest were connected to companies such as AOL and Microsoft (which are themselves now considered media firms).

By 2005 the Project for Excellence in Journalism (2005) found that 60% of the most popular news websites were owned by just 20 media companies. It concluded that, 'in short, despite the attention paid to blogs and the openness of the internet, when it comes to sheer numbers, online news appears dominated by a handful of traditional big media sites, and for now that domination appears to be increasing.' The Pew Internet and American Life Project (2006) found that in the US only 12% of internet users have visited a foreign news website, 9% visited blogs and only 6% visited what could be classed as 'alternative' news websites. By 2008 the Project reported that 33% of internet users say they read blogs but only 12% had ever had their own blog. By 2010 the Project (2010a) reported a significant decline in the number of young adult bloggers – from 28% of 18–29 year olds in 2006 to 15%. In 2009 the European Union's Office for Statistics (2008) reported that 15% of Europeans use the internet to read blogs. By 2008 (Project for Excellence in Journalism, 2009) two of the five most popular websites in the US – CNN and AOL News – were both owned by the largest media company in the world, Time Warner. The others were owned by Yahoo, NBC Universal and *The New York Times*. Overall, the ten richest companies owned 28% of the most popular news sites. In 2010 the Project listed the most popular news websites in the US and their owners. The list showed clear corporate domination with Yahoo, MSNBC, CNN, USA Today, AOL, Fox News, *The New York Times*, *LA Times*, Google and National Public Radio dominating the top ten places.

3 Digitally Challenged Business Models

Selling the Crown Jewels

In 2006, Jeff Jarvis wrote an article congratulating *The Guardian* newspaper for its bravery. What attracted the accolade was a decision to post stories on the web before they appeared in print. Jarvis dubbed this 'handing your crown jewels to the future', applauding a progressive business strategy that recognised online readers as the primary source of future income. 'It takes guts', he said, to change the timing, delivery and geography of a newspaper and 'also its very definition' (Jarvis, 2006).

This coincided with a year of great optimism in the newspaper industry both in the UK and US and *The Guardian*'s 'brave' decision was part of print journalism's collective move into the 'free news' model for journalism online. Many businesses had become infatuated with the potential of the worldwide web for creating new markets and satisfying news customers online. It may have seemed antithetical to 'give away' an expensive product for free, but the pundits were adamant that 'free' was the only way to go and that those seeking to erect paywalls (charging readers for online content) would lose in the long term. In contrast to the precipitous decline in newspaper circulations across Europe and America, the future for online ad revenue appeared rosy. Ambitious organisations heavily invested in the web were poised to reap the rewards of their aggressive cyber-business strategies.

Online display advertising, in its infancy at the start of the new millennium, was thought to be the future of revenue generation. Ten years later, as print struggled with falling circulations, a drop in display advertising and the near annihilation of its classified ad revenue – a market lost to the entrepreneurial fleet-footed web market – advertising online could not fill the void.

In desperation, Walter Isaacson, former managing editor of *Time*, led a rearguard action to turn back the clock and start charging online users for content:

> This is not a business model that makes sense. Perhaps it appeared to when Web advertising was booming and every half-sentient publisher could pretend to be among the clan who 'got it' by chanting the mantra that the ad-supported Web was 'the future.' But when Web advertising declined in the fourth quarter of 2008, free felt like the future of journalism only in the sense that a steep cliff is the future for a herd of lemmings. (Isaacson, 2009)

As we saw in the previous chapter, the concept of display advertising had underwritten print news business models for centuries. Advertisers paid for readers' attention that drifted from news articles to advertising columns and back again. This revenue combined with subscriptions and classified advertising made a newspaper's business model sustainable and profitable. As new media, such as commercial radio and television, came on stream throughout the twentieth century, there were concerns that the amount of advertising available to newspapers would shrivel; but, these worries proved unfounded.

The World of Broadcast Abundance

Policies concerning the analogue world of terrestrial television signals ensured that only a very few companies were allowed to operate and only two of these (ITV and later Channel 4) were permitted to sell advertising. And yet, it was evident even as far back as the 1970s and 1980s that the media ecology was changing: it would soon become possible for units of broadcasting (programmes) to be delivered to the public just like products in the supermarket. Companies were already experimenting with digital transmission and these experiments would later manifest with products like 'video-on-demand', 'pay-per-view' and the BBC's 'i-Player'.

It was relatively easy to sell audiences to advertisers in the pre-digital world. So long as there was spectrum scarcity, free market conditions in broadcasting could not exist and there was a quasi-legitimate reason for the operation to be run with strict regulatory controls within what was effectively a duopoly (ITV and BBC). This resulted in what was often called 'a licence to print money' for the commercially funded ITV network. When media went digital, this was no longer sustainable.

Back in the 1980s an economist, Alan Peacock, was invited by Margaret Thatcher's Conservative government to imagine a world unfettered by spectrum scarcity. He envisaged a full broadcasting market where the consumer was sovereign, there was no licence fee and broadcasters were held to account through purchasing decisions:

Eventually we hope to reach a position where the mystique is taken out of broadcasting and it becomes no more special than publishing once the world became used to living with the printing press. (Home Office, 1986: 711)

This vision unnerved many in the political and social establishment and, yet, as the latter part of the twentieth century heralded the introduction of digital plenty and the number of digital channels grew and the number of online sites offering free programme downloads expanded exponentially, a new model for financing broadcast news was needed.

Peacock's vision of a fully market-led broadcast ecology did not materialise as quickly as the free-market advocates might have liked, and 20 years on, the BBC had used its position as a publically subsidised broadcaster to gain market dominance in national and international online news delivery. James Murdoch, non-executive director of Sky Television in the UK and son of Rupert Murdoch, chose the prestigious UK MacTaggart lecture (2009) to deliver a resounding attack on what he saw as the authoritarian nature of news funding in the UK. He suggested that state-funded news, in whatever form, was an aberration and undemocratic. Specifically, he accused the BBC of dumping free, state-sponsored online news onto the market making it difficult for journalism to flourish on the internet. 'It is essential for the future of independent digital journalism', Murdoch claimed, 'that a fair price can be charged for news to people who value it' (J. Murdoch, 2009).

This attack was broadly welcomed by a UK press that saw free online content, delivered by such a mammoth and well-respected organisation, as one of the major barriers to its own online news profitability. In Europe overall, falls in print circulation and advertising revenue had commonly been matched by gains online (Sparks, 2010). The UK was the exception to this, and the reason most often cited for the problems with British online news profitability was the BBC's market dominance.

New Media Pennies

Historically journalism, with the exception of state-funded operations, had largely been defined by its place in the capitalist economy – a commodity bought and sold at the price the market was willing or able to pay. By 2010 the product was not attracting buyers at the prices it used to command. The worldwide web had ushered in systemic change to news corporations' business models.

The press were blamed for a failure to respond quickly enough to this new reality with a lack of foresight and management talent and an inability to comprehend the strategic significance of the web. The fundamental problem for newspapers was that advertising was moving online. Traditionally printed newspapers contained bundles of content with display advertising supplementing the cover price. Online, these

Table 3.1 UK newspaper falls in circulation 2009–10 (Luft, 2010)

	Average circulation	Year-on-year decline
National morning popular	5,452,310	– 4.21%
National morning mid market	2,781,710	– 4.5%
National morning quality	2,115,729	– 12.46%
National Sunday popular	5,344,301	– 7.56%
National Sunday mid market	2,848,936	– 6.29%
National Sunday quality	2,134,871	– 12.84%

bundles split apart and offered advertisers little incentive to take out generic display ads when they could target customers through performance rated, direct marketing techniques that were shown to be more efficient and cheaper. Companies like Google and Facebook enjoyed the volume and scale necessary to take advantage of this new 'purposeful use of the internet' but it was harder for individual publishers to enjoy the benefits as the new darling for advertisers was search-based advertising which grew very fast and was dominated by one provider, Google, with over 90% of the search market in Europe (Sparks, 2010).

This reality left newspapers scrambling to develop new economic models less reliant on traditional display advertising. The problem was that most attempts to shift business online were commercial failures as they traded 'old media dollars for new media pennies' (Nichols and McChesney, 2009). Media economists calculated that in 2010 an online reader was worth approximately 1.2 Euro a year, and a freesheet reader 18 Euro a year, but circulations stubbornly refused to rise and, with each passing year, newspapers were unable to arrest the decline in readership.

These declines were partially offset by dramatic rises in internet news reach over the same period. For example, the UK's *Guardian Unlimited* increased traffic to its online news pages by 22% in the same year as it lost 16% of its print readers.

Yet, because online eyeballs were worth a fraction of their print counterparts, the numbers simply did not add up. Newspapers on both sides of the Atlantic were closing, merging and making drastic cutbacks in order to stay solvent. It became uncomfortably obvious that old business models were failing and that figuring out how to pay people to create journalism was no longer easy and in many cases impossible.

Having failed to charge for online content on a subscription basis when their websites were first introduced ten years previously, businesses found it difficult to impose a tariff on customers accustomed to a free service. Research indicated that only 1–5% of readers would be prepared to pay for news online. They had, in effect, already let the genie out of the bottle and resources for journalism across Europe and the US were disappearing faster than the new media could create them.

The increasing competition for readers online also served to undercut the ability of news media organisations to charge for content and, as US academic Paul Starr observed, it undermined the ability of the press to cross-subsidise the production of public service journalism as, 'The metropolitan dailies no longer occupy the strategic position between buyers and sellers they once did'. The explicit warning Starr sounded was that the news media will fail in their principal role of holding power to account because of their failing economic strength (Starr, 2009: 28). For the first time it wasn't difficult to imagine a 'doomsday scenario' where some major cities would no longer have any newspapers and the number of working journalists would drop to a small fraction of their turn-of-the-century highs.

It is important to remember that newspapers were facing problems before the internet (see Chapter 2) and there was a tendency to conflate the future of the newspaper industry with the health of journalism generally and to see declines in newspaper circulations, often brought about by poor and unresponsive management, as symptomatic of a decline in journalism's civic function. Panic ensued over the decline in the profitability of this journalistic medium, but, there was no suggestion that newspapers couldn't still be profitable, just not on quite the scales enjoyed prior to the 1990s.

Yet given that, as discussed in Chapter 2, 'good journalism costs money', the value created in the journalism supply chain needed to be reclaimed at some point. Historically, those who had access to the means of publication were few and thus the value chain was easy to control; but, when the means of production were opened up through the internet, traditional news providers needed to become far more creative in marketing and monetising their products.

Digital Disruption

The Project for Excellence in Journalism in the US noted at the end of 2008 that, 'the newspaper industry exited a harrowing 2008 and entered 2009 in something perilously close to free fall. Perhaps some parachutes will deploy, and maybe some tree limbs will cushion the descent, but for a third consecutive year the bottom is not in sight' (Pew Research Centre, 2009). By 2010 it reported that the US news industry had lost $1.6 billion in annual reporting and editing capacity since 2000 – over a third of the industry's total worth (Pew Research Centre, 2010a).

It described how newsroom executives felt 'broadly unprepared for the changes sweeping over them' and most significantly just 5% said they were very confident of their ability to predict what their newsrooms would look like in five years time.

The study, by US journalist Tyler Marshall, painted a picture of an industry caught between two competing priorities, the first being to save money at all costs to ensure the viability of the business and the second contradictory priority was to invest in their future through innovative new forms of journalism. He concluded that round upon round of debilitating cutbacks over two years with the backdrop of the 2007 recession and sharp declines in advertising revenue had stifled the very innovation needed to survive into the future. A similar trend has been documented in the UK and Europe. Veteran journalists were leaving and were replaced by junior staff. Other cost cutting measures included outsourcing, an increasing reliance on press releases, advertorials and fake-localism symbolising a move away from local content towards generalised content with a grafted-on superficial local angle (see Pilling, 1998; Davies, 2008). This cost cutting was best summed up by US researchers in 2008:

> Meet the American daily newspaper of 2008. It has fewer pages than three years ago, the paper stock is thinner, and the stories are shorter. There is less foreign and national news, less space devoted to science, the arts, features and a range of specialized subjects. Business coverage is either packaged in an increasingly thin stand-alone section or collapsed into another part of the paper...The newsroom staff producing the paper is also smaller, younger, more tech-savvy, and more oriented to serving the demands of both print and web. The staff is under greater pressure, has less institutional memory, less knowledge of the community, of how to gather news and the history of individual beats. There are fewer editors to catch mistakes. (Pew Research Centre, 2009)

It was clear to see how cost cutting, although essential for survival, might become a self-defeating strategy. Some well known US papers such as the *San Francisco Chronicle* adopted 'content farming' to help lower costs. This is an algorithm-based strategy that uses the number of hits (also known as the clickstream as discussed further in Chapter 7) to commission content. Freelance writers who responded first with the 'story' were being paid 'peanuts' for their work (Sparks, 2010). The risk was that readers would ask, why pay for publications that are pale shadows of themselves? 'It is the daily newspaper death dance-cum-funeral march', announced Nichols and McChesney (2009). When trouble hits, businesses cut costs. In this case the costs were taken directly from the newsroom affecting the value of the product. The problem then became trying to make money selling a weaker product into a weaker market.

This phenomenon was not isolated to the US or to print. In the UK observers were writing about the effects of 'rational irrationalism' where business models were imposed 'with relentless vigour' to the rationalisation of the newsroom, with management driving down costs, streamlining news gathering and 'stripping every morsel of information for its maximum value'. One study of the UK Press Association Group concluded that the:

rational utilisation of new technologies to embrace the multi-platform news age in organisations such as PA will see the practice of journalism grow progressively irrational, as copy checks are diluted, hard news themes partly displaced, and bite sized chunks of celebrity and sport news, rendered and circulated in their place. (Manning, 2008)

Although not the cause of the precipitous decline in newspaper profitability, the financial instability created by the worst global recession in generations had sped up the rate of decline and magnified the underlying problems with the old print business model in a networked digital age.[1] With profits dropping by a quarter, businesses needed to either raise more capital by borrowing or by issuing new shares. This proved impossible in the recessionary climate with stock values plummeting in some cases by 90%. Despite the relatively high profit margins of the past (20–30% was not uncommon) many newspapers had made ill-advised acquisitions taking on huge debts in 2006 and 2007 ensuring that they had no room to manoeuvre in the lean years.

In 2009, Matthew Engel wrote a poignant obituary for Britain's local press that began with the statement, 'If the local press is to be saved, it cannot be left in the hands of the groups whose obscene profit demands have wrecked real journalism' (Engel, 2009: 55). He described how the 'Gannett Corporation business model' was exported to the UK in the 1990s, a model which treated the local press as a cash cow with an 'utter indifference to journalism', where a journalist's first priority was not simply to make money but to 'make more money' (Engel, 2009: 59). By the turn of the millennium, after a great deal of consolidation, the big four players in local UK newspapers were Johnston, Northcliffe, Trinity Mirror, a subsidiary of Gannett, and Newsquest. In 2005–6, Johnston made an operating profit of 35% with others close to that level. 'The City was impressed at first. The shares, valued at 350p as late as mid 2007, were, by early 2009, worth about a swig of Irn Bru' (Engel, 2009: 59). These handsome profits were invested in ill-judged new ventures and the industry was badly over-leveraged when the financial crisis hit. Online investment had been patchily implemented and poorly engineered and couldn't provide any form of salvation. As a result journalists lost their jobs, and papers folded.

The economic downturn also triggered an intensification of the international trend towards consolidation and changes in ownership, described in Chapter 2, along with calls to governments to loosen their legislative grip on cross ownership (Fenez and van der Donk, 2009: 41). Roy Greenslade, former editor of the UK's *Daily Mirror*, led a chorus of lobbyists pushing for a relaxation in the cross media ownership laws in the UK to help competitiveness. The 2009 'Digital Britain' report hinted that ownership laws may be relaxed because the evidence-based regime will be able to assess competitive constraints between different types of media, when investigating local or regional media mergers. 'It is quite possible that print advertising faces sufficient competitive pressure from advertising on other media, especially the internet, to protect consumers (readers and advertisers) in the face of a merger' (Carter, 2009: 152).

Once the Coalition Government took power in June 2010, it quickly moved to publicise a series of deregulation measures permitting local media mergers across radio, television and online with the 2011 Communications Bill aiming to consolidate these changes.

Decoupling

On both sides of the Atlantic, then, newspapers had very little money to finance the rapid business transformation needed to cope with the new digital competition. Industry leaders were accused of lacking the business creativity needed to turn things around and begin monetising the link economy.

One main problem newspapers faced was that upstart internet industries such as Google had been very successful in developing 'search advertising' facilitated through content aggregation. (See Chapter 2 for a detailed discussion on the impact of internet search engines such as Google.) Google news-related searches account for around 10% of its advertising (although little of this is returned to the news producers), and it was rising healthily through the recession as conventional display advertising crumbled.[2] The fundamentals of print display advertising are based on a scarcity model. Scarcity is less of an issue in online display advertising, and thus the rate that an advertiser is prepared to pay shrinks relative to the abundance of space. The other problem is that 79% of US online news users said they never or hardly ever click on the display advertisements effectively devaluing them even further (Pew Research Centre, 2010b).

Once news providers online decided collectively in the 1990s that they were going to provide their content for free it enabled search engines and aggregators to piggyback on that content and attract significant ad revenue. In 2009 two-thirds of all US internet searches were put through Google. Each searcher is exposed to a customised and highly targeted advert and billions can be made from the sheer volume of searches that go through its system. At the same time that Google was expanding and perfecting its search advertising, web display advertising, intended to prop up the news online business models, began to lose credibility. It was seen as too crude a way of delivering readers to advertisers when more sophisticated, highly targeted models were on offer. The harsh reality was that online advertising had decoupled from news content:

> In fact, the jury is very much out on how well online ads running alongside news content work for users. Many readers dip in and out of sites quickly; many considering

a product or service go straight to a search or shopping site and probably are just as happy that no news is getting in the way of what they're looking for. (Tyler Marshall, 2009)

There was also evidence that news consumers, especially the younger generation, were happily 'grazing' or 'skimming' their way through news content. The hope was that once a reader arrived at a news story through search, they would stay there a while and move on to read other articles within the same site. Research from 2010 showed that this was not happening. Instead many readers ended their encounter after just reading the 'headline, by-line and first sentence of text. In short, news consumers young and old get a good idea of news without ever clicking on the story. If this cursory read is deemed valuable – or valuable enough – it could send content producers back to the drawing board for both their content and financial strategies' (Pew Research Centre, 2010a). Rightscom, a company specialising in intellectual property rights, estimated that a headline was worth 60%, the summary 30–35% and the body copy 10%.

Larger established newspapers such as *The New York Times* claimed that 10% of its $3.2 billion annual revenue came from the web in 2007, climbing to 11% in 2008. It said that it had around ten times the number of readers for its website than its print edition; however, the advertising revenue for its newspaper is ten times its revenue for its website. Although these figures were healthier than most, they weren't nearly high enough to support its international news gathering operation. If a paper this well resourced failed to monetise the web effectively, it was not surprising that smaller newspaper brands struggled. At this juncture, traditional circulation continued to be critical to business success.

Whilst 'native' companies such as Yahoo, Google and Craigslist had developed successful business models from the outset, the legacy news providers were compelled to look to creative partnerships for survival such as financial advice, holidays, syndication, games and entertainment, classifieds and bespoke shopping such as 'reader offers'.

Micropayments come in and out of vogue, but experiments were often unsuccessful. Szabo (1996) made the argument against micropayments suggesting they presented customers with a 'mental accounting barrier' – meaning that it is not worth the mental investment to calculate whether it is worth paying a tiny amount for something. This barrier is even higher when readers cannot see first what they're buying, and when similar products are available for free in dozens of other locations.

At the same time the legacy publishers were growing increasingly uncomfortable with Google's ability to link and index with impunity, yet paradoxically they valued the traffic it created. Google was dubbed a 'frenemy', half friend and half enemy. Some publishers 'willingly opened their walled gardens to Google's indexing "bots" (web robots), whilst others continued to restrict access – notably, by adopting the model of "first click free"' (Currah, 2009: 85). Rupert Murdoch's News Corporation (NewsCorp) threatened to withdraw all its content from Google searches but finally chose in the end to erect paywalls around its content.

Despite the fact that news providers had willingly submitted products to the 'link economy', the need to shore-up the bottom line through the deep recession forced them to reconsider. The fight for survival went hand in hand with a deep animosity towards the harvesting of news content by news aggregators such as Google and other blogging portals. They were accused of 'scraping' content from news gathering sites and exploiting it for free. This prevented the so called 'legitimate' news organisations from capturing more of the revenue from the work they did. Google News, launched in 2002, was achieving more than 11 million monthly unique visitors in 2008 according to the ratings agency Nielsen. Given that Google News produces little to no original content, it was accused of deriving a disproportionate share of the value from the content it harvested. Legal measures were investigated in 2009 by two leading US industry players, Associated Press and *The Wall Street Journal* to determine whether news aggregation was indeed theft and whether the copyright holder could legitimately claim money back in recognition that traditional news gathering operations created value along the supply chain. They wanted to exercise some control over the practice and profit of 'news scraping'. Their key targets were Google, Yahoo and other aggregators such as the Drudge Report. William Singleton, CEO of MediaNews, said, 'We can no longer stand by and watch others walk off with our work under misguided legal theories' (Osnos, 2009).

News providers had to decide whether it was feasible to erect paywalls around their content. Inspiration for changing to a pay-per-click business model came from other web innovators such as Apple's Steve Jobs who was credited with successfully weaning Napster users from the popular free (albeit illegal) service onto his pay-per-download service (iTunes) where users became habituated into paying for what they had previously taken for free. Publications such as *Slate* or *The Independent* flirted with pay-for content, yet these were dangerous flirtations. *Slate* lost a number of readers as a result, and *The Independent* quickly abandoned registration for its online content.

Rupert Murdoch's NewsCorp chose 2009 to erect paywalls after years of advocating free access. His UK titles, which include *The Times* and *The Sun*, faced major economic challenges with significant drops in advertising revenues year on year, and Murdoch saw an overwhelming business case to raise new funds by starting to charge readers for online content. His son, James Murdoch's MacTaggart lecture was well timed to reignite the debate on charging. UK newspapers were concerned that they would lose their online readers to the free BBC service should they build paywalls. Murdoch led a rallying cry to all online news providers to be brave and join with him in a new pay-per-click model. It was an ideological stance he was promoting. He wanted the UK regulators (Ofcom and The BBC Trust) to force the BBC to charge too. The right path, he asserted was, 'about embracing private enterprise and profit as a driver of investment, innovation and independence and the dramatic reduction of the activities of the state in our sector' (R. Murdoch, 2009).

Although all newspaper businesses were looking for ways to more effectively monetise their intellectual capital, not all chose Murdoch's path. Some preferred to wait it out to see how the NewsCorp experiment worked; others, like UK Trinity Mirror chief executive Sly Bailey, chose to keep her paper's online content free, despite suffering similar revenue declines:

> The important thing for us is to develop the brand with the right content that engages a passionate audience…Whether that gives you the opportunity to think about whether there are areas you can charge for, that's an open discussion – but you have to create the content in order to have that option. (Andrews, 2009)

Specialists in media economics, Enders Analysis, produced research suggesting that paywalls can't possibly compensate for declining print revenues. In a research paper, they concluded that a paywall subscriber was only worth a quarter of a print reader:

> Even if every single Times print buyer were instantly moved to the paid iPad app or to the paywall and the offline operations vanished in a puff of smoke along with all the problems of terminating print operations, The Times could not maintain its current scale of operations profitably. (Evans, 2010)

They claim that going totally digital by abandoning the printing presses and distribution costs would come with savings of 25%, but this could never compensate for the smaller online income. The differential would have to be made up by charging large sums for online access, which looked very unrealistic.

Instead hopes were being pinned on the new mobile frontier and news operations were looking hungrily at the exponential rise in the uptake of mobile news applications (apps) through which it was hoped they might get a second chance to monetise their content effectively. (See Chapter 8 for an expanded discussion on how mobile news has changed the way journalism is consumed.)

Information Wants to be Free

Jeff Jarvis, Associate Professor of New York's City University, has been a long-term advocate for free online content. He was disdainful of any moves to build online paywalls and in response to the threats of law suits against news aggregators, he wrote:

I think it's saber-rattling; and, I think it's deflection. There's a fundamental misunderstanding on both sides of the discussion. We're seeing the shift from the content economy to the link economy. In the content economy, you could sell multiple copies of a piece of work, whether it was a book or a newspaper or a syndicated article. Online, you need only one copy of anything and it is the links to it that add value. So the tragic irony of this discussion is that newspapers are acting as if Google is stealing their value when indeed Google is giving them great value. (Jarvis, 2009c)

The old business model required media companies to act as gatekeepers to information. This is traditionally how they made their money. The internet, on the other hand, promoted the elimination of the middle man. The right to be a gatekeeper was partially revoked when the news products went online, where a culture of information-sharing was already established. The new reality meant that news companies needed to see Google as both a partner and a competitor. Steven Johnson argued that to best understand the significance of this change the media should be seen as an eco system in the way it circulates information as opposed to outdated notions of the mass media as top down and centralised. 'The new world is more diverse and inter connected, a system in which information flows more freely'(Johnson and Starr, 2009: 26).

This highlighted the double-edged sword that is news aggregation: 'Putting content behind a wall cuts it off from search and links; cuts off your Googlejuice' (Jarvis, 2009a) and with free content so abundant online consumers were saying that they were more likely to choose a free offer with comparable quality or sufficient quality than one they had to pay for (Fenez and van der Donk, 2009: 21).

Yet, much attention was being paid to developing new financial models that shared the riches between news originators and news aggregators. 'There was a growing sense among the "legacy media", at least, that Google facilitates a corrosive move away from paying content providers for their work', wrote Peter Osnos in the *Columbia Journalism Review*. He proposed a model in which all stakeholders would have their share in the link economy, advocating concepts of 'fair conduct', 'fair use' and 'fair compensation'. These fairness concepts for the internet age, he argued, will help meet 'society's fundamental demand for news that supports itself' (Osnos, 2009).

Freemium

Certainly not an advocate of paywalls, Chris Anderson, editor of *Wired Magazine*, wrote a book *Free! The Future of a Radical Price*, which espoused an economic model where the cost of certain products inevitably drifts to zero in a digital economy. Once the audience is hooked on what's free, they can be up-sold and charge for the specialist product range – freemium. 'You're going to have to compete with people out there who are offering your product for free', he announced. Instead of withdrawing from the free link economy, he challenged businesses to be clever by using 'free' as a form of marketing to promote 'freemium' (Anderson, 2009b).

Anderson had built his own journalism fiefdom applying these rules. He advocated giving away the abundance and charging for the scarcity. He knew that the physical products (part of the scarcity economy) such as the print copy of his magazine *Wired* which required expensive resources such as trees, ink and distribution were fundamentally different from the cyber-based products like his website (Wired.com) which, as part of the abundance economy, costs far less to produce. Both are needed, he suggested, because you can only make money from scarcity (the physical product) with the marketing value derived from the free product.

Anderson's print magazine brought in the lion's share of revenue through its cover price combined with the elevated cost its display advertising commanded. The website operated at a loss. Anderson described the online space as a 'sort of playspace':

> We have a very different editorial process online. In the magazine, every page is golden, every page is expensive. It has to be perfect. I have to say no to everything. On the web site we have an infinite number of pages and if we make a mistake we can correct it. We can say yes to almost everything including non professionals... we don't edit them, we don't fact check them, (fact checking is naturally built into online) we don't tell them what to do and out comes this miracle. (Anderson, 2009c)

The corollary in the music industry is that a performer might give away the CD to promote the freemium concert tour. Google operationalised this model very successfully. In 2009, of its approximately 300 products, 290 of them were free and the people who paid for the premium or 'freemium' products (advertising or enriched search profiles) paid for the rest to consume the standard offer (basic searches).

Niche Success

Anderson's success with *Wired* magazine was built on high-end, niche print magazine sales, a model proven very robust in the new digital economy. Sales data on niche publications that target mums, cars, boats, finance etc. found a far more resilient market throughout the period (Pew Research Centre, 2009). This success was not enjoyed by all publications. For example, in the summer of 2009 *Newsweek* and *Time* magazine both adopted emergency measures to survive the double blow of a recessionary sales environment coupled with competition from online news sources.

Newsweek decided to reposition itself as a high-end magazine selling in-depth commentary and reportage. After 76 years as a successful generalist news digest it needed to stop being all things to all people because the internet was doing that. Instead it dropped its circulation by half and appealed instead to the few willing to pay for what they couldn't get free and on-demand through the web.

Both *Time* and *Newsweek* needed to find relevance to a smaller customer base and adopted similar strategies. One commentator noted how this was in response to accelerating news cycles and the changing purpose of newspapers which 'have effectively become newsweekly-style digests themselves, turning to muddy "news analysis" now that the actual news has hit us on multiple platforms before we even open our front door in the morning' (Hirschorn, 2009: 50). This example supports the overarching principle of remediation (see Bolter and Grusin, 1999) that new media don't necessarily supplant old media but act as a catalyst for reform in instances where attractiveness or relevance fades. It is worth remembering that US newspaper circulation had been declining per capita at a constant rate since 1965 when new media such as television and radio began eroding news print's monopoly on our attention.

To give more credence to the idea that specialty or niche sold better in the new digital economy, the print edition of *The Economist* bucked the downward trend in 2008 and 2009 with increased advertising revenues and healthy circulations. This highbrow international news digest had been able to position itself as still relevant with intelligent analysis and critique. Thus it remained primarily a highly valued print product and with a circulation of 800,000, it was thriving in 2009. 'The Economist sits primly apart from the orgy of link love elsewhere on the Web' (Hirschorn, 2009: 55).

Two other obvious examples of niche success were *The Wall Street Journal* in New York and London's *Financial Times*. Both had been able to hold their own in print sales and also manage to cultivate 'freemium' web products to support their revenue streams. *The Wall Street Journal* still gave away its most popular content to generate the traffic needed to command higher advertising rates. Only the more niche content on specific industry domains is paid for (Anderson, 2009b). This view was backed up by an international Price Waterhouse Coopers report on the 'Outlook for Newspapers in the Digital Age'. It discovered in 2009 that, 'both consumers and advertisers have demonstrated a willingness to pay more for high value, topic specific publications than they would for newspapers providing general news only.' (Fenez and van der Donk, 2009: 15). They found it was critical that newspapers were able to earn their reader's trust and loyalty with 'the core principles of deep analysis and trusted editorial.' In this way they concluded 'the medium is secondary to the brand' (Fenez and van der Donk, 2009: 4). The trend was for most news organisations – new or old – to 'become niche operations, more specific in focus, brand and appeal and narrower, necessarily, in ambition' (Pew Research Centre, 2010a).

Platform Agnostics Saving the Bacon

With each passing year studies showed that the immediacy and flexibility of online and mobile news was shifting news-seeking behaviour away from print, radio and TV. This trend was most advanced in the US:

On a typical day, 61% of Americans get news online, which puts the internet just behind television as a news source and ahead of newspapers. And more than a quarter of adults now commonly access the internet on their phones and PDAs, adding yet another layer of change in consumers' relationship with news. (Pew Research Centre, 2010a)

The more farsighted newspaper businesses had taken measures to adapt to this change in news-seeking behaviour by making changes to the way they managed their businesses. In 2006, one of the UK's best known broadsheet newspapers, *The Daily Telegraph*, decided that it was no longer going to be feasible to define itself primarily as a paper-based news supplier and invested heavily in redesigning its newsroom to accommodate multimedia production.

It wanted to be 'customer focused' and provide news when people wanted it during the day at regular convenient intervals. Media commentator Professor Roy Greenslade believed that the long-term circulation success for newspapers lay in viewing the printed paper as the 'core brand' on which to build a host of digital 'products':

> Though we journalists may blanche at those terms and possibly recoil from the concept, we have to appreciate that our future is tied to wooing an audience that is gradually turning its back on our inky output. And we have to do it fast. (Greenslade, 2005: 8)

Chris Lloyd, head of business development for *The Daily Telegraph*, wanted customers to buy the news in print in the morning and then come back during the day to 'nip and snack' on news content in the form of video, audio and text packages (Lloyd, 2008). The consequent demand was for 'platform agnostic' journalists to work across all media. Research had shown that the use of video in online news sites in particular gave the feel of a 'TV-like' experience, which was said to be peoples' favourite way of engaging with news (Fenez and van der Donk, 2009: 18). *The Telegraph* still claimed to put the newspaper at 'the heart' of operations while acknowledging the tough marketplace for UK 'paid for' circulations in steady decline. Lloyd credited this progressive multimedia strategy for his paper's relative success: 'A large part of this success is down to encouraging our web readers to come to our newspapers as much as our newspaper readers coming to our web site' (Lloyd, 2008). *The Telegraph* had also been successful in getting its audiences to pay for access to games, fantasy football and cricket services while also selling its puzzles at a premium. Dubbed e-commerce, this type of business is less cyclical and more infotainment based.

As the print medium began muscling in on broadcast's traditional territory, the broadcasters lost no time in ensuring that they too had an equally powerful multimedia mix to woo online users. One Sky News (UK) trainee journalist recalls a typical day on the job:

Over the past 15 months at Sky News I've worked online writing and shooting video. I produce live web shows and have worked on the mainstream TV output. A typical day for me at Sky News might start at 7 or 8 am. I might start by writing a news story for the web site. Or I might be asked to embed a video in a blog. Then I will be tasked to research the latest YouTube hits for the evening TV strand or I might leave the office to film some web video. Perhaps I'd go to a press conference and use the text message tool called Twitter to update a story on Sky News online. (Barnett, 2008)

The fluidity with which news seekers grazed across media needed to be catered for.

Both generic boundaries and media boundaries were breaking down. There was no longer a TV news market separate from a newspaper market separate from a publishing market and people shopped around for news within a broader infotainment environment. The digital revolution had left a permanent mark.

Muscling in Online – the Cult of the Amateur

Another significant marker for change in journalism was the massive proliferation of news blogging. The divide between amateur and professional journalist was placed in sharp relief as technology lowered the barriers to entry for publication and opened up multiple portals for the 'non professional' to practice (see Chapter 6). In 2009, *The Wall Street Journal* reported that just under 10% of American adults (20 million) blogged with 1.7 million profiting from the work and 452,000 using blogging as their primary source of income. This led one commentator to declare that: 'The information age has spawned many new professionals, but blogging could well be the one with the most profound effect on our culture. If journalists were the Fourth Estate, bloggers are becoming the Fifth Estate' (Penn and Zalesne, 2009). In the same article the author observed that there were 79% fewer DC-based employees of major newspapers than there were a few years ago and predicted that the value of *The Huffington Post*, a political news blog dating back to 2005, would shortly exceed the value of *The Washington Post*. *HuffPost* had 50 staff in 2008 compared to 700 newsroom staff at *The Washington Post* – down from 900 the year before.

The Huffington Post is often cited as one of the leading blogging success stories. Founded by a Greek-born, well connected socialite, Arianna Huffington, it has been credited with revolutionising US political news. In 2008 it had 5.5 million unique monthly viewers and a £80 million valuation. Andrew Keen credited it with 'changing the economics of public intellectual life' (Keen, 2008: 51).

Huffington didn't use conventional news business models. For a start, she didn't pay her writers and only rarely edited contributors' work. Big name political celebrities and popular academic thinkers were happy to write for free because it gave them standing and exposure in a way that money couldn't buy, providing valuable attention within the 'attention economy'. Goldhaber first coined the term 'attention economy' describing a cacophony of voices all competing for recognition. He argued back in 1997 that if the web and the net can be viewed as spaces in which we will increasingly live our lives, the economic laws have to be natural to this new space and what counts most is what is most scarce, namely attention (Goldhaber, 1997). 'Huffington's genius', Keen argues, 'is to have understood this shift in the value of content and to have crowned herself queen of the attention economy before most of us even knew of its existence' (Keen, 2008: 52).

Yet, there were very definite downsides to this celebrity style journalism. At first sight it appears that everyone is a winner with 'interesting free opinion from a glittery array of writers'. Yet, as Keen is quick to point out:

> The problem is that the free information economy of HuffPost is actually very costly when it comes to reliable knowledge about the world. As professional journalists are replaced by opinionated celebrities competing for recognition in the attention economy, how will an Arianna Huffington, blogging from her home in Brentford, LA, know what's happening in Tehran and Washington? As newspapers shut down their foreign desks – something that is already happening – how will we Huffington readers know whether to trust the accuracy of her work? (Keen, 2008: 52)

This complaint levied against 'the cult of the amateur' echoed from numerous sources. The new media-rich world allowed for experimentation on many different levels. The granddaddy of profit-making blogging sites, much admired and feared, was the Drudge Report, famous for breaking the Clinton–Lewinsky scandal. It set the template for other partisan sites with little compunction when it came to printing unsubstantiated rumour. *Newsweek* had the Lewinsky story first, but turned it down. The Drudge Report started in 1994 as a right-wing news aggregation site, with some original content. More recently in 2008 it published pictures of Prince Harry of Wales in Afghanistan, the first major news portal to do so and at a time when the mainstream press were under a self-imposed embargo to protect the Prince's life. Chapter 4 examines this phenomenon further in relation to audience trust and transparency.

Making 'Citizen Media' Pay

As we will investigate further in Chapter 6 on local media, the digital ecology heralded a renaissance in citizen media throughout the 1990s and 2000s.

Although Drudge and Huffington were good examples of profiteering blogging sites, there were thousands of 'citizen media' experiments being conducted at the time which were not natural money-spinners. Dan Gillmor, author of an influential book, *We the Media* (2004), chronicled the ways in which 'non-professional' journalists could use the internet to publish successfully. Shortly after publication he tried his hand at developing his own profit-making community online news site. He left a secure job at the *San Jose Mercury News* to pursue what he termed his passion for 'citizen media' (Gillmor, 2006).

The project which served the San Francisco Bay area failed to fund itself and Gillmor was forced to abandon it in less than a year. What was interesting about this particular failure (one of countless many) was Gillmor's own insights into why it wasn't economically viable. He wrote:

> I erred, in retrospect, by taking the standard Silicon Valley route. I was trying to figure out how to make this new phenomenon pay its own way out of the gate, just as the traditional, still deep pocketed media, super energized entrepreneurs and legions of talented 'amateurs' – a word I use in the most positive sense here – were starting to jump seriously into the fray.... I concluded that I could do more for the citizen journalism movement by forming a non profit enterprise. (Gillmor, 2006)

His mistake, if you can call it that, was to harbour an ambition to produce local community citizen journalism as a viable business. He wanted to be able to provide its investors and citizen contributors with clear financial incentives for participation, but, instead had to rely on their commitment to the cause rather than the purse (see Chapter 6). Gillmor's decision to move from a dot.com model to a dot.org model acknowledged how hard it can be to monetise this form of journalism. Yet, he believed that a more democratised media was crucial to the country's common future even if the numbers didn't add up.

Since this 2005 experiment, there have been a multitude of similar attempts to build businesses on the back of citizen media, but the majority of for-profit local sites have failed. One remarkable exception to this has been OhmyNews in Korea. A lot has been written about this amazing experiment in citizen media (see Allan, 2006: 129–38) which was seen as influential in determining the outcome of the South Korean presidential elections in 2002. At the beginning it was able to employ staff writers and to pay many of its regular freelancers; however, after the initial shine of the early years had worn away, it became clear that its business model was not viable.

Seven years later, the news website still had millions of daily page views but the display advertising revenue was not enough to support the business. It had been in the red for three years and had lost $400,000 in the first six months of 2009. 'We have made significant experiments so far,' said its founder, 'Now we have to introduce a sustainable model' (Ihlwan, 2009).

The 'sustainable' model referred to was the introduction of paid subscriptions and a push for charitable donations. What is clear from this innovative experiment in community-based media is the need for constant reinvention. Korea's largest advertising agency pointed out that OhmyNews' citizen journalism, 'emerged as a significant media outlet early this decade, when it served as a rare alternative to conventional news organizations that largely reflected conservative views and portrayed Roh (the election winner) as a dangerous leftist. "We live in a different environment now, with numerous blogging sites and social media catering to a wide variety of viewpoints and values, OhmyNews is no longer a novelty"' (Ihlwan, 2009).

There were many success stories amongst the failures. In the US in 2009 online newsrooms such as voiceofSandiego.org, MinnPost and Crosscut.com were thriving non-profit organisations helping to break investigative news stories using raw, new talent funded by charitable foundations (Brennan, 2009: 301). The UK's Investigations Fund was also set up by a charitable grant of £2 million dedicated to investigative journalism in the public interest,[3] aiming to be a counterweight to the decline of traditional media investigations.

Crowdfunding models such as the innovative Spot.Us site asked a large number of readers to contribute to its investigative journalism by putting small amounts of their own money towards the content. This model had some success in the US which had no tradition of publically funded news, but was less successful in Europe where a tax on television ownership was common to support public broadcasting. The network of Indymedia sites (Chapter 4) was funded through an initial investment from a charitable foundation supplemented by donations and subscriptions and also more old-fashioned fund-raising initiatives such as selling t-shirts, badges and hosting screenings and festivals.

The longevity of all these non-profit funding initiatives has yet to be tested. The first aggressive expansionary citizen media phase had passed by the end of 2010 and the novelty of these sites had been lost to their abundance in the attention economy of the internet.

A Hundred Online Flowers May Bloom

In 1921 a New York friend said radio – a funny little box – would kill newspapers. If this radio thing is going to be a menace to newspapers, then maybe we should own the menace (Barker, 2008).

It took 90 more years and the proliferation of journalism online for the threat of new media to seriously compromise the future of the printed news word. History will most likely conclude that the period from 1990 to 2010 was a critical time during which the news business experimented with numerous survival strategies with many casualties, readjusting, as it had done so before, to the threat of yet another new medium.

In 2010 newspapers still dominated internationally, yet, their epitaph had already been written with many seeing them as a nineteenth century product in the twenty-first century. The newspaper industry was facing a long-term structural challenge, forced to redefine itself and rethink its entire business model to stay in play. As the industry eagerly embraced the link economy and then woke up to financial bankruptcy, it was forced to realign itself in order for news gatherers to once again enjoy the fruits of their labour. As this rebalancing act was taking place many emerging business models were collapsing and reinventing themselves. What had yet to be understood in this new economy was how to put a value on the cost of journalism. News work has an economic but also a social and cultural value not always taken into consideration. Cultures with a strong tradition of public service news paid for through taxes or licences were in a stronger position, and countries with a weaker tradition of state intervention in market failure were left scrambling for new public subsidy models (see Chapter 5).

Territories outside the Western hemisphere did not follow exactly the same path as their Western counterparts. In other parts of the world pay-content sites have been more successful as a result of the social and political conditions in which they operate. For example, in Malaysia Malaysiakini charges $40 per year for access, which the CEO of the company believes Malaysians are willing to pay because the legal restrictions on television and newspaper journalism in the country make online the only medium in which people can access good quality disinterested journalism (Bärthlein, 2008). At this juncture, those most successful in monetising online content appeared to be Asian news companies such as Malaysiakini, which never let its paywall down and enjoyed significant revenues through its subscription base (Chandran, 2009). Similarly, Folha, Brazil's number one news portal could boast almost 2 million paid subscribers as part of what appeared to be a very healthy media mix.

So was Jarvis right to celebrate *The Guardian* newspaper's decision to sell its crown jewels to the future? Was it the correct strategy? The process of remediation is never straightforward and the enduring successful business models in a digital news age have yet to be formerly recognised. People will always pay for news they see as essential to their personal wellbeing. If the news is accurate, trustworthy and targeted enough, it should sell at a premium. How it's delivered and how the original costs of production are underwritten will undoubtedly cause Murdoch and his ilk many future sleepless nights. This time of chaos, as in all previously tumultuous times of change, might prove as Brian McNair predicted, 'creative and liberating', while also 'confusing and destructive' (McNair, 2009a: 349).

The great nostalgia for the quality of the old printed word has not lessened. One commentator wrote in an emotive piece entitled 'Build the Wall'.

The fledgling efforts of new media to replicate the scope. competence and consistency of a healthy daily paper have so far yielded little in the way of genuine competition. A blog here, a citizen journalist there, a news web site getting under way in places where newspaper is diminished – some of it is quite good, but none of it so far begins to achieve consistently what a vibrant newspaper, staffed with competent, paid beat reporters and editors, once offered. New media entities are not yet able to cover – day after day – the society, culture and politics of cities, states and nations. And until new models emerge that are capable of paying reporters and editors to do such work – in effect becoming online newspapers with all the gravitas that implies – they are not going to get us anywhere close to professional journalism's potential. (Simon, 2009)

Entrenched attitudes such as this will always find a voice as old companies die and new ones created, and the loss of past normative journalistic standards grieved. Yet, the future of journalism online may well be better than our printed 'golden age'. Online journalism has the potential to be characterised by increasingly distributed profits, more collaboration and more accountability through the magic of algorithms capable of calculating each story's reliability and source as well as its popularity. Perhaps in the continued wrangle over who has the right to call themselves a journalist, money may provide the most simple answer. Arguably a journalist is someone who makes a living out of the activity regardless of previously recognised professional norms, experience or proven craft technique. This definition, however, immediately dismisses the thousands of contributors to non-profit, open-source sites around the world.

In the meantime, as one observer noted, 'it's wonderful to see a hundred online flowers bloom; this is worth cheering about' (Schudson, 2009: 370); and another reminded us that we shouldn't ignore the history of capitalism and the story of industrial revolutions, 'A technology is invented, it spreads, a thousand flowers bloom, and then someone finds a way to own it, locking out others. It happens every time' (Anderson, 2010).

Endnotes

1 Total news industry advertising in the US dropped by 23% between 2006 and 2008 with further declines in 2009 (Pew Research Center, 2009).
2 Pew Research Center reported that 'Search, by far the largest piece of online ad revenue, was projected to increase 3% to $10.8 billion (US Market) in 2009' (Pew Research Center, 2010).
3 See www.investigationsfund.org/?p=624

4 Truth, Trust, Transparency

It is frightful that someone who is no one ... can set any error into circulation with no thought of responsibility and with the aid of this dreadful disproportioned means of communication. (Nineteenth century philosopher, Søren Kierkegaard, writing about newspapers (in Kierkegaard, 1967))

Throughout this study we consider the claims made by journalists about what they perceive as 'online journalism'. A version of this was expressed by Andrew Muller (2000) in *The Sunday Times*. Muller informed us:

> Until recently, consumers of news have relied ... on a rigid and time-honoured structure of filters to present them with a workable approximation of the truth: these are the newspapers of free societies, or trusted national broadcasters such as the BBC and ITN.

> The internet has made a fundamental change to the relationship between the media and its consumers, so that we no longer have to depend on the established arbiters of truth to make sense of the world for us. All the news-gathering resources that have, for years, been available only to journalists are now available to anyone with a computer and a phone line.

> ... The fact that consumers can now access an immense variety of unfiltered news sources raises issues of trust and credibility. Most newspapers and broadcasters are anchored in both history and accountability, and a great many websites have neither.

Muller's argument here was based on two assumptions, first that 'traditional' journalists develop a 'workable approximation of the truth' and second that citizens had hitherto been unable to access certain information. The consequence of this supposed change, as Muller put it, was that truth may suffer, as we saw so many commentators charge in the first chapter.

One of the key concerns of such critics is with the 'amateurism' of non-institutional journalists discussed in more detail in Chapter 6. The lament of journalists about these new kids on the block was loud. Yet amateurism was not a phenomenon confined to journalism. Indeed in 2004 the British think tank Demos investigated what they called 'The Pro-Am Revolution', through which we can understand much of the 'new amateurism' driving digital journalism. Their point was that the amateurism of the late twentieth and early twenty-first century was distinct from that of previous decades:

> The twentieth century was shaped by the rise of professionals in most walks of life ... formerly amateur activities became more organised, and knowledge and procedures were codified and regulated. As professionalism grew, often with hierarchical organisations and formal systems for accrediting knowledge, so amateurs came to be seen as second-rate. Amateurism came to be to a term of derision. Professionalism was a mark of seriousness and high standards. (Demos, 2004: 12)

In contrast to this, from the 1990s onwards:

> a new breed of amateur ... emerged: the Pro-Am, amateurs who work to professional standards. These are not the gentlemanly amateurs of old – George Orwell's blimpocracy, the men in blazers who sustained amateur cricket and athletics clubs. The Pro-Ams are knowledgeable, educated, committed and networked, by new technology. The twentieth century was shaped by large hierarchical organisations with professionals at the top. Pro-Ams are creating new, distributed organisational models that will be innovative, adaptive and low-cost. (Demos, 2004: 12)

According to the Demos report, the Pro-Ams 'work at their leisure, regard consumption as a productive activity and set professional standards to judge their amateur efforts'. They show commitment, skill and effort in their 'leisurely' pursuits, or what Demos refers to as 'active' leisure. This active leisure 'requires the physical or mental engagement of participants (and) should be distinguished from more "passive" forms of leisure, in which consumers are recipients of entertainment' (Demos, 2004: 23).

It is this Pro-Am paradigm that is perhaps most challenging to modern journalism. It is this paradigm that is reconfiguring the relations between journalists, audiences and sources, to which we will pay particular attention in the remaining chapters.

The reservations about this reconfiguration harboured by professional journalists that we highlighted above and in the previous chapter, are often based on an understanding of amateurism as deeply inferior. However, as we shall see in a number of situations, the Pro-Am is not necessarily an inferior journalist. Pro-Ams can contribute knowledge and expertise that professional journalists may lack. It is the contention here that if professional journalists fail to recognise the value of participatory practice and the new relations of production in the news industry, they stand to miss a crucial opportunity for renewal.

As we have seen, it is not the contention that professional journalists are unnecessary or that journalism is dead, but that some elements of journalism can be improved through this sort of engagement.

The notion that 'time-honoured structures' have been adequate for journalists to arrive at a 'workable approximation of the truth' is not universally shared. As we saw in the first chapter, 'journalists' and 'journalism' refer to a broad range of activities. For example, it is unlikely that a reasonable person would consider Fox News, *The Sun*, *Sunday Sport* or the *National Enquirer* to be 'arbiters of truth'. Even more 'serious' journalistic enterprises have been exposed as problematic insofar as ideology and discursive structures lead them to help establish and reinforce 'regimes of truth'. This is to say that so often power comes to dictate what is considered 'truth' (see Allan, 2004: Chapters 3 and 4).

Crucially for this argument, citizens do not always share the trust claimed by traditional journalism (which is contrasted with the claimed untrustworthiness of online journalism). Each year the British polling organisation Ipsos MORI conducts a poll of trust in the professions, and each year journalists vie with politicians to take the mantle of least trusted profession – with only 22% of the population trusting journalists to tell the truth, which is the highest proportion since the poll began in 1983! A staggering 72% of respondents 'trust' journalists not to tell the truth. (Mori, 2005)

The Reader's Digest 2010 Trusted Brands survey, which measures opinion across Europe, found the average proportion of the population that trusts 'the press' is 43%, with the UK at 23%, Russia at 17% and Finland at 68%.

The Pew Research Center for the People and the Press (2009) found that in the US as of 2009, the US public's perception of the accuracy of news stories in the corporate media[1] was lower than at any point in the preceding 20 years, with only 29% of people believing that traditional news organisations generally get facts right.

The situation becomes complicated when we consider internet users as a specific group. Research on press performance between 1985 and 2007 by the Pew Research Center will be uncomfortable reading for journalists who expect citizens to share their concerns about the accuracy and truth of online information. The research looked at audience perceptions of the performance of corporate news organisations, such as CNN, Fox News and MSNBC. It found that a large majority of US citizens criticise such news organsiatons for 'political bias, inaccuracy and failing to acknowledge mistakes'. However, of particular interest is that 'some of the harshest indictments of the press now come from the growing segment that relies on the internet as its main source for national and international news' (Pew Research Center, 2007).

Perhaps because of its early adoption in educational and research institutions, the internet audience has always been somewhat younger and better educated than the general population. This fact that may help explain why the research found that twice as many people who cite the internet as their main news source express unfavourable opinions of mainstream news as those who cite television as their main source of news (Pew Research Centre, 2007). One might deduce that internet audiences are actually less naïve and carry a healthy scepticism of established news organisations.

In South Korea, citizens' disaffection with the press has been widespread for a long time, and the internet has been seen as a more trustworthy medium. As Kim and Johnson (2009: 299) put it, 'Korean online users tend to distrust the conventional media system, which has for so long played a major role in establishing the highly conservative and centralized structure of communication in Korea's political culture. Instead, they have turned to the internet for more up-to-date and reliable political information'.

Print and broadcast journalism is not as well trusted as journalists might like to think, and internet users are far more media-savvy than they assume. The most significant point, however, is that the dichotomy between 'traditional' and 'new' media simply cannot be maintained, especially as material and conventions overlap and merge so much.

Who Are You Looking At?

The belief that the internet provides inaccurate and untrustworthy information is largely based on beliefs about the quality and accuracy of corporate journalism that seem not to be true. Axel Bruns' (2005) book, *Gatewatching: Collaborative Online News Production*, makes precisely this point. Bruns' starting point for developing his concept of journalism as gatewatching is that the 'gatekeeping' function usually associated with journalism faced a significant challenge. According to Bruns gatekeeping has never entailed upholding democratic media standards. Rather, gatekeeping subjects information to a commercially and institutionally driven filtration process in which huge amounts of information are systematically excluded. Bruns suggests that the rise of propaganda, public relations and professional communications intensifies these problems.

For Bruns, though, the real challenge to gatekeeping comes from the potential of internet technologies. He suggests that the gatekeeping function and the forms and conventions of news writing stem from technological limitations: especially the limited space and bandwidth of newspapers and television, and the associated difficulty of accessing and distributing information. As Bruns (2008) puts it:

News coverage in traditional news media is always limited by the technical and commercial limitations of broadcast and print news channels; hence the need for journalists and editors to combine the reports of various news sources into a single news story following the 'inverted pyramid' style (and thus prepared for further truncation if the available channel space further decreases due to breaking news). The same scarcity of channels also places significant responsibility on the proprietors of such channels: since the threshold of entry to such news media is prohibitively high, journalists working in the resulting small number of channels are obliged to report objectively and impartially.

With the internet all this changes. The impossible orientation to 'objectivity' can be abandoned as spectrum scarcity becomes a thing of the past. Instead, Bruns calls for 'multi-perspectival' journalism.

The lower cost of production online means that journalists could cover more 'marginal' stories that are often considered uneconomical. Moreover, with the use of hyperlinks, the journalist as gatekeeper or interpreter may be challenged as direct links to information are provided. This further lends itself to multi-perspectivism, by allowing numerous sources entry to the public sphere without (mis)representation.

The interactive possibilities afforded by the internet are said by Bruns to potentially lead to more open journalism, not just with the use of links, but also by transforming the audience into active producers. They become producers by selecting and editing information from a range of sources.

The multi-perspectival elements of Bruns' model and the notion of direct links may well assist in achieving greater transparency in online journalism. As the role of the journalist slightly shifts and the sources of information can be made more transparent, so the mystique of journalism recedes.

Effectively Bruns' argument for multi-perspectival journalism is based on a liberal–discursive conception of truth, which draws implicitly on John Stuart Mill's argument in his book *On Liberty*. Mill contends that free expression from a multiplicity of perspectives better enables a society to grasp the truth of matters. For Mill, if a person is, 'unable to refute the reasons of the opposite side; if he does not so much as know what they are, he has no grounds for preferring either opinion'. For any reasonable judgement to be made those opinions should rather be presented in their most 'plausible and persuasive form' by persons who believe them to be true and 'who defend them in earnest' (Mill, 1996: 38). For Mill, 'even in revolution of opinion, one part of the truth usually sets while another rises. Even progress… for the most part only substitutes, one partial and incomplete truth for another' (Mill, 1996: 47). Thus the only way to test and validate received truths is to hold them up to what Habermas (1989) refers to as the court of public opinion.

Perspectives on Perspectives

Bruns' considerations of the potential of the internet for reconfiguring journalism may sound optimistic, but they do point to new possibilities that are still marginal to journalism. Where new forms of subjectivity and new opportunities for multi-perspectivism might have arisen, other scholars have pointed to disturbing trends in new forms of journalism. Allan (2006) points to the availability to online journalists of the 'collective intelligence' of bloggers. However, Allan is cautious about the development of blogging. He writes:

> This 'collective intelligence', it needs to be acknowledged, is frequently politicized ... along fiercely partisan lines. Few would dispute that the blogosphere has been sharply skewed to the political right. (Allan, 2006: 87–8)

Allan's concerns are well placed – he refers to this politicised blogging as 'politics by other means'. Indeed, a number of the concerns of journalists may have a point not that the internet is necessarily full of lies, but that there's a lot of material that is very much slanted to one particular view or another. However, it is perhaps best to consider journalism bloggers as akin to columnists. As has been seen throughout this book, there are many different journalistic practices and no single one has been able to claim advantage over the others. Thus, partiality and journalism are not mutually exclusive.

Concerns about the pernicious leanings of some bloggers are ameliorated, as Allan points towards, by the fact that often baseless political opinion has been a feature of newspapers (for example *The Sun*), television (Fox News in the US) and radio (with commentators such as Rush Limbaugh) for a long time. Indeed some writers have accused commentators working for Fox News, for instance, simply as liars (Franken, 2003).

Two of the most significant challenges to the shortcomings of corporate news' claims to objectivity can be seen in the collaborative online journalism projects, Wikinews and Indymedia.

Multiperspectival Journalism: Wikinews and Indymedia

Wikinews was first developed between 2003 and 2005. Its appeal lay in the technology it used, the Wiki. A Wiki is a format that allows users to create and edit web pages whilst they are online. This means that users are able to contribute to web pages without any necessary web-editing skills, and that their contributions are 'live' – updates can be immediate. The Wiki format lends itself to collaborative working, and as such the Wikinews founders saw an opportunity to develop collaborative or participatory journalism.

Wikinews is open to contributions from anybody wishing to write news reports. The reports themselves tend to be produced collaboratively and remain open to editing and correction after 'publication'. As Thorsen (2008) puts it, 'News articles are typically a synthesis of other news sources, but also can be based on original reporting or a combination of the two methods. News items are protected from further development after two weeks, after which they are only open to non-content amendments carried out by administrators'. The articles cover current affairs of interest to its users locally, nationally and internationally, covering issues that may be excluded from corporate media.

In addition to participating in writing, participants can also help formulate policy, which they do via the website, internet relay chat and email groups. Akin to historical radical media projects, participation in Wikinews is organised on the basis of a formally horizontal structure in which formal hierarchy is rejected. However, the editorial policies of Wikinews resemble those of corporate media insofar as they claim to adhere to strong neutrality in reporting.

Wikinews claims to offer not objectivity, but a 'neutral point of view' in its new reports. The site allows anyone to contribute stories, providing an open, participatory platform. The openness of the site is mitigated by its editorial policy, which instructs participants not to promote any particular viewpoint, to be transparent by citing sources, to revise articles a maximum of three times per day, to respect copyright laws and to be respectful of other participants. The ability to participate is also mitigated by the necessary hierarchy amongst the team of participants insofar as one has to be registered to vote and administrators have technical privileges that are not held by all.

Although Bruns is critical of Wikinews, it seems to chime with his normative suggestions in some respects, mainly in terms of its commitment to multi-perspectivalism. Wikinews proposes that 'texts that present multiple viewpoints fairly, without demanding that the reader accept any one of them, are liberating' (Wikinews, cited in Thorsen, 2008: 939).

Thorsen (2008: 950) finds that 'Wikinews articles were given an objective, formal and dispassionate tone by its contributors. That is, they encompassed a pragmatic representation of events and their actants, supposedly balanced according to their proportional representation within the given discursive sphere'. In this sense, 'it is not far from traditional interpretations and implementations of objectivity' (2008: 952). Thus in some respects Wikinews' adherence to the 'neutral point of view' leads it to fall back on something akin to objectivity, thus masking ideological presuppositions that may underpin decision-making. This route for these presuppositions, according to Thorsen (2008: 950), is set out by Wikinews 'asking contributors to use "common sense" in their application of policies and guidelines'. Consequently, the 'current implementation of the neutral point of view is clearly inconsistent and more likely to reflect the individual contributors' interpretation than a unified concept'.

An alternative to the 'neutral' multi-perspectivism pursued by Wikinews is the subjective journalism advocated by Indymedia or Independent Media Centres (IMCs). IMCs were developed in 1999 to counteract the inadequate and biased coverage corporate news had given to protest movements of various sorts – usually of the left. IMCs are generally used by activists to report on their actions, thus copy is subjectively produced from within rather than about movements and actions. In this sense, Indymedias have adopted a deep subjectivity, akin to much of the radical media projects of the 1960s (Atton, 2001; Downing, 2001).

The first IMC was established in 1999 for the purpose of providing grassroots coverage of the anti-World Trade Organisation protests in Seattle in 1999, acting 'as a clearinghouse of information for journalists' (IMC, 2003). Although the Seattle IMC focused on the internet, they made use of other media, with the former used as the central coordinating medium. To this end, satellite was used after the Seattle demonstration to distribute documentaries about the WTO and the protests throughout the US to public access television stations:

> The center also produced its own newspaper, distributed throughout Seattle and to other cities via the internet, as well as hundreds of audio segments, transmitted through the Web and Studio X, a 24-hour micro and internet radio station based in Seattle. The site, which uses a democratic open-publishing system, logged more than 2 million hits... Through a decentralized and autonomous network, hundreds of media activists setup [sic] independent media centers in London, Canada, Mexico City, Prague, Belgium, France, and Italy over the next year. IMCs have since been established on every continent, with more to come. (IMC, 2003)

IMCs clearly position themselves in relation to mainstream media, facilitating a form of autonomous communication network, which is not only independent of systemic ownership and control, but also of the 'logics and languages of the mainstream stenographers to power' (IMC, 2004: 14).

IMCs rapidly expanded beyond Seattle, now covering scores of sites from South Africa to Brazil and Palestine to Burma. At the same time as IMCs have internationalised, they have also localised. As such, within any national site there may be many local sites, such as Chiapas Indymedia or Leeds Indymedia, forming an international network. New IMCs can be proposed at any time to focus on a locale or an issue. As long as it is willing to subscribe to the IMC's Principles of Unity the new IMC will be integrated to the network, and participants will be able to use the IMC's software, servers and domain name (for example, la.indymedia.org or ecuador.indymedia.org).

Each new IMC has to adhere to the Principles of Unity of Indymedia, though each has autonomy in terms of the details of its local mission.

The Principles of Unity act as a type of editorial policy or overall mission that impacts on the sort of coverage IMCs promote. The IMC network should operate upon principles of 'equality, decentralization and local autonomy'. The IMCs must be not-for-profit and must not be 'derived from a bureaucratic process, but from the self-organisation of autonomous collectives'. To this end, they must develop non-hierarchical and anti-authoritarian relationships and must 'recognize the importance of process to social change, from interpersonal relationships to group dynamics… be committed to the principle of consensus decision making and the development of a direct, participatory democratic process that is transparent to its membership'. IMCs and participants should consider open exchange of and open access to information a prerequisite to the building of a more free and just society, and as such they should utilise 'open publishing', allowing 'individuals, groups and organisations to express their views, anonymously if desired'. Each IMC should be made up of people who are committed to caring for one another and their respective communities both collectively and as individuals. IMCs should promote the sharing of resources including knowledge, skills and equipment and should use free source code software to 'increase the independence of the network' – each IMC may use different software for servers, database operation and operating systems, or even use similar software to another, but customised to their needs. Finally, all IMCs should be committed to the principle of human equality, and should not discriminate on the basis of race, gender, age, class or sexual orientation (IMC, 2002).

The platform remains open, with reports being produced either by individual citizens or collaboratively, via an email list. There is no prior restraint on content, with material being removed only if it contravenes the local editorial policy. When material is removed, it is 'hidden' rather than deleted so that decisions remain transparent. In fact most decisions take place either on archived email lists, internet chat or physical meetings. As with Wikinews, although there is formal equality in IMCs, some individuals have more power (by virtue of knowledge, technical skill and so on) than others.

Crucially, because of its oppositional orientation the Indymedia network requires that contributors are able to participate anonymously – thus raising questions of transparency, trust and responsibility (see Jones and Royston, 2007).

On Thorsen's (and Bruns') analysis Wikinews frequently deals with 'controversy' by 'removing value-laden words and minimizing modal expressions. Words, sentences and paragraphs in dispute were either rewritten or removed' (Thorsen, 2008: 950). In contrast, IMCs see themselves as situated in a broader media landscape in which they add balance to the dominant 'corporate' worldview by taking an 'oppositional' stance (Salter, 2008, 2011). IMC UK, for instance, exists to report 'from the struggles for a world based on freedom, cooperation, justice and solidarity, and against environmental degradation, neoliberal exploitation, racism and patriarchy'. Its focus on grassroots politics, actions and campaigns is justified because they believe that:

> Inherent in the mainstream corporate media is a strong bias towards Capitalism's power structures, and it is an important tool in propagating these structures around the globe. While the mainstream media conceal their manifold biases and alignments, we clearly state our position. Indymedia UK does not attempt to take an objective and impartial standpoint: Indymedia UK clearly states its subjectivity. (IMC, 2010)

Thus Indymedia is best understood from the perspective of a broad discursive conception of truth in which it provides not objective or neutral information, but information that is not provided elsewhere. It does not feign to provide 'all the news that's fit to print', an authoritative news source, or a 'neutral point of view'. As a consequence, the type and range of coverage offered by IMCs fills a gap in online news.

Platon and Deuze suggest that authority at Indymedia is not derived, as in conventional news culture, through the use of experts and elite commentators, but rather from the collective. 'Truth is not seen as an absolute but an infinite sampling of perspectives of a given situation' (Platon and Deuze, 2003: 34). Indymedia participants claim this authority through reporting directly, thus neutralising the fear of the gatekeeper. Indeed, Jones and Royston's (2007) research into Indymedia clearly outlines the beliefs of Indymedia participants: 'The issue is, is truth free or does it cost?'; 'the mainstream media is being viewed as untrustworthy by ever larger numbers of people as awareness of its failings spread via the Web. My mother trusts my impression of a protest far more than the nightly news. Corporate media started dying the day the internet was invented' (Indymedia participants cited in Jones, 2008).

Perhaps the greatest problem for IMCs is that the anonymity they facilitate may mitigate against trust – as anybody can contribute, and as there are no editorial processes, on what basis can a reader trust what is written? As Kierkegaard feared of the nineteenth century press, so too Indymedia allows anybody who is nobody to set an error into circulation with no sense of responsibility. The solution may be, however, that to establish trust Indymedia participants have to provide stronger evidence (and links to it), on the basis of which trust can be established.

Whilst it is clear that IMCs differ from Wikinews in their adherence to subjective reporting, their value lies not in communicating the whole truth, but in supplying perspectives normally excluded from corporate news and even some 'alternative' projects, such as Wikinews. It is not that such projects have been able to access the truth more directly but that they move away from the claim of older forms of journalism to present an unencumbered window on the world, and towards recognition of their own partiality and subjectivity. The increase in the depth and scope of journalism in a digital world means that together the multitude of perspectives may enable audiences to have a better overall picture. The audience becomes much more active in the creation of news by participating in production and seeking out sources.

Watching the Watchers

As deeper participation in news production is made possible online, there seems to be a consensus that more traditional forms of journalism are still necessary. However, traditional journalism has, of course, not been left untouched.

Indeed much of the online journalism-related activity addresses in traditional journalism precisely the sorts of issues that traditional journalists have raised in respect of online journalism: truth and accuracy. Indeed, one of the main features of blogs has been to scrutinise the corporate media. Cooper (2006) referred to bloggers as a 'fifth estate' that watches over the watchdogs. In fact, citing many cases in which bloggers have exposed significant errors in corporate news output and caused the downfall of journalists as well as politicians, Cooper argues that bloggers as media critics matured into a social institution.

What we may witness here then, contrary to the arguments of so many journalists, is that bloggers in particular – whatever their political leanings – are trying to hold corporate media to account in a way that has never occurred before. On this account it is the journalists in corporate media organisations who are not trusted, and the internet that provides the opportunity for scrutinising them and holding them to account.

Whilst Allan (2006) has pointed to examples of essentially right-wing bloggers attacking what they perceive to be the 'liberal media', which he shows to be a 'bizarre' accusation, there has also been a flourishing of more sober media watchers offering coherent criticism of systematic ideological bias and exposure of factual errors.

Taking their prompt from the critical research of Edward Herman and particularly Noam Chomsky, MediaLens has utilised Herman and Chomsky's (1994) propaganda model to analyse corporate news coverage. As they put it, their function is to correct 'the distorted vision of the corporate media'. As such they employ a form of discourse analysis to evaluate the ideological underpinnings of what they perceive to be 'dominant establishment views' in news reporting. They elaborate:

In reality it is not possible for journalists to be neutral – regardless of whether we do or do not overtly give our personal opinion, that opinion is always reflected in the facts we choose to highlight or ignore. While we seek to correct corporate distortions as honestly as possible, our concern is not to affect some spurious 'objectivity' but to engage with the world to do whatever we can to reduce suffering and to resist the forces that seek to subordinate human well-being to profit. We do not believe that passively observing human misery without attempting to intervene constitutes 'neutrality'. We do not believe that 'neutrality' can ever be deemed more important than doing all in our power to help others. (Medialens, 2010)

To do this they analyse news reports largely in the UK's 'liberal media'– *The Guardian*, *The Independent* and on the BBC. As opposed to the right-wing bloggers, they do not attempt to expose a left-wing bias, but a system of propaganda, propagating the ideas of a corporate-capitalist system that serves a small elite.

Typically, Medialens analysts will analyse a news article to look at what information is included and excluded, who speaks, how they speak, and what emphases are given in the article. The analysis is published on the website, and distributed to an email list of subscribers. In criticising the report, the analysis will draw on information on the subject published around the web sometimes by other journalists, but more often drawing on information published online by international organisation such as the United Nations, World Trade Organisations, pressure groups such as Greenpeace and NGOs such as Amnesty International.

In accord with Bruns' exhortation to multi-perspectivalism, Medialens uses this additional information with the aim of providing an '"alternative" perspective' to that of the corporate media (Medialens, 2010). This alternative is produced not just by Medialens analysts but also by citizens encouraged to participate in analysis.

Often the analysis will be forwarded to the journalist for response, and the response will be published in full on the website. This method differs from those of right-wing bloggers, as Medialens claims to 'encourage the general population to challenge media managers, editors and journalists who set news agendas that traditionally reflect establishment/elite interests' (Medialens, 2010). As such they encourage polite engagement with journalists and editors, which must always be based on clear, reasonable evidence. They have engaged a number of top journalists including Donald Macintyre of *The Independent*, Jeremy Bowen, Mark Urban and many others from the BBC, Justin Webb writing in the *Daily Mail*, Martin Durkin of Channel 4, and many others. On occasion the engagement with journalists has been productive, though on other occasions the engagement seems to merely antagonise journalists, leading to dismissive responses. However, even then Medialens can certainly claim to have raised public consciousness of systemic problems in journalism.

Such projects have flourished on the internet. In the US, Fairness and Accuracy In Reporting (FAIR) has been analysing news coverage since 1986, initially distributing commentary via its magazine. Since it established a presence on the internet, the distribution of its analyses has expanded massively, with an email list numbering 50,000 people.

Sites such as prwatch.org, spinwatch.org and sourcewatch.org can help journalists and audiences read behind the news by finding out who various speakers, think tanks and pressure groups really are. They have established wiki sites, reports and databases that report on the origins of stories, the background of sources, and the backers of various industry front-groups. Most of these sites are open, and all encourage public participation in various forms. They also encourage industry insiders, and 'whistleblowers' to participate. Other online watchdogs include snopes.com, which began by seeking to debunk false 'urban legends', but has since moved to evaluate a broad variety of claims in the public sphere.

Factcheck.org is run by the Annenberg Public Police Centre in the US, and describes itself as:

> a nonpartisan, nonprofit 'consumer advocate' for voters that aims to reduce the level of deception and confusion in U.S. politics. We monitor the factual accuracy of what is said by major U.S. political players in the form of TV ads, debates, speeches, interviews and news releases. Our goal is to apply the best practices of both journalism and scholarship, and to increase public knowledge and understanding. (Factcheck.org, 2010)

Factcheck provides a wealth of information online including analytical and investigative articles, podcasts, graphs, databases and charts. It also offers information on the backgrounds, funding and orientation of various 'movements' and campaign groups.

It also offers the audience a degree of engagement by encouraging citizens to email questions. A more participatory factchecking project, TruthSquad, is run by NewsTrust.net, with the help of Factcheck.org. TruthSquad is a crowdsourcing project and describes itself as a 'community fact-checking experiment' in which editors provide questions for citizens to find information on. The information is then uploaded to the website and participants are expected to consider and revise conclusions in the light of new information.

NewsTrust itself works to do what traditional journalists might regard as their own function. It 'provides quality news feeds and review tools to help people make more informed decisions as citizens'. The site 'features a daily feed of news and opinions from mainstream and independent sources, based on ratings from our reviewers. Our web review tools enable people to rate stories for facts, fairness, context and other core journalistic principles — and become more discriminating news consumers in the process' (NewsTrust, 2010).

The Media Standards Trust (MST) in the UK is a more traditional form of organisation that believes 'high standards of news and information ... are being challenged by the enormous, revolutionary changes in the production, funding, packaging, delivery and consumption of news and information'. They highlight a number of changes that we have drawn attention to in Chapter 2, including 'more frequent inaccuracies in reporting', and 'escalation in the use of manufactured news', an 'increase in self-censorship', a 'growth of subjective over objective reporting' and a 'reduction in sustained, in-depth reporting on the ground, particularly investigative reporting' (Media Standards Trust, 2010).

Besides the more traditional advocacy functions the Trust undertakes is the innovative website, Journalisted.com. Journalisted.com collects information on journalists and lists the stories they write 'to make it easier for you, the public, to find out more about journalists and what they write about' (Journalisted.com, 2010). Journalisted is the Trust's project to increase transparency in journalism by making available a public database of journalists, their writing and biographical and contact details.

Another Media Standards Trust project worthy of note is Value Added News (VAN – valueaddednews.org) which the MST refers to as its 'Transparency Initiative'. VAN works with the key innovator of the web, Tim Berners-Lee to explore and develop 'ways to make online news more transparent, thereby helping the public in their search and assessment of news content on the web'. Interestingly, VAN applies some of the fundamentals of journalistic reporting – who, what, where, when – to actual news articles. To this end, besides basic identification, it provides audiences with information on who wrote an article, who published it, what source it comes from, what journalistic codes it adheres to, and when it was changed since publication (VAN, 2010).

Newssniffer.co.uk services this latter task in relation to BBC News Online, by automatically monitoring the various iterations of a particular story over its lifetime. The site lists links to stories, which can be clicked on to show the various versions. The site automatically highlights changed sections.

News-watch projects have placed sufficient pressure on corporate news organisations to self-monitor. For example, the BBC's NewsWatch facilitates complaints and criticism, though it all too much resembles a traditional complaints system mediated by the web. Its sister site, The Editors allows the audience to better understand the decisions of editors, by providing a blog through which editors justify decision-making at BBC News. Although these are fair attempts at institutional transparency, the emphasis of both sites is to give BBC journalists and editors a voice to explain and the public to merely complain.

The engagement of news organisations with readers' criticisms has expanded, so that newspapers and news websites as far afield as the US (*The New York Times*, *The*

Washington Post) and India (*The Hindu, Hindustan Times*) have employed readers' editors and ombudsmen.

In a strange sense, for all of its problems, the online environment has perhaps given a much greater rather than lesser sense of truth-seeking and transparency. As a result the online public sphere is as confusingly complex as reality itself.

Am I Worth It?

In Chapter 1 we argued that the question of whether 'blogs' are journalism or not is now a false one. However, scepticism remains about the veracity of them. Blogs have been praised by new media enthusiasts but have been much maligned by professional journalists – as we saw in Chapter 1 they are often seen as purveyors of rumour, falsehood and lies. This assertion rests on an assumption that blogs carry with them a lackadaisical attitude, amateurish culture and inadequate practical engagement.

However blogs are a medium – a mode of display, not content or process. Indeed, Alfred Hermida's (2009a) research into the use of blogs at the BBC confirms this. Hermida analysed the use of blogs at the BBC between 2001 and 2008, focusing on their employment in the institutional context of the BBC. He also considered how the BBC reflected upon its use within reports and blogs of those responsible for implementation, supplementing this information with interview data.

Hermida refers to the initial scepticism about blogs within the organisation. The initial impression was based on the common idea that 'with none of the traditional journalistic checks, [blogging] spawns errors, hoaxes and downright lies which can be right round the world before the truth has its boots on' (Douglas, cited in Hermida, 2009: 6). With the success of the blogs of political editor Nick Robinson and city editor Robert Peston, they could no longer be ignored, but despite these success stories, blogs were adopted only slowly at the BBC, due to a perceived incompatibility between the supposed culture of blogging and the institutional culture of the BBC (see Chapter 5).

However, rather than reject blogs out of hand, they have, as with all technological innovations been slowly adopted and adapted to fit with the values of the institution in which they are used. Indeed, once journalists, editors and executives realised blogs in no way necessarily imposed particular uses or practices, their adoption became inevitable. Indeed, Hermida's (2009a: 13) study found that 'correspondents do not view blogging as a significant departure from existing forms of journalism', and that 'senior correspondents have embraced the notion of the blog as a delivery system for journalistic elements that do not fit within established broadcast news' (Hermida, 2009a: 12). He goes on to report:

Instead blogging is seen as a platform for delivering content that complements broadcast output, albeit in a more personal and informal tone. In this sense, the difference between broadcast and blogging seems to be more about the style, rather than the substance, of reporting (Hermida, 2009a: 13)

For Hermida, the BBC case shows how:

news blogs can be seen as a new genre of journalism offered by the corporation, but it is one that has been largely defined by established professional parameters. The BBC experience suggests established news organisations may be taming the 'black market journalism' aspects of blogging (Wall, 2004) by subduing it within journalistic norms and practices. (Hermida, 2009a: 13)

Whilst the BBC is right to see blogging as an adaptable platform with few necessary properties, Hermida complains that the BBC's desire to integrate blogs into its institutional culture meant that it failed to utilise the potential of the blog as an interactive platform. As he puts it, 'if it is considered as a process that involves both the author and the audience in an exchange of ideas, then BBC News blogs fall short' (Hermida, 2009a: 13). We will investigate more of the difficulties the BBC faced with blogs in the following chapter.

Einar Thorsen (2009) has shown how other attempts by the BBC to engage the audience have also fallen short of what may be understood as necessary qualities of online journalism. His research on the development, use and moderation of BBC message boards, the 'Have Your Say' sections, has shown how the same institutional logic has restricted their use (see Chapter 5).

Limiting Perspectives

Much as critics of corporate media are right to point to the pernicious effects of commodifiction on journalism and news, as noted in Chapter 2 resources and means of sustenance are necessary to enable journalists to do their work. Furthermore, unpaid journalism – perhaps the defining feature of Pro-Am journalism – can actually restrict participation. Although there is a strong middle-class bias in journalism staffing in corporate media organisations, the fact that it provides paid employment, a job, means that persons from less well-off backgrounds have the potential to sustain themselves through journalism.

In contrast, although some may claim Pro-Am or amateur journalism may allow persons to avoid the problems of political economy and organisational structure that may distort truth, those with greater personal material wealth are better able to take part in unpaid journalism; running a blog or a news website is a time-consuming business. Poorer persons have by circumstance less time and money to participate in online journalism, regardless of how insightful they may be.

Thus we return to the contours of market power (rather than truth) as a determiner of what gets published – those blogs that appeal to a more consumer-orientated audience with purchasing power (and inclination) will be more likely to succeed.

For example, one of the most popular blogs in the world (the 426th most visited website in the US) is the Drudge Report. Its right-wing populist and far-right content and emphasis has meant that it has established a sizable audience. *The Daily Telegraph* (2008), which referred to Drudge as 'the most powerful journalist in the world' estimated that the site attracted 600 million hits per month at its height. Alexia.com reports that the demographic of Drudge's audience shows it is particularly popular in traditionally conservative areas, such as Denver, Phoenix and Atlanta. Alexia.com also reports that its users are 'disproportionately Caucasian, and they tend to be higher-income, moderately educated men over the age of 35 (especially upwards of 65 years) who have more children' than average' (Alexia.com 2010).

The audience of the Drudge Report seems to be drawn from a section of society with significant disposable income. The site is funded almost entirely by advertising revenue. To get a sense of how much advertising money such a large group of reasonably wealthy readers can draw, CNN Money (2003) estimated that even in its early days the site drew in excess of $800,000 per year, which was, per worker, ten times what *The New York Times* website drew. Drudge was also able to secure lucrative television and radio deals, not least due to his political leanings.

Some commentators have criticised citizen journalism more generally from the viewpoint of resourcing. An editorial in *The Digital Journalist* (2009) notes:

> You will not see many citizen journalists wandering around the battlefields of Afghanistan. It takes a lot of money to pay for travel, the gear, the armor vests, translators and so on. Why should a military unit 'embed' a so-called citizen journalist? Because you think it is a cool idea? Wrong. Every unit takes on a professional photo journalist with some degree of skepticism. Because a false move by someone not schooled in warfare endangers the lives of every man and woman in the unit, the military evaluates that person. That is why the journalists who do this have bona fides from legitimate agencies. Who will the citizen journalist get to accredit him or her?

The questions of recognition also arise here. However, the writer seems to be missing a central point about citizen journalism. As Allan (2006) makes clear in News Online, citizen journalism is not about a professional journalist residing in the UK travelling to embed with a military unit. Indeed for critics like Allan, the embedding process is precisely the problem, as it embeds outsiders into a particular military view of a conflict. Rather Allan suggests that citizen journalism allows ordinary citizens on the ground (in this case Afghanis and perhaps aid workers and the like) to report what they see, from their perspective. Nevertheless, we can see an elementary question of political economy here – which Afghanis or Iraqis have sufficient electricity, access to computers, access to the internet, literacy, technical know how and so on? Again we see a division reflected in online journalism.

Thus as trends develop issues of trust and transparency change their complexion and it becomes increasingly difficult for traditional news organisations to navigate the complexities of top down, authorial journalism with the need to encourage participation on many levels. The BBC provides an interesting case in point, as the next chapter elucidates.

Endnote

1   Corporate media refers to media organisations that are legally incorporated to form a legal body. This concept refers to both commercial and state media organisations.

Public Service News

Passing the Public Value Test in a Digital World

The first decade of the twenty-first century wrought havoc with the systems that supported and nurtured the journalism industry, challenging many of the sacred cows that underpinned the modern practice of reporting news. Old ways of working, supported by a long history of liminal analogue broadcasting frequencies together with a secure cost base for printed news, became increasingly obsolete while new supply models remained nascent and untested.

The worst global economic contraction since the Great Depression alongside the rapid growth in the number of news outlets quickly reduced the scope for the news industry's typical high yielding returns and left the private sector scrambling for new ways to monetise content as investors took flight. As we have seen, these events served to undermine the business models that had underpinned news gathering and dissemination for two centuries as print weeklies and dailies, national and local, struggled to retain both readers and advertising.

Within the realm of broadcast, as analogue switch-off across Europe gave way to digital supply, public service broadcasters and their flagship news and current affairs services were caught in the eye of the same digital storm. News services that the public paid for through taxes or licences were exposed to 'credit crunch' politics, and this, combined with a new era of austerity, created a cocktail of instability. It was perhaps counter intuitive to regard organisations such as the BBC as vulnerable given that its powerful global branding and reputation as a trusted news source made it one of the few safe ports in an unpredictable squall; but, a newly elected Coalition Government less sympathetic to unrestrained BBC growth and more receptive to the lobbying forces of private industry put the Corporation on the back foot. The effect of a sharp drop in advertising revenues across the whole media sector, whether cyclical or systemic, gave commercial news operators a chance to cry foul as hostilities between the private and public sector (never far from the surface even in good times) intensified. This meant that as the second decade of the twenty-first century began, Britain's main public service broadcaster, the BBC, with its guaranteed income of £3,600 million a year, became a visible target for its privately funded competitors and right-wing communications regulators.

Hence, more than ever since its foundation in 1926, this publically subsidised organisation needed to prove that it continued to pass the critical public value test that underpinned its generous funding.

Cultural Variations in Publicly Funded News

Commonly described as the fourth estate, the place of journalism within a market economy has often been the subject of debate. The fundamental reason for the existence of public service broadcasters (PSBs) in a European context had been to serve the public by broadcasting news that informs their role as citizens within a democracy. This is based on the assumption that the market would fail to do this as 'serious' news has always been an unreliable profit-making genre.

The public service-driven European system, led by the UK's massive injection of public funds into broadcasting over the last 90 years, contrasted starkly with the US model which had mostly rejected the idea of public service journalism for fear that it would break the first amendment commitment to freedom of speech. The provenance of publicly funded news over commercially funded news is culturally specific and highly dependent on the nation of origin with many democratic societies running a dual economy of state and privately supported output. The debate on where functions that serve the public interest, such as journalism, properly belong in democratic societies, has deep historical roots. The democratic position, perhaps best represented by Mahatma Ghandi, advocated a total separation of enterprise from news reporting:

> It is wrong to use newspaper as a means of earning a living. There are certain spheres of work which are of such consequence and have such bearing on welfare that to undertake them for earning one's livelihood will defeat the primary aim behind them. When a newspaper is treated as a means of making profits, the result is likely to be serious malpractices. (Ghandi, circa 1910)

This animosity Ghandi describes between content creation and revenue production in the news business was reignited through the recessionary dip, as many commercial news enterprises failed to flourish and governments refused to maintain levels of public expenditure in news.

On either side of the Atlantic there were culturally specific reactions to the perceived 'crisis' in journalism's ability to sustain itself. In Europe, there was regulatory and commercial pressure to reign-in the power of the public news providers while in the US, arguments were being made to increase the government's role in financing public journalism.

The US system had always promoted the free market as the best home for journalism to thrive; yet, the great global recession in 2007 acted as a catalyst to revisit the role of the state in news production. Tod Gitlin, a well respected voice in US academic circles, chose 2009 to announce that proposals to shore up newspapers in the US rested on interventionist public policy, the first time in Gitlin's life that this became a discussible subject given that the US was 'allergic' to government interference in this sector. Gitlin signposted that 'a fundamental sea change' was under way and that journalism as a public good required the state to intervene. Strikingly, he concluded that, 'the PSB approach is likely to be more resilient than the US market-based model' (Gitlin, 2009).

Statistical evidence available in 2008–10 suggested that although many of the news industry's woes were attributable to the economic downturn, long-term structural problems associated with the digital economy also had a part to play (see Chapter 3). Where markets fail, governments may choose to intervene and as Hallin observed in the US:

> ...with the economic model that once sustained the public service role of the media clearly in question, as newspapers and broadcasters cut their news staffs, who knows? Perhaps it is possible to imagine that there would be calls eventually for greater state involvement. (Hallin, 2009: 334)

Significantly, in Europe, a weakening private news sector solicited the opposite regulatory response – that of de-regulation. Yet, the US situation was potentially far graver given the rate of newspaper insolvencies without the compensatory effect of a public service broadcaster. In 2009, the UK invested 60 times more per capita into its public news operations than America, and Finland and Denmark 75 times more (Nichols and McChesney, 2009). Thus, highly dependent on the market, and with news gathering and reporting operations not attracting sufficient returns on investment, financial underpinning for this activity in the US was severely compromised. Many solutions were tried to fill the funding gap: micropayments, where the reader pays pennies per story; philanthropists and foundations who make the decision to underwrite investigative journalism; citizen donations and crowdfunding; creative use of the taxation systems; and volunteer labour all played their part but none seemed able to provide long term solutions to the democratic deficit resulting from the loss of the traditional news print industries.

All this ensured that, in 2009, the role of the US government in supporting the press was seriously debated within its political establishment. Dubbed, 'The Uncle Sam Solution' by *Columbia Journalism Review* writer, Bree Nordenson (Nordenson, 2007), proposers of state-funded journalism argued that only government can implement policies and subsidies large enough to provide a local and national framework for quality journalism to thrive.

In a market driven media economy such as the US this was the equivalent of heresy as government intervention was equated with government control. With many Americans largely unsympathetic to state funded European models of broadcasting, there was deep suspicion that news might no longer be adequately insulated from state intervention. Nichols and McChesney attempted to counter this fear in an article 'The death and life of great American newspapers', arguing that government policies and subsidies already defined the US press system, arguing that historically the strength of the American free press in the 1830s was due to 'massive newspaper subsidies through printing contracts and the paid publication of government notices, all with the intent of expanding the number and variety of news papers.' They advocated the introduction of a tax credit system for regular subscribers to local and national dailies on the basis that journalism is a public good that has broad social benefits (Nichols and McChesney, 2009).

Although the authors made a compelling argument, in some respects it was based on the assumption that 'press is best', conflating the future of journalism with the future of any one journalistic medium. This view was predicated on the assumption that online news models could never sustain themselves as they needed to operate parasitically on press organs producing original, 'quality' work. The idea that the death of newspapers is synonymous with the death of journalism is discussed more fully in Chapters 1, 2, 3 and 6.

The British Case 2010

Tensions between the BBC and commercial news operators come into sharp relief over the battleground of the internet in 2010. Licence fee money supported the UK's largest online news content site – news.bbc.co.uk – and there was evidence that the regulators were softening to the lobbying forces of private business. In 2009 Lord Carter concluded in the Digital Britain Report that, 'Free is very difficult for any paid-for business models to compete with' (Carter, 2009: 140). Yet, the report did not depart too radically from its predecessors, arguing that a weakening of the commercial environment still made:

a strong, confident and independent BBC more vital than ever. The market intervention which sustains the BBC is and should remain the most significant intervention for public service content. (2009: 18)

Embedded in the report's narrative was the critical importance of plurality and 'content partners' in an age where the money supply was dwindling. The report focused on the implications of the potential demise of commercial-sector ITV regional news coverage and the need to ensure continued plurality of provision, 'central to democracy and the holding of public institutions to account' (2009: 19).

The Digital Economy Bill (2010) building on Lord Carter's 2009 report was the principal source of political disagreement between the British mainstream left- and right-wing parties. It sought to increase the regulatory power of Ofcom and in keeping with traditional ideological divides, the newly appointed Conservative Minister, Jeremy Hunt, described any increase in regulatory power as 'the biggest possible deterrent to private sector investment in innovation in the online space. The possibility of a British Google is killed stone dead'(Hunt, 2010).

Hunt's preference was to relax regulation and allow private enterprise to 'flourish'. The Conservatives believed that the market alone could support plurality ensuring that everyone had access to the kind of regional news and financial information they needed and deserved. (Chapter 6 discusses the means in which Hunt planned to achieve this.) The political uncertainty was compounded by the intervention of one of the UK's biggest commercial news operators James Murdoch, Chief Executive of Sky Broadcasting in the UK, led the commercial sector in a direct attack on the BBC targeting its online service, the most popular online news source in the UK with over 13 million unique online users each week.

Dumping free state sponsored news on the market makes it incredibly difficult for journalism to flourish on the internet yet it is essential that a fair price can be charged for news to people who value it. We seem to have decided as a society to let independence and plurality wither to let the BBC throttle the news market and then to get bigger to compensate. (J. Murdoch, 2009)

It is worth noting that Murdoch's assumptions about the link between independence, plurality, quality and the private sector is problematic to say the least – it is widely known that NewsCorp's news outlets are invariably right-wing (every single one of Murdoch senior's newspapers around the world supported the invasion of Iraq in 2003, for instance, and NewsCorp's lead 'brands' consist of Fox News, *The Sun* newspaper and the *New York Post* which are usually regarded as some of the most guttural right-wing news outlets available in their respective countries).

Indeed, many commentators have accused Murdoch as leading a 'race to the bottom' in terms of journalistic standards.

This attack from the Corporation's arch enemy came at a time when the international Murdoch media empire was erecting paywalls around its online content and other commercial operators were watching this move very carefully. Murdoch hoped that it would just be a matter of time before the majority of news consumers would be paying for online journalism content which, until 2010, they had been accustomed to getting for free (see Chapter 3).

Murdoch's attack wasn't limited to the typical agitating about unfair competition as the public sector encroached too far on commercial territory; it was equally focused on a neo-liberal platform attacking the very legitimacy of public funded news in a democratic state in favour of 'consumer sovereignty' (see also Chapter 7).

> The greatest divergence between the rest of the media and broadcasting is the unspoken approach to the customer. In the regulated world of PSB, the customer does not exist; he or she is a passive creature – a viewer – in need of protection. In other parts of the media world – including pay television and newspapers – the customer is just that; someone whose very freedom to choose makes them important. And because they have power they are treated with great seriousness and respect, as people who are perfectly capable of making informed judgements about what to buy, read, and go and see. (J. Murdoch, 2009)

This impassioned plea for the supremacy of the market in news production, and for the reduction or elimination of government or regulatory control in media affairs, were central to the Murdoch family's campaign anticipating that a new right-wing government might be willing to see the licence fee as an anachronism from a bygone era of analogue scarcity.

Not all newspaper publishers supported the view that the BBC needed to be drastically reduced in size. Alan Rusbridger, Editor of *The Guardian* in 2010, looked across the Atlantic to the US where the newspaper industry was in deep trouble despite having no public service broadcaster to compete with:

> You could do an awful lot of damage to the BBC and still find you had not solved the problem of newspapers ... as a citizen rather than a competitor, I'm afraid to admit that I really like, admire and respect the BBC – including even its website. (Rusbridger, 2010)

This admission came despite a potential loss in revenue for *The Guardian*'s own website (the tenth biggest in Britain and the second most-read English-language newspaper in the world) from such a powerful free-to-market competitor.

Proving its Value

Up until 2010, the BBC had always been the only direct beneficiary of the UK licence fee. Yet, the political fallout from a change in government in 2010 put the BBC on the defensive, needing to ensure that it continued to pass the all-important 'public value test'. The broadcasters' activities were closely scrutinised in response to the powerful lobbying force of commercial operators criticising the way public money was being used to cross subsidise incursions into alleged commercial territory.

The BBC had already refuted suggestions made in Carter's Digital Britain Report (2009) that it should necessarily scale back its involvement in areas such as providing free news on the internet and argued against the proposal that the licence fee should be top-sliced and money given to its PSB competitors saying this wouldn't be good for 'high quality public service content.' This would, 'weaken the BBC, threaten its independence and reduce accountability to licence fee payers' asserted the BBC Trust's Chairman, Sir Michael Lyons (Lyons, 2009).

The Trust was rightly nervous of impending threats and needed to argue that everything the BBC did was relevant in the new media economy. Its opponents believed it had become 'too big for its own good' growing massively over the previous 20 years from being the provider of two TV channels, four national radio stations and a local radio network to a 'media giant with a world-leading online presence and a commercial publishing arm' (Bradshaw, 2009). The previous year it had stopped the implementation of a BBC hyper-local news network citing the negative impact on the commercial sector outweighing the potential public value created by its introduction. It had also been at the forefront of a national de-investment in broadcast news and current affairs across the BBC, ITV and Channels 4 and 5 amounting to a 13.5 % reduction in four years (Ofcom, 2009).

To help shore up the importance of public service journalism, a case had to be made that moving away from PSB and into a commercially-led environment would lead to a less informed citizenry, and thus a democratic deficit. This wasn't always easy to establish as many important news stories tended to be available first through non-BBC sources:

> When a story takes off on the internet, as they have many times in respect of the credit crunch over the past couple of years, it's a massive worldwide explosion. But it's not just business or economic stories. Think about how TMZ's disclosure of the death of Michael Jackson went from internet scoop to global TV news within minutes. (Peston, 2009)

It was the Corporation's policy to trade accuracy for speed, and as a consequence, people were almost guaranteed to get their primary exposure to a breaking story from a competing source. This became even more problematic as mobile news applications grew in popularity (see Chapter 8).

Indeed the BBC is quite able to break some of the biggest stories, not just in its news services, but also in its current affairs documentary programmes, which then become the basis of news reports worldwide. For example it is unlikely that any commercial service would risk the ire of FIFA by exposing alleged corruption among members of the World Cup bid selection team, as the BBC did in November 2010. Similarly with the BBC's breaking of the seminal Northern Rock story – BBC Business Editor, Robert Peston became a household name in 2007 when he broke the story of Northern Rock's insolvency problems on his BBC blog, resulting in the first run on a British Bank in almost a century. He argued in his keynote address to the Edinburgh Festival (2009) that his detailed investigative research into the very non-sexy area of news could have only been properly supported through PSB and that only the BBC, a trusted public sector news provider, could inform and educate the public on a grand scale so that, 'there is democratic participation in big decisions about the future of capitalism' (Peston, 2009).

Peston believed that news about a bank's spreadsheet woes at the height of the financial boom was a fundamentally important issue and history has since endorsed this view; however, it was not high-up on the agenda of most newsrooms. He warned that information on GDP, banking liabilities and economic regulation risked being relegated to the 'back pages' in a totally commercialised news environment (Peston, 2009).

Demographic changes and audience migration and fragmentation were also major concerns for the BBC. Surveys revealed that news-seeking migration from TV to the internet sped up considerably around the time of the international economic collapse – 84% still turned to TV first, but 53% used the internet and 52% newspapers. For younger news consumers, this was even more skewed in favour of the web at 61%.

The general shift from TV viewership to web news-seeking created a situation where younger citizens, in particular, were not habituated into consuming news (Patterson, 2007). This led to much soul searching by the BBC as its traditional news and current affairs audiences were getting older and a new generation of licence fee payers were failing to engage with its content. It was essential for the BBC to reverse this trend and they saw the internet and mobile news as the central battleground. 'If the news is important, it will find me', became an important mantra and the Corporation lost little time attempting to exploit the new opportunities that came from mobile applications. It recognised that, for the younger iPad generation, the place to reach its audience was on the move. 12 years after the launch of BBC Online, the BBC was primed to launch a range of new smartphone news applications in 2010, despite howls of protest from its commercial competitors.

'We are putting technology to work to create greater public value' the BBC's Director of Future Media and Technology declared: 'It will give users flexibility in how they personalise their news experience' (Ponsford, 2010). The mobile application launch was halted one week before its unveiling as a nervous BBC Trust decided that the climate was too politically sensitive to introduce yet another 'free-to-air' product to compete with commercial rivals.

Top Down to Bottom-up

To help justify its public relevance, the Corporation recognised the importance of being seen to engage with the public so it continued to invest its energies into evolving a more interactive and participatory digital news culture.

This was helped enormously by the BBC's early strategic web development through the 1990s. It was either serendipity or long-sightedness that drove then Director General, John Birt to channel resources into an untried an untested 'new media' (see Jones and Royston, 2007: 190). This left it in a very strong position to drive digital participation and gave the BBC an edge over its competitors in engaging online users.

Examining the function of journalism within a democratic nation state, theoreticians have isolated a number of operational modes of delivery. As we covered in this book's introduction, journalists, under what has been described as 'the elite model', are charged with facilitating or organising participation of the public in the political process from the top, whereas the alternative 'deliberative model' is more closely identified with the Habermasian notion of the public sphere where the press works with the public to accomplish the same goal.

The crisis dialogue that permeated journalism at the end of the noughties tended to presume that the elite model was the one that deserved to be saved and nurtured because this dominant social and political frame reinforced mainstream journalists' own conceptions of their work and also sustained the economic model within which they were used to working (see Benson, 2009). Yet, networked digital news had the potential to change the patterns of communication flow upsetting the balance between the elitist and pluralist models and allowing for a more pluralistic, bottom-up dynamic creating the possibility of a revitalised critical public culture. The problem was that these new voices needed to be loud enough and credible enough to catch the attention of the institutional gatekeepers, as we will examine in greater depth in Chapter 6.

Sustaining citizenship and civil society was cited as the first and most important criteria in the Department of Culture, Media and Sport's review of the BBC's Charter in 2005 (DCMS, 2005: 5). The suggestion was that the Corporation's survival might well depend on its success in engaging diverse publics, bringing them together through the latent power of new media and providing the legitimacy it needed to continue its present funding regime past its 2016 charter review. The vision was of a newly revitalised BBC central to hosting an online 'civic commons' that would inspire and facilitate public participation in government.

The 2006 BBC Creative Future document (BBC, 2006) celebrated, 'a new editorial blueprint designed to deliver more value to audiences'. It was what Peter Horrocks (then head of BBC Television News) described as an 'anti-elitist revolution' leaving behind an age when broadcasters told the public what to think and embracing the chance to host citizen's debate (Horrocks, 2006). Shortly afterward the BBC announced in November 2008 that it was reorganising BBC News to put the web and user generated content, 'close to the middle of the operation' (Horrocks, 2008). This was hailed as part of a cultural, structural and physical transformation that would put the audience at the centre of BBC activity. This internet-led 'self-styled' reinvention was intended to fundamentally change the way the BBC interacted with its digital news audiences.

The problem was that in the world of conventional news there exists a core consensus on who has the right to speak. But within the new digital environment, this privileged stance came under attack. The rise of bloggers and user-generated content rendered it difficult to define who counts as a reporter entitled to invoke this right (see also Chapters 4 and 6).

The BBC's News Quandary

> Journalism matters not simply because it is a manifestation of dissent but because it is an expression of plurality. Open societies not only tolerate alternative views; they understand that different poles of opinion are the lifeblood of a healthy democracy based on representative government. (Barber, 2009)

The voice of the listener and viewer were deemed largely irrelevant in the first few decades of the BBC's dominance of the airwaves. Studies of audience participation in BBC programmes concluded that it only allowed for what McNair (1999) described as 'access by proxy', a form that ensured the programme makers were largely free of any obligation to confront the public on its own terms. Holding its audience at bay in this way was seen as a means of protect its brand as an impartial supplier of news.

Since the 1920s, UK media regulators have charged broadcast news with upholding impartiality at all costs, whereas the press maintained its right to partiality and newspapers in the UK were renowned for their transparently political leanings.

When benchmarked across the globe, these regulatory distinctions contrast widely with other European and North American norms and might be interpreted as a cultural hangover from the 1920s launch of BBC Radio in a state-centred, restricted analogue environment with little relevance to 21st century realities.

In a converged environment where the traditional distinctions between television, radio, print and online journalists have all but evaporated, PSB and its regulatory masters had to be prepared to redraw the lines that previously, conveniently, separated the two.

This critical point didn't go unnoticed by James Murdoch in his 2009 Edinburgh Festival address:

> … the system is concerned with imposing what it calls impartiality in broadcast news. It should be hardly necessary to point out that the mere selection of stories and their place in the running order is in itself a process of unacknowledged partiality. The effect of the system is not to curb bias – bias is present in all news media – but simply to disguise it. (J. Murdoch, 2009)

The fact that selectiveness is tantamount to partiality and that news and truth are not necessarily the same thing is not a new idea within the rubric of journalism studies. News is inherently selective, dependent on editors' as well as readers' tastes. The problem was that the rise of the internet ensured that this notion was exposed to intense public scrutiny.

The comments actively solicited by the BBC under the umbrella of 'public participation journalism' had the potential to introduce fresh voices into the national discourse. Yet, BBC journalism is hidebound by its cultural heritage and operating practices and its ability to adhere to a firmly established set of editorial standards, and it was forced to carefully reconsider the case for and against impartiality within its service.

The values of egalitarianism and subjectivity compete with control, filtering and impartiality. Incorporating citizen voices within a regulated commitment to impartiality proved a tremendous challenge, as we illustrated in the previous chapter. Horrocks (2008) acknowledged this in a public speech. He described how the BBC was caught in a quandary where it remained afraid to gatekeep, but just as nervous about what might happen if the gates were allowed to open. On the one hand he endorsed the notion of radical impartiality, where the BBC is allowed to host variant voices:

> I have argued previously that the traditional model – safe, middle of the road, balancing neutrality – is now outdated and that we need to embrace the idea of 'radical impartiality', that is of a much broader range of views than before. (Horrocks, 2008)

Yet, it proved a very difficult task to make the BBC content meaningfully dialogical. The risk was too great. Forays into this form of output simply risked becoming another form of public display, 'an extension of the presentational mode of communication, as in ... a television, newsletter or an advertisement' (Jackson, 1997).

Often such dilemmas, i.e. incorporating citizen voices within a regulated commitment to impartiality, prove transformational for organisations. The question was, Would this be the case for the BBC? In its Creative Futures Report (BBC, 2006) the BBC acknowledged the need to forge innovative relationships between producers, texts and audiences that take advantage of new technology to realise its stated 'public value' goals – that of building a new civic commons and an active and informed citizenship. The report identified opportunities and challenges created by the disruptive wave of digital technologies and talked of 'seismic shifts in public expectations, lifestyle and behaviours'. It stressed that unidirectional, linear discourses were not interesting for younger citizens (those that the BBC must attract to survive). The assumption was that those under 35 would prefer to interact, to change and add content or ideas and the rise of blogging in the first decade of the 21st century was seen as testament to this.

The Prod-user

Picone prefers to use the word prod-user (producer-user) to describe the activities that define interactive journalism activity. As the production of news becomes part of the consumption of news, the user's role is reconceptualised. 'He does not merely consume news, but also shares it, rates it, searches it and produces it' (Picone, 2007: 104). This has the potential to upset the power base and editorial decision procedures of any traditionally run news organisation. The BBC needed to decide to what extent audience participation should be exploited, how it should be exploited, and what commitment there might be to integrating audiences into the production process – into the very formation of news.

Initial experiments with the adoption of user instigated material created problems for the BBC as illustrated vividly in a speech by its then head of Multi Media News entitled, 'The value of citizen journalism' (Horrocks, 2008). He described what happened when the public's voice is harnessed within a traditional news culture that necessarily militates against equality of voices being heard. Horrocks discussed BBC forays into what he called 'participatory journalism', whereby users contribute images, thoughts, stories and opinions through its website.[1] Underpinning his speech was a profound ambivalence towards participatory journalism. His remonstrations suggested that the Corporation remained uncomfortable fully embracing audiences as producers of news:

> I want to argue that the somewhat messianic and starry-eyed way in which public participation journalism is argued for needs some very careful consideration.... We cannot

just take the views that we receive via emails and texts and let them dictate our agenda. Nor should they give us a slant around which we should orient our take on a story.

Horrocks gave many excellent reasons for this discomfort including issues of quality, impartiality, cyber-bullying, lobbying and professionalism. He relayed a powerful dilemma his news team faced just after the Pakistani Parliamentary Candidate, Benazir Bhutto was assassinated in January 2008. The newsroom quickly launched a, 'Have Your Say' forum which is a facility for users to post and recommend comments. They were deluged by reactionary, racist posts condemning the Islamic religion. As a consequence a nervous BBC considered turning off the comment recommendation facility on the BBC News website. Horrocks said:

> It was only a fleeting suggestion, but that we could consider, however briefly, freezing this important part of BBC News' service tells you something about the power and the potential danger of the new intensity of the interaction between the contributing public, journalists and audiences. And it raises the question of how much attention and resources news organisations should devote to this rapidly burgeoning aspect of our journalism. The vehemence and the unanimity of these opinions against the Muslim religion were striking. So why did we briefly consider freezing this forum? A small part of our thinking was that in the context of the death of a significant international figure, who was herself Muslim, we thought that the weight of remarks could be offensive to some users of the BBC News website. Might some readers believe that such views as 'most recommended' represented an editorial line by BBC News? I suspect not, but there was at least that danger. But our real question concerned the editorial value of the comments and how far they should influence our coverage more widely. And the answers to that were: very little and hardly at all.

This shows the tensions between a genuine desire to make use of contributions from the public and host a civic debate and the need to control that debate. The racist messages were not palatable for a state broadcaster to relay and yet it could not cut off the flow of feedback without being accused of censorship. The BBC had charged itself with growing and nurturing the community it serves, but, Horrocks voices his discomfort in opening the gates too widely, allowing disparate voices to be heard. Instead, the normative functions of the BBC newsroom struggle to re-assert themselves against this unwelcome tide of 'bilious vitriol' from its public. Yet, once the dissolution of boundaries is underway and once expectations are created that the public has a voice, it may be difficult to quiet. Despite this, user-generated content at BBC News has grown significantly over a relatively short time, raising expectations within the BBC's news audiences that a serious paradigm shift is underway that might genuinely dissolve boundaries between those that make the news and those that consume it.

Techno-optimism

Hierarchical routines with top-down, one-way communications are difficult habits to break. The tension created between the need to adopt new ways of dealing with its public and its need to maintain impartiality had to be worked out on the coalface of programme making at the BBC.

When Kevin Marsh took over as Editor of the BBC's flagship Radio 4 News and current affairs programme, Today in 2002, two things struck him. First he noticed that 50,000 a year 'well-argued' emails arrived in his email box with no promise of publication in any form. Secondly, what he called the 'accidental' popularity of the message board on the Today website. There were 18,000 original threads developed between 2001 and 2006 with some containing up to 3,000 posts.

The challenge, as he saw it, was to use these voices to enrich the public discourse without jeopardising or compromising his programme. In response to this largely unsolicited groundswell of public comment, Marsh sought to experiment with this new public force. He calculated ways in which he could open the programme to its citizen audience. These included guest editors, listener's reports, listener-led interviews and mining emails and the message board for agendas and expertise (Marsh, 2010).

Marsh worked with his team to devise and hone highly specialised filtering devices to ensure the proprietary of the programme was not compromised. His most prized experimental outcome was 'the listeners law' where he tested how far he could go by linking citizens with legislators through the medium of journalism. Listeners wrote in to suggest a new law they would like to place on the UK statute books. One was finally selected – to reinforce home owners' rights to defend their properties – but, it eventually fell foul of parliamentary procedure. Marsh concluded that:

> ...it's difficult to see how the process could be scaled up without it either collapsing under its own weight or its outputs becoming reduced to a few simple denuanced 'knee-jerk' concepts around which sharp arguments could be assembled (Marsh, 2009: 113)

At the end of the day, only a very small handful of citizens were truly engaged in these experiments, although it kept listeners riveted and made for a popular talking point within the national press. One producer commented, 'if this is a talking cure for the problems of democracy I doubt it will work: you can't re-engage people two dozen at a time' (Billington, 2010: 114).

Even though the BBC website received thousands of user comments, these contributions often come from just 0.05% of the site's daily unique audience. Despite the obvious tokenism of such efforts, Marsh concluded that if the Today Programme hadn't at least tried, then the millions of voices crying out for attention on the web will be, 'little more then background radiation of our civic universe' (Marsh, 2010: 114).

Indeed, there may be larger benefits to entering into even a superficial dialogue with audiences. In discussions with industry players, Hermida and Thurman noted that for some editors, the number of people who contribute doesn't necessarily matter, as a small number can make a UGC (user generated content) format 'worthwhile' (2007).

How far down the path of 'bottom-up' democratic production the BBC is willing or able to go is dependent on public trust which up until recently has been built top-down through authority and credibility and disseminated through a strong corporate ethos of impartiality. But, trust and audiences are both diminishing (Horrocks, 2006) and it remains to be seen whether trust might be enhanced through these experiments in digital crowdsourcing.

The BBC's Belated Blogging Revolution

Blogs have been described as, 'evidence of journalism's attempts to rethink its values and relations with its publics' (Matheson, 2004: 462). There were well over 100 million bloggers in 2008 gradually infiltrating the mainstream press' operational domain having been successfully co-opted from the alternative sphere.

When the BBC first tentatively entered the blogging market, it used blogs to paint a picture of life behind the scenes of the newsroom – a privileged glimpse and what was previously forbidden was suddenly encouraged. The Editor's blog became one of the most popular sites.[2] Its stated aim was to explain the editorial decisions and dilemmas faced by the teams running the BBC's news service and a different tone of communication was encouraged, more informal, honest and personal seen as part of the post-Hutton climate of restoring faith in the BBC's journalism. This was described by then Controller of BBC2, Roly Keating, as, 'proactive candour, with senior figures admitting to varying degrees of error or cock-up, usually before the outside world has even noticed' (Keating, 2010: 313).

In theory the BBC was well placed to develop an expansive blogging culture providing an open link to all communities of people with no commercial interest or paywalls to hold it back while free to maximise the potential value of the internet's immediacy and hyper-textual qualities, in what *The Guardian* Editor Alan Rusbridger called a collaborative-as-well-as-competitive approach which usually gets to the truth of things faster:

> Journalists have never before been able to tell stories so effectively, bouncing off each other, linking to each other (as the most generous and open minded do), linking out,

citing sources, allowing response – harnessing the best qualities of text, print, date, sound and visual media. If ever there was a route to building audience trust and relevance, it is by embracing all the capabilities of this new world, not walling yourself away from them. (Rusbridger, 2010)

Embracing and linking openly to users and fellow journalists is risky. Journalism as practice needs to change root and branch as discussed in Chapters 1 and 6. Kevin Marsh, having moved to run the BBC's College of Journalism seemed to take this to heart when he announced in 2010 that the use of blogs by BBC journalists was the 'biggest change to journalism' fundamentally reinventing the way that the BBC delivers news:

> blogging has done more to change the way journalism works than anything else thus far…without really intending to have, it has pulled us away from the idea that a story isn't a story until it appears on the 10 o'clock news. (Marsh, 2010)

He repeated the mantra adopted by advocates of open source journalism saying that there needed to be a live, continuous conversation so that stories were never finally written and put to bed and to re-educate any of his journalists who might still believe in the idea that, 'a story isn't a story until it appears on the 10 [O'Clock News]'. He said that the BBC was responding to 'bottom-up' change and reinforced the importance of 'story communities' which grow up around a story in the way Facebook communities do. He impressed on his audience that the BBC news culture was changing rapidly 'from within'. The BBC wanted to be seen as being proactive in seeking these contributions and advertised that, 'A deep understanding of, and involvement in, the blog world should now be a requirement for all our journalism.'

In the months that followed, many BBC journalists embraced limited interactivity through hyperlinks, raw footage, background links and immediate feedback. The consensus was that with the right craftsmanship, stories could be richer, more detailed and instant. They found this new format surprisingly flexible and were happy with the more relaxed tone and greater discursive possibilities it allowed, helping to convey, 'not just stories, but what we think of them and how we get them' (Hermida, 2009b: 11) High profile BBC Bloggers such as Robert Peston and Nick Robinson increasingly came to see their blogs as the 'spine' of what they did at the BBC. It allowed for detail, comment, interaction. It was the source of good stories and a way to gauge their accuracy and interest to the readers.

But there were problems. As with the 'Have Your Say' function embedded within the BBC News site, the sheer volume of posts became an issue. After only 11 weeks of operation, Rory Cellan-Jones' blog 'Dotlife' proved too popular to maintain and this led BBC News website editor, Steve Hermann to recognise that, 'responding to comments consistently across the blogs continues to be one of the greatest challenges for all concerned'. With seven million monthly visits to BBC blogs by October 2007, the BBC became a victim of its own success (Hermann, 2009: 312)

It became more and more evident that the principal challenge faced by all large institutions (media or otherwise) when opening the tap for interactive digital communication, was how well they could manage this dialogue without weakening relations with audiences. Research with British Members of Parliament revealed that even before the internet they could barely keep up with the old-fashioned post bag; however, once email communication was encouraged they were soon swamped with suggestions too plentiful to handle meaningfully. There was also evidence that the democratisation of the NHS through soliciting online comments with its own 'Have Your Say' site, so overwhelmed the institution that no meaningful attempt could be made to respond to the communications turning the exercise into a facade rather than a practical means of improving the service (Davis, 2009: 133).

The BBC chose to incorporate blogging as a platform for greater accountability and transparency, part of a larger trend of the mainstream media's desire to co-opt this emergent format. Its conversion to the power of blogging was arguably a little late and not entirely heartfelt (Hermida, 2009b: 307). Just like its flirtations with user-generated content, the Corporation's need to filter the content to protect its brand of impartiality made the discursive and iterative nature of blogging a difficult format for its journalists to fully embrace.

Professional Tastemakers

The ascendancy of digital journalism challenged some important precepts on which public service broadcasting had been built in the UK from 1922 to 2010. Mark Thompson (2009), BBC Director General, declared that licence fee funding, 'probably makes more sense in a digital age than at any other time in the BBC's history', but questions remained about its political sustainability as analogue scarcity gave way to digital plenty.(Thompson, 2009: 58). Despite Thompson's affirmation, as the BBC's hold over analogue spectrum waned, the Corporation was left struggling to find relevance in the lead up to the 2016 charter review in an environment of hyper-digital competitiveness.

The move to digital was as David Lloyd described, the first breach of the, 'adamantine wall that has since 1922 held against any raid on its licence fee' (Lloyd, 2009: 54). 'The era where channels were doled out by government to commercial companies in exchange for commitments to provide public service programming was, in retrospect, a kind of regulatory and capitalist heaven', Lloyd argued. All that changed with the digital world of plenty.

The BBC's survival depended on it winning the argument that the market alone couldn't deliver the plural sources and high standards of independent and impartial news and current affairs our democracy needed to stay in good health and its struggle to come to terms with various forms of social news from 2003–10 was an important part of its battle to find relevance in this new media ecology. Technological solutions for filtering content were explored in order to strike the right balance between hosting disparate and maverick voices and projecting authoritative news. It had to learn quickly how to filter the 'noise' effectively. The advanced filtration systems the BBC developed became the defining legacy of this transitional period. Filtration systems ensured the BBC could maintain its position as a world-leading and trusted brand in news delivery while also crowdsourcing its content. The transition was slow – incremental change at best – but the Corporation's ethos stayed intact as it strategically absorbed and used the contributions donated online by its constituent base.

Many argued that, as media fragmented, trusted international brands like the BBC were poised to become more, not less, valued and perhaps it might have asked too much of this cultural institution to move too quickly to embrace open source journalism in a way that might fundamentally change its culture. The rhetoric of its directors idealising participatory journalism, challenged it to recognise and host new voices, but also to carefully manage them. Not everyone celebrated interactive news cultures and there were many cautionary voices raised against letting a wide range of views proliferate. One notable critic, Andrew Keen, suggested that the key challenge for professional news people was to learn to, 'emancipate themselves from the mass humility and noble amateurism', throttling good journalism:

> At least the mainstream media has professional filters which, if not ideal, certainly get rid of some of the dross and finds some jewels … But, I prefer to have my culture served up to me by professional tastemakers than an algorithm or by anonymous people on the internet acting in the name of the virtuous crowd. (Keen, 2007: 10)

This view was not an uncommon one and the support for content curated by experts was often expressed in editorials and public comment of the time, challenging the assumption that audiences would automatically welcome moves towards democratising the news agenda.

These representative public posts, following the online publication of a speech delivered by Peter Horrocks on the rise of social news at the BBC were almost unanimous in wanting the BBC to abandon attempts to democratise the newsroom:

> 'I think that the inclusion of such a high proportion of user-generated content and especially comment is a mistaken path for the BBC to be following.'

'We pay a licence fee to the BBC partly so that it can gather and present the news to us, and sometimes to analyse it. I trust its journalists and editors to be experts. Why is user opinion necessary at all in this process?'

'As someone who relies on BBC news on the radio and web for your (usually very good) coverage of the world, I don't feel included or empowered by this aspect of the site, but rather patronised and irritated by it. Just because the web can be more inter-active than older media doesn't mean it should be.'

'I'd like to see an end to all this interactive rubbish. I pay my license fee to learn stuff from trained journalists and genuine experts. I don't want to hear the knee jerk bigotry of anonymous texters.' (Horrocks, 2008)

These responses were crying out for authority and reliability, not asking for a voice or any part in this brave new interactive world. This phenomenon had been observed in other studies (Picone, 2007: 105) and was testimony to the enduring forces that cultivate continuity and limit change within the context of remediation. Nothing has yet, 'destabilised the ascendancy of dominant news brands', Fenton concluded in her series of empirical news studies from 2009 and the internet (Fenton, 2009: 15).

The BBC unquestionably values contributions from its listeners and viewers; but stops short of investing them with any real social or cultural capital. The constraining filter is so strong; the topic is pre-selected, the contributors are chosen (one in a thousand) and the place in the line-up is dictated so that the contribution conforms to the rigid format within which it sits. The audience's contributions still have the feel of the 'and finally' section of a news bulletin where the news turns into entertainment and loses some of its gravitas.

Thus, with the Corporation's expertise primarily focused on perfecting its journalists' curatorial and weeding skills its initial flirtations with audiences tended to be more symbolic than fundamental. It wasn't surprising that the BBC's attempts to change its corporate culture weren't immediately transformational; however, there were undeniable benefits to opening the door even a little, as pressure from outside voices had the effect of keeping it on its toes rendering its construction more transparent.

Endnotes

1   The rise of participatory journalism can be traced back to the prominence of citizen journalism images that accompanied both the 9/11 terrorist attacks in New York and the 7 July 2005 terrorist bombings of the London Underground. Stuart Allan refers to these contributions as being from 'digital citizens' (Allan, 2006: 144).
2   www.bbc.co.uk/blogs/theeditors/2006/05/welcome_to_the_editors.html

6   Local Digital Journalism

What's clear is that the old-school of journalism can no longer continue as before. There is a future – and a potentially prosperous one – where amateurs and professionals work together to tread the difficult line between quality and extensiveness. (Carnegie Trust, 2010:108)

The first decade of the 21st century saw a significant, although partly cyclical, decline in revenue and circulation amongst local and regional news operators across the Western world. This contraction of local news gathering operations was seen as a direct consequence of the maturation of the digital economy, leaving pundits, publishers and regulators arguing about whether this was a systemic or structural change and whether once the short term financial problems connected to the banking crisis of 2007 were resolved, the newspaper industry could ever rebuild itself to its former prominence (see Chapter 3):

> ...it is an ineluctable truth that many provincial newspapers and some nationals are now in a near-terminal economic condition....If our critics spent as much zeal trying to help reverse this tragic situation and work out how good journalism – which is, by its nature, expensive – is going to survive financially in an internet age, then democracy and the public's right to know would be much better served. (Dacre, 2010)

Thus lamented the UK's *Daily Mail* editor Paul Dacre in his 2010 annual report as chairman of the UK Editor's Code Committee. There was general agreement that the local print and broadcast monopoly of information had been profoundly disrupted; but there was very little consensus on how to solve this problem.

The Local Scrutiny Gap

There's a real concern that the news media may be forced along a path that may erode the scope and efficacy of its collective civic function. (Currah, 2009: 119–20)

There was a net contraction in the reach and capabilities of news gathering across the local regions of the UK from 2007–10. The economic foundations of news publishing weakened as over 100 local and regional press titles folded and ITV wobbled dangerously on the brink of abandoning its commitment to regional news. There was hope that the proliferation of media on the web would make it easier for civil society to find a voice locally; yet, concerns about plurality in news supply remained.

In 2010, James Curran challenged an audience of academics to consider the following two eventualities:

1 The current crisis is creating opportunities for new green shoots to emerge. A legion of citizen journalists will till the space vacated by tired, dead wood professionals.
2 The current crisis in news print is a blessing in disguise. It will lead to the renaissance of journalism in a new, more inclusive, more participatory, self-generative form. In other words things will get better because they're getting worse. (Curran, 2010)

The utopian vision of innovative participatory and collaborative cultures bypassing traditional gatekeepers and redrawing the lines between amateur and professional, harnessing technology and reinventing journalism from the bottom-up proved compelling. Curran, however, could not endorse this vision, suggesting that they were the wrong way of looking at the problem as newspapers weren't facing Armageddon, or a Schumpeterian purge, but, 'merely a continuation of a cumulative process of decline.' His concern was that local newspapers were closing, and journalists were being fired at unprecedented rates. He concluded by saying that we should be seeking not just to arrest the decline of local journalism, but identifying ways of regenerating local journalism and that we should be cautious about abandoning traditional models in favour of untried and untested iterative, self-correcting 'non-professional' solutions. While many suggested that, 'it's journalism that needs saving, not the newspapers', Curran feared that digital disruption might kill the golden goose before its offspring had a chance to mature.

Structural Changes Circa 2010

The problem was that the sudden demise of the UK commercial regional news sector (television and press) in 2008 came as a shock to regulators who had meticulously planned digital switchover to help release the analogue spectrum and wean audiences from the analogue age. Local media had to keep pace and move gracefully from digital adolescence to maturity but old structures were being demolished faster than new ones were coming of age (Digital Britain, 2009: 151).

Ofcom, the independent regulator for the UK communications industry, published research in 2009 suggesting that the local media sector was facing major structural challenges, driven by the growing take-up and use of the internet as people changed the way they access and consume local and regional media (Ofcom, 2009: 1.19). 'Newspaper circulations have been in slow and consistent decline for the last 30 years', it reported, and 'more recently there have been reductions in the consumption of regional television and local radio' (2009: 1.20).

Another structural threat to the local press was the rise of local government news from 1997 to 2010 (see O'Neill and O'Connor, 2008). Glossy newspaper-like weeklies and increasingly comprehensive digital offerings ensured that government at both a local and national level was infringing on areas traditionally the domain of a free press. Councils often went beyond informing their citizens about services such as recycling and rubbish pick-ups and started to use their public relations departments to produce slick dummy papers indistinguishable from a local paper including lifestyle articles, TV listings and film reviews disguising their partisanship nature. These publications represented another thorn in the side of the struggling local commercial press which lobbied hard for Councils to cease using tax payers' money to propagandise to their communities.

At the same time the internet was becoming an increasingly important part of the local media mix. Although local audiences weren't abandoning traditional media in droves, there were many signs of the users shifting towards more interactive, mobile and immediate sources of news. A third of adults with broadband access claimed to use local websites at least weekly, with consumers saying they valued the internet for accessibility, convenience and quality of information. However, as the decade closed, television was still the most popular source for regional and local news for 72% of the UK's population with 26% turning to a local newspaper or magazine and 17% using the radio to stay informed (DCMS, 2009).

Yet, this trend was changing and age was an important factor influencing people's favourite news medium. Audiences for mainstream news bulletins tended to come from the older sections of the population. In 2003, 39% of the audience for the main public service broadcast news bulletins was over 65 and by 2010 that figure had risen to 41%. The younger news consumers were increasingly going online.

Stewart Purvis, Ofcom partner for Content and Standards, echoed the industry's uncertainty about television's future capacity to draw news audiences in a digital age:

> The long-term and still-to-be-answered question is whether the current young heavy users of digital media – and rejecters of TV news – will, like the generations before them, learn to love catching up on the day's events in front of the TV or will they become life-long rejecters of TV news. (Purvis, 2010)

New Local Journalistic Frameworks

Very large news organisations had been built over the 20th century when margins were high and the shareholders enjoyed characteristic returns of 30–35% on their investments. As we saw in Chapter 2 and 3, 'nothing fails like success', and these large conglomerates' licences to print money were looking very out of date. A leading media economist diagnosed their problem as 'path dependency', rendering many large corporations immobile as social media changed the way millions accessed news (Picard, 2010). This left openings for fleet-footed, entrepreneurial operators most evident on a local level where the barriers to entry for journalists were lowest.

As introduced in Chapter 2, economics and culture expert, Clay Shirky, believes we no longer needed large corporations to organise journalism effectively. Shirky argues that society is best informed outside the professional framework of journalism, and that it makes no sense to take a professional metaphor and apply it to this distributed class:

> The printing press precipitated 200 years of chaos. I'm predicting 50 years of chaos in which loosely coordinated groups are going to be given increasingly high leverage and the more that these groups forgo traditional institutional imperatives like deciding in advance what's going to happen or the profit motive – the more leverage they're going to get. (Shirky, 2005)

If we agree with Shirky's view that 'loosely coordinated groups' relying predominately on crowdsourcing will outnumber and outrank traditional institutions and that cooperative frameworks are going to force a massive readjustment across all sectors of our lives – starting with journalism – this suggests that institutions that manage themselves rigidly and rely on informational monopolies are going to come under greater pressure as communications structures reinvent themselves. The vision of legions of citizen journalists, 'filling the space vacated by tired, dead wood professionals' may be overstating the change; yet, there was certainly evidence of a new mixed economy journalism emerging at a local level.

Shirky's ideas around the 'distributed class' resonated with Habermas' notions of the public sphere, a useful normative concept that helps to evaluate trends in journalistic production such as those discussed here.

Habermas was concerned about the way in which bureaucratic organisations and economic interests used technologies that took them ever further away from the public, always threatening democracy. For Habermasians, a democratic use of media technologies would entail reducing the distance between audiences and media producers and removing the distance between citizens via media technologies.

This organising principle was behind many new ultra-local news sites such as 'MumsNet' in the US and 'Netmums' in the UK. These powerful new 'bottom-up' networks with growing political clout were started by stay-at-home mums in suburbanised, duel-income Western societies. They were attempting to recapture the sense of community lost in the cultural shift toward suburban isolation. The sites were successful in creating a digital network of support reproducing the connectivity of small-scale neighbourhoods – communities of interest reinvented using internet tools. These networked news blogs reproduced themselves many times over, ensuring that news that materially makes people's lives better, could be found in amateur circles.

We saw in Chapter 2 how the renegotiation of boundaries between professional and amateur journalists alongside a change in the configuration of the public sphere were creating what Bourdieu called 'noble amateurs', credited with cultural and social capital. Anyone might gain a seat at the table where they had previously been excluded within the elitist concept of journalistic production (Bourdieu, 1983: 29–73). This form of community-generated news, facilitated through the web, represented a significant change in the way human affairs were arranged and at its core was a profound question of how democracies handle public knowledge and civic engagement. 'Generative' news of this kind was central to the redefinition of the digital journalistic mission – a mission often lost when it inherited its institutional journalistic baggage.

An Emergent Hyper-local Tier

New web-based platforms emerging on the local level are what Barnett calls, 'exciting, innovative, open and non-hierarchical initiatives which can play a significant role in binding communities together, keeping them informed and helping them to resolve everyday local issues'. Yet, Barnett is not confident that they can fulfil the vital civic function of journalism, claiming that they, 'cannot interrogate, they cannot report in depth, nor can they properly represent given the generally small number of people participating in such sites' (Barnett, 2009). This rather negative assessment of the new emergent tier of local sites emerges from a fear of losing the institutional props for this kind of work. Yet, as we saw earlier in the book (Chapters 2 and 4) it is reasonable to assume that within the emergent digital public sphere both old and new forms will coexist and the professional class of journalist will continue to play a vital part in this evolutionary process (see also Barnett, 2009; Gitlin, 2009).

Barnett's concerns reflect a deep-seated position presupposing that trained, professional journalists, drawing a wage and supported by reputable institutions, are essential for the proper maintenance of civic journalism. However, the notion of 'enhanced localness' suggests that local stories grounded in local, hermeneutic knowledge often represent a more accurate picture and have more depth, accuracy and community context. This advantage cannot fully be exploited by professional broadcast news gathering teams and regional presses that find it difficult to keep close tabs on local stories as the territories they serve are increasingly large, broad and diverse. The established local press has a big area to cover and community-based and smaller commercially based sites help plug these gaps. For example, if a knifing happens in the patch and a community journalist can get pictures and interviews moments after it happens, why send a BBC reporter with only an outsider's perspective the day after?

Hyper-local news publishers and local community media pioneers and bloggers passionate about their local area, are a potentially rich and truthful source of local news. What's more, these local and ultra-local operations generate a large seam of stories that normally never see the light of day:

> Local websites of all shapes and sizes are providing community news and information to hundreds of thousands of people. Most of these sites are volunteer run, using free publishing platforms like 'www.wordpress.com' with no hard costs. They show that grass roots media can provide an accurate, reliable popular source of news and information without regulation or subsidy. Their news values and thresholds are new, reflecting grass roots interests and priorities. (Digital Britain, 2009: 150)

Another advantage to community-based news organisations is that they have always offered a good recruitment start for those currently least likely to enter journalism because of class barriers which, as we discussed in Chapter 4, have consistently been a long term impediment to inclusive and unbiased journalism. They represent an opportunity to create a more diverse workforce of local reporters – and potentially support the development of new audiences and communities of interest as well as geographic communities. With a clearly defined set of core standards and values, this tier can make a meaningful contribution. With basic legal, compliance and investigative training at their disposal, this burgeoning army of volunteers has the potential to provide a reliable reporting base filling the local scrutiny gap identified in the UK in 2010.

A Labour of Love

What is interesting structurally is that a mid-tier of bottom-up news content is being created – an organised semi-professional layer inbetween the professional and the so-called 'noise' of user-generated content. These news sites often operate around one postal code area with an editor working from home writing two or three stories a day scouring notice boards for their news. They sometimes generate enough income to pay for themselves through advertorials, classifieds and restaurant reservations. Others are driven by the need to campaign and be at the heart of community activism, proud of the way they keep tabs on what's going on at their local councils and, in the case of community radio, keen to develop social cohesion and promote cross cultural understanding in their broadcast areas.

A sense of pride and civic responsibility drives many news bloggers and community media activists to put the time into researching, writing and maintaining their sites and the social gain, non-profit set-up enshrined in the UK Community Radio Order of 2004 and also in the principles underlying the US National Public Radio network, provide a useful model for the future of digitally produced and distributed local news.

Theorising how social production might transform markets in a networked society, Yochai Benkler focused on the psychological gratification that comes from social connectedness as an alternative to the recognition that comes from the market exchange of labour. He suggested that peer production of information, knowledge and culture can often be more efficient than market-based systems (Benkler, 2006: 115). He concluded that, 'transacting within the price system may either increase or decrease the social-psychological rewards' associated with the activity and that social standing, self-esteem and mutual recognition were all equally compelling reasons to participate or add value to social production (2006: 96). In other words, money isn't the only reason people like to communicate and the presence of money in a transactional framework could even be de-motivating.

Nurturing the Bottom of the News Pyramid

One of the main problems facing the development of any new local journalism venture is how to nurture the talent at the bottom of the pyramid. When citizen journalism first emerged as an important source of news post 9/11 (see Allan, 2006) the concern was primarily focused on verification and mediation of third party material to be spliced into professional news reports (see Chapter 5). Corporate producers such as *The Guardian* and the BBC successfully developed strategies for harvesting this kind of user-generated content on their own terms; but strategies for dealing with content in a co-production environment remained elusive and a little scary.

'Professional' news people were acculturated to being at the top of a cast system where only paid employees working for established media companies could rightfully call themselves 'journalists'. This had the effect of creating a de-professionalised zone where talent and expertise wasn't effectively recognised or successfully nurtured by those at the top. Prejudice based upon the desire to uphold standards of quality and impartiality, and also to maintain the professional status associated with pay and conditions, mitigated against turning the news chain upside down and encouraging reverse publication. It was also the case that the constraints of political economy restricted the ability of journalists to cover the full range of stories. Yet a new tier of local journalists were at the heart of pushing the boundaries between professional and amateur in an attempt to validate new voices in the public sphere. The emergence of this new tier of amateurs and semi-professionals was affecting a digital upset challenging the entrenched occupational ideology. The professional journalist's self-understanding (see also Chapter 1) set up a false dichotomy represented in Table 6.1, a binary internalised by most working journalists.

The 'traditional and safe' sector was fearful of anything too polarised and the concept of deliberately iterative news, whereby stories were post-moderated or had an interactive life after publication, was seen as a threat to credibility and impartiality. This binary was at the core of objections to expanding any co-production activity or embracing reverse publishing and dispersed circulation.

William Perrin, founder of the King's Cross ultra-local community news blog[1] considered 'relevance' and 'trust' to be more useful defining features of his work. He used his website to campaign for the community, taking on big players like Network Rail and winning. The site reported stories that the local paper didn't think worth reporting, 'unearthing interesting angles that the papers missed'. Their patch was only a mile long by half a mile wide and, with just four people writing for the site as volunteers, they were able to produce more than 800 stories in their first four years. Perrin referred to himself as a community activist and resolved the question of 'professionalism' in his own mind by refusing to take on the title 'journalist':

> We have a very strong community of people who work for us and send us stuff. None of the people who work for us are journalists. We're not journalists; it's a name I actually resist (Perrin, 2010a)

It could be argued that this self-attribution does not necessarily resolve the question of, 'who is a journalist?' as laid out in Chapters 2 and 4; it is more a deflection of the

Table 6.1 Digital upset

Traditional and safe	Different and scary
Pre-moderated	Post-moderated or iterative
Objective	Subjective/polarised
Mediated/processed/packaged	Unmediated/raw
Polished	Rough
High quality	Low quality
Robust	Insecure
Top-down	Bottom-up
Professional	Amateur

Source: adapted from notes and discussions with Stuart Allan, 2006 issue, a way of avoiding the difficult questions of occupational ideology. Perrin gives himself a licence to reinvent the rules of journalism, but refuses to wear the mantle of office. For example, his experience running the successful Kings Cross website made him a firm believer in 'the wisdom of crowds' or the value of iterative news. In theory, he argued, all sites are self-correcting:

> We have to have the courage to let go. We're producing detailed, impartial and correct output on Kings Cross. Our public correct us constantly. It's more accurate than most newspapers. (Perrin, 2010b)

It may be acceptable for post-moderation of content to be used as a means of fact checking and correction, hoping that the reader will iteratively hone the online stories. Yet, this form of moderation is institutionally unacceptable for traditional news suppliers such as the BBC.

In Perrin's view the role of the professionals in this new digital news ecology should be to formulate 'kitemarks' that certify the legitimacy and trustworthiness of alternative news websites. This would allow them to link with impunity and to host a plurality of voices by taking on the role of curator. Stories of regional and national significance also have the potential to be reverse published or fed through the system upwards. We saw in Chapter 2 how a reliance on PR or agency copy for an increasing number of stories replaced the need for original investigations and coverage. Reporters under time and cost pressures became more dependent on secondary sources for information and reverse publishing or 'venacular rearticulation' had the potential to present an important new source of stories to combat this trend towards 'churnalism'. The hope was that this nascent resource would brighten the civic discourse and allow journalism to fight a rear guard action against the ascendancy of PR so well documented in journalism studies through the first decade of the 21st century.

The Value of a Local Meta-mediating Role

In order for the digital local news ecology to grow and develop, synergies between amateur and professional needed to be nurtured for the betterment of both, and for the audience.

> Journalism must perform a meta-mediating function, not only connecting people to public knowledge, but helping them cope with fractured and fragmented sources of such knowledge. (Coleman et al., 2009: 45)

The vision of the changing role of the professional journalist whose job it is to harvest content from volunteers and act as curator, correcting and editing copy, presented a significant break from the past. The obvious advantage of the professional zone taking on a curatorial role was that it might ensure a comfortable distance between organisations such as the BBC and this emergent semi-professional ticr. To make this happen, journalists needed to become more comfortable as content aggregators respectful of the potential value this new tier of local content adds to the system. Digital tagging, digital anchoring (see Currah, 2009), navigation and cross referencing of stories with their stakeholders were all ways being investigated to help align the new forces behind local journalism. It wasn't envisaged that this new rapidly expanding tier would be able to provide a structural alternative to the mainstream national news media serving mass audiences, but, it had the potential to offer a substantial new thread promoting civic dialogue and interaction. Director General, Mark Thompson applauded this strategy recommending in his introduction to the BBC Strategy Review in April 2010 that:

> ...the BBC should become a catalyst and connector within the public space. It is uniquely well placed to help other institutions and groups reach and enrich the public. (BBC Strategy Review, 2010: 3)

Funding for Local News

Regional news has been a core public service obligation of ITV since its launch in 1955. Its regional news franchises were part of its public service broadcasting obligations in return for the rare analogue frequency it owned for over half a century.

Digital switchover, to be completed in 2012, meant that ITV no longer needed this Faustian pact as it could happily market itself digitally. As regional news was a major loss maker, it made its future on ITV unsustainable. Quality television news costs money and this left ITV on the brink of abandoning its regional news commitments in 2010. It claimed annual potential losses of £64 million for all 15 of its regional news franchises (Barnett, 2010: 4).

In anticipation of a major gap arising in local news production and to guarantee that the BBC would continue to have some competition in this arena, the government floated the idea that community media might fill the void left by a weakened professional tier. Fore grounded as part of the UK Coalition Government's 2010 media reform agenda it moved to deregulate local media markets allowing cross-media ownership of local news gathering operations for the first time. The idea was to create 'Local Media Companies' (LMCs) staffed by amateurs and semi-professionals alongside established, professional news operators:

> This would foster a 'bottom-up' approach to local news through judicious use of local volunteers and unpaid participants. New business models suggested that quality did

not pay on a local level[2] suggesting that production values would be 'different' from those traditionally associated with regional or national television, with regulation kept to a bare minimum. (Barnett, 2010: 7)

The LMCs were initially predicated on the principle of 'zero public subsidy'. The hope was that the cross-media advertising platforms and partnerships with local newspaper groups would make them commercially sustainable; although, there were many who were doubtful that these companies could turn a profit even under the new regulatory regime (Enders Analysis, 2010). Despite this, Jeremy Hunt, Minister of Culture, was determined not to raise a whole new generation of subsidy junkies:

Using the licence fee to prop up regional news simply casts a failed regional TV model in aspic. It would actively prevent the emergence of new, local media models, making broadcasters focus their energies on satisfying politicians not reaching viewers. (Hunt, 2010)

After the Schott report in January 2011, it was agreed that the BBC would fund the roll-out of these new local TV services by top-slicing £25 million from its licence fee. Despite this last minute injection of funds, the questions dominating the development of local news structures focused on the cost-benefit equation. Government policy relied on amateur or low-paid contributions as the engine of these news services suggesting that this new development needed to piggy-back on the gift economy at a community level. The hope was that the same economics that drove down the costs of cameras and computers empowering many more prod-users with the desire to create content and stream video, sound or images, could be turned to advantage. Public acceptance and familiarity with new categories of public media such as Wikipedia, Twitter and YouTube had also changed the grammar associated with media images making low grade and amateurish quality more acceptable. The idea was that the Conservative Party's much touted 'Big Society' ambitions[3] when blended with the fourth estate, would produce something valuable and sustainable without public money.

Critics of this new way of working argued against 'journalism on the cheap'; yet, advocates claim that broadcasting 'quality' is a luxury in local journalism if it fails to garner a significantly greater viewing audience. In the UK, the only organisation that could afford to produce 'high-end' video quality was the licence fee funded BBC. The ITV regional news model collapsed along with the analogue scarcity that supported it. William Perrin argued that local public service news can and should be constructed cheaply. He advocated the content farming method made popular in the US, whereby, 'if a councillor says something stupid' a brief is sent out to the local stringers and the first one to get an interview and embed the video in Google gets paid. 'The money will be small, maybe £150 a story' (Perrin, 2010b).

From an audience perspective it remains unclear at what point 'video on the cheap' fails to pass the quality threshold for credibility and authority. Unquestionably the proliferation of citizen journalism content on sites such as Facebook and YouTube has changed the aesthetic of visual news and has also radically changed the way people source news; but further studies need to be done on news audiences' perceptions of the relationship between quality, reliability and accessibility of amateur content.

Another major concern was the impact of deregulation on local news:

> Although other factors contribute to producing homogeneity in the media, ownership and ownership structures are key. The critical mechanism to ensure plurality in the media is regulation. (Carnegie Report, 2010: 108)

Those opposed to the LMCs argued co-produced community-based journalism didn't mix well with the relentless pursuit of profits. Past experience had shown that when local media is owned centrally its localness is neutered. Consolidation, although pragmatic for economies of scale, has a tendency to dilute local character and local commercial monopolies owned by a few national conglomerates might homogenise the multiplicity of voices and opinions. A network of strong, independent, diverse local voices is more likely to be resilient in the face of this possibility. Yet, the underpinning Government policy on local media was a hope that there was commercial value in this form of news and that it could be realised through market investment.

The Commercial Value of the Hyper-local News Economy

Half of us live half an hour's drive from where we grew up and the commercial value of local information produced and distributed digitally through ultra-local sites was being realised by a diverse range of companies experimenting with new financial models. The vast majority of those working on the coal face of this new 'industry' contributed their time for nothing, but others found ways to make it pay.

Companies were quick to see how to make money from the rise of ultra-local news sites. One such international company, Fwix, aggregated local news and information available from blogs, news sites, and social media sites. Consumers could read this aggregated news in the form of daily 'paperboy' emails or on third party websites that had commercial agreements with the company. Metrics measuring the reader's level of interest in each cutting personalised the service further, making it more or less likely that that type of story would appear again in their customised digest.

Other companies brokered advertising on behalf of their hyper-local clients. In 2009, 30 million pounds was spent in the UK on hyper-local online advertising.

In commercial terms, hyper-local was defined as communities of interest – where you work, socialise – or by postal code area. In advertising terms it was commonly defined as a five mile radius around where the customer lived. One company, Oxbury Media services, acted as a media buying agency for 10,000 ultra-local publications reporting that 3,000 local 'geo-tagged' customers were needed at minimum to make each site valid. The money was funnelled by linking national brands and hyper-local media. It created generic, downloadable advertising that could be localised.

James Mawer of Oxbury Media Services, suggested that hyper-local is filling a vacuum as the regional press weaken and centralise. They reverse-published stories from the ultra-local sites back to the national news aggregators, syndicating content outwards to regional and national publications. Mawer suggested this trend was on the increase as there was plenty of demand for monetising user-generated content in this way as it represented a different form of content harvesting (Mawer, 2010).

'Neighbour net' provided another interesting commercial revenue model. A profit-making news network relying primarily on stay-at-home spouses to staff, this network used proprietary software to franchise to ultra-local areas based on the principal that the pothole outside your own house is much more interesting than the one two miles away. Editors must live locally and work in their own homes providing holiday cover for those in the network. Audiences build slowly and as the digital reader is low profit, the traffic has to be relatively high to attract enough advertising. Whilst from the ethical perspective they are deeply problematic, from the business and management perspective, advertorial stories have a strong role to play in this commercial model (Prophet, 2010).

On a larger scale, local newspaper chains were also experimenting with a network of local sites linked to their newspapers. In 2010, the *Daily Mail* and General Trust announced an expansion of its network of 100 plus hyper-local sites built around postal code areas. It paid its community editors approximately £5,000 a year to run the sites and these people were described as part time journalists and part time community organisers. They weren't looking for professional journalists or even journalism graduates, just people with a keen interest in and connection to their communities. The *Teeside Evening Gazette* claimed that 85% of its 20 hyper-local postal code sites were fully sponsored within a year of launch. Editor Darren Thwaites credited this success to the basic law of localness. 'What chance has news on your street got to be covered in the local paper?' he asked, 'Perhaps one story in ten years and that doesn't satisfy the demand that's out there.' He also reported how the best stories from the sites were commonly reversed-published back to the printed paper (Thwaites, 2010).

In the US one high profile local news chain, the Journal Register Company, used citizen journalists to help broaden its coverage. It claimed to reach 14 million people a month through its 324 multi-platform news providers.

We recognise that news is now created and consumed in remarkably different ways. We need to partner with our audiences, our communities and others if we are to be successful. (Paton, 2010)

The idea behind this initiative was to provide local bloggers with the tools they needed to become successful – journalism and marketing skills – so their material could be content harvested for the main sites and papers. The company was taking Clay Shirky's advice recognising that content harvesting was cheaper and claiming that, 'an incredible amount of great local journalism comes from independent local blogs and sites' that need to be supported for this grassroots content to seed.

Not all newspaper barons looked to digital journalism to sustain their businesses. Some like Sir Ray Tindle, the UK's regional newspaper elder statesman and owner of the Tindle Newspaper Group came through the economic downturn, 'without losing a single title or making a single journalist redundant' (Tindle, 2010).

He was confident in the continued ascendancy of printed local weeklies and claimed that, 'many local papers lost their way (in the recession) by diluting their local brand. He recounted an apocryphal story of saving the local Tenby paper from bankruptcy in 1970. Its revenues dried up when it overextended its footprint and diluted its patch and effectively stopped being local. Tindle came in when the staff were clearing their desks and challenged them to start anew. 'A cat must not have kittens in Tenby without the readers knowing', he decreed. 'Stop targeting all of West Wales and focus locally'. He had the paper back in profit within a year.

Built on similar principles of 'enhanced localness', but without expanding into the digital space, Tindle Newspaper Group were able to weather the economic downturn surprisingly well. As its competitors were closing titles, it launched 12 new local weeklies. Its health was also ensured by a lack of 'shareholders demanding obscene profits' and no expansion into loss making areas' (Tindle, 2010).

This section has focused on new alignments of productive power and distributive capacity suggesting how professionals and amateurs might work together on local news fostering an 'enhanced localness'. Chapter 4 explored how traditional journalists, trained as gatekeepers rather than 'gatewatchers' (Bruns, 2005), have been accustomed to relying on their editorial authority and professional craft skills to perform their role and any redistribution of agency represented a challenge to their integrity and professionalism. Yet, as Fenton reminds us once the social actors involved in the construction of news expand and extend outside of the newsroom this eventually leads to an 'expansion of the locus of production' (Fenton, 2009: 11).

A significant amount of literature from the last two decades has outlined the crisis of trust in news (see Chapter 4) and it will be interesting to see how any redistribution of agency at a local level might contribute to addressing this problem. At the core of any discussions on local news is the question of how democracies handle public knowledge and civic engagement. Central to this is the definition of the journalistic mission. Journalism for the 21st century is being reinvented and that reinvention will be led at a local level. As Coleman et al. conclude in their investigation into public trust in news looking at the importance of news as a civic resource, 'journalism can no longer be conceived in the paternalistic terms of early public service broadcasting, when the myth of a homogeneous public sphere was in vogue' (Coleman et al., 2009: 43).

The community hyper-local sites will depend on building trust within their communities of interest. Media saturation and diffusion of attention mean that the audiences will be small and it is still unclear if the type of self-correcting mechanisms Perrin referred to earlier in this section will be enough to ensure quality. Users may adapt and learn to surf with discrimination, and the development of branded 'kite marks' certifying the legitimacy and trustworthiness of site content will also help to legitimise sources allowing users to swim in the sea of information and consume intelligently.

Working as institutional actors, professional journalists might consider switching tactics and provide what Currah describes as a 'digital anchoring' service aggregating content around a 'brand voice' and capturing what's good in 'the digital tsunami' of web news.

> The next generation news media have the capacity to recast themselves as a professional hub within a broader, more distributed and transparent network of quasi-news suppliers, stretching from the sophistication of the public relations industrial complex to the raw energy of citizen journalism. (Currah, 2009: 142)

The problem of how to reconcile oppositional practices into the mainstream commercial production of news will be central to the evolving process of change. The traditional model of journalism will no doubt survive and be reinforced and legitimised as part of the process of remediating news digitally. Yet, the so called legitimate practice of journalism will no longer be restricted to a handful of 'organisationally validated professionals' (Atton, 2008: 144).

> In an age of pervasive media interactivity, institutional legitimacy cannot be maintained in splendid isolation from an ongoing conversation with the public....Journalism needs to play a key role in facilitating and moderating intelligent and meaningful interaction between the public and their representative. (Coleman et al., 2009: 44)

Finally it helps to invoke Riepl's (1913) classic law – and as we argue throughout this study – that innovations in media almost always add to what went before rather than replace them. Fenton entreats us not to ignore our communications technology history reminding us that although:

innovative content and forms of production have the tendency to appear in the early stages of a new technology and offer a potential for radical change, this is more often than not cancelled out or appropriated by the most powerful institutions operating within dominant technological and socio-political paradigms. (Fenton, 2009: 13)

Yet, the journalistic mission does seem to be changing and despite the conservative tendencies for media to revert to type and old structures to maintain their grip on the means of production, it is likely that, when old and new learn to work side-by-side, a complementary news ecology will emerge allowing digital journalism to flourish on both a civic and commercial basis.

Endnotes

1   www.kingscrossenvironment.com
2   MTV, Manchester's local TV station folded in 2010 after problems with financing 'quality' broadcast output. It left many believing that local TV was unsustainable using traditional business models.
3   'The Big Society is about a huge culture change......where people, in their everyday lives, in their homes, in their neighbourhoods, in their workplace......don't always turn to officials, local authorities or central government for answers to the problems they face ......but instead feel both free and powerful enough to help themselves and their own communities.' (David Cameron, Speech, July 2010)

News Customisation

The 'Daily Me'

Throughout this book, we have looked at challenges to the professional identity of journalists as the division between spheres of journalistic production and consumption became less defined, challenging the hegemony of mainstream and traditional news in the public sphere (see also McNair, 2006: 37–49). The space occupied by professional journalists working in their capacity as gatekeepers to information has been challenged by digitally enabled journalism in two very distinct ways.

Firstly, there was the competition for the audience's attention as news sites multiplied and traditional markets fragmented. Secondly, and the subject of this chapter, is the increased use of 'metrics' to measure and assess the popularity of individual news stories and the targeted ability to customise news delivery services into what Nicholas Negroponte described as, 'The Daily Me' (Negroponte, 1995). Digital media technologies offered new potential to 'filter' news and this process of personalisation made it possible for readers to limit their exposure to ideas, stories and contrasting world views that weren't of their own choosing. The fear is that the more news is consumed *à la carte*, the more likely we are to descend into, 'customised echo chambers', where, 'popularity engines are emerging as principal gatekeepers between news and the citizen' (Currah, 2009: 150).

Technologically Driven Change

To understand the significance of the move to news customisation it's useful to examine the trend through the lens of the social adoption of new technology.

Technology has done a lot to individualise communication processes and this can be deeply unsettling, but it can also be liberating. Researchers struggle with the creation of the right formula for studying the impact of any new technological innovation. There exists a classic, but not always resolvable, 'chicken or egg' question about the role technology plays in the development of new journalistic forms. Key analyses suggest a complicated relationship between the interplay of journalistic routines and technology, a kind of push–pull dynamic, which allows for individual take-up and adoption in different institutional contexts (Boczkowski, 2004; Deuze, 2007; Thurman, 2008). The hypothesis of this book is that journalism and technology shape each other, as we discussed in Chapter 1

> If we accept that the social contexts within which technologies are taken up are critical to their development, as a consequence, 'the evolution of technology is not predefined or foreseeable' (Paterson and Domingo, 2008: 21). A comprehensive analysis of the social adoption process of a technological innovation such as the internet requires the understanding of technologies as a socially constructed multifaceted reality, and not a monolithic element that appears from nowhere and imposes its own logic to social actors such as media companies (Ibid: 19).

In other words, what's interesting about technology is what people and institutions do with it. Winston describes the process of social adoption in terms of the push and pull tensions likening them to 'accelerators or brakes'. Accelerators push forward technological innovation and social adoption whereas brakes are normally actions of specific social actors that try to slow down the social adoption (Winston, 1996: 21–5). Brakes are often applied when there's potential for major disruption to social and economic models of production. Often, powerful vested interests wish to maintain a status quo that serves those interests. When new technology threatens to disrupt the status quo there is a tendency for many actors, be they academic commentators or industry players, to paint a doomsday scenario strongly advocating that social brakes be applied to the adoption process.

In the case of the development of news accommodation systems, there is evidence of this kind of resistance. It comes from two quarters: journalists, who see their professional editorial identities superseded, and news businesses, which struggle to maintain their brand identities as consumers increasingly cherry-pick their 'Daily Me'.

Who Sets the News Agenda?

People have enjoyed the ability to digitally navigate their way to a story online ever since search engines developed sophisticated algorithms for this purpose circa 1990. Web users are now accustomed to selecting stories through searches and random hyperlinks often stumbling on the unexpected or serendipitous in the process.

Although 70% of Americans went online specifically to get news or information at least a few times a week in 2010, 80% said they came across news serendipitously while doing other things (Pew Research Centre, 2010b). Google News and other news aggregators – websites that aggregate news from other news sources – have been able to take commercial advantage of this behaviour by encouraging customers to engage with their customised news interfaces.

This form of customisation allows news seekers to input key search words and by doing so they collectively indicate how popular any one news story is on the day. This is called 'click-through' monitoring. The information is tracked and used commercially to privilege the production of a greater number of stories in popular areas through content farming (see Chapter 6) or through the redesign of home pages. As an example, once it became clear that Naomi Campbell's 2010 testimony at the war crimes trial of former Liberian President Charles Taylor was attracting the attention of the clickstream, it didn't take long before the front pages were changed to cover what had been, up until that point, an important but under reported story:

> Congratulations murdered and mutilated Sierra Leoneans! You finally have a celebrity angle, meaning your obscure little story has been given its brief moment in the limelight, before being reassigned the sort of news value that couldn't hope to trump a Cesc Fabregas transfer rumour. (Hyde, 2010)

The media's obsession with celebrity stories is nothing new and even before search engine's algorithmic secrets were exposed, news organisations were keen to copy from each other and magnify the popular. The difference here is that editors enjoyed instantaneous feedback on the traffic each story received which certainly changes their news priorities. The influence of the clickstream is necessarily dependent on the type of news outlet in question. For example, news aggregators don't have an editorial brand to protect; but, reputable news producers have to navigate the tricky terrain between being popular and being credible.

Yet, even the most authoritative news sources were quick to capitalise on the granularity offered through the clickstream. Thurman studied how a variety of national US and UK news providers were adapting to this news accommodation technology and found that the BBC and NYTimes.com had the most elaborate homepage customisation. Even an institution such as the BBC, strongly branded with an ethos of quality and impartiality, had a long history of flirting with news customisation beginning in 2005 when it spent £15 million on a pilot project, 'My News Now'. Thurman described how its Director of News defended the development of user-centred approaches as an appropriate response to audiences' increasing expectations for 'a high level of personalisation' (Thurman, 2011). The BBC's 'most popular stories section' reflects high levels of clickstream activity:

On a day when the BBC News web page lead was 'Africa turns the heat on Zimbabwe', the most popular story was 'Foot mystery baffles Mounties' – the macabre mystery of five severed human feet washing up on the shores of British Columbia. (Lee-Wright, 2009: 77)

The BBC was naturally reluctant to admit that these potentially popularist measures drove editorial decision making. It preferred to use the clickstream as a way of, 'informing editors' choices', recognising that it is a blunt tool reflecting the number of people tempted to click through from a headline written to maximise traffic but not indicating the reader's actual engagement with the story (for example, appreciation index, length of time viewing, etc.).

Many of the forms of personalisation described in Thurman's study function quite independently of both users and producers of journalism suggesting we should be looking specifically at the logic of computer algorithms to extend our gatekeeping theory. He developed a useful taxonomy of personalisation strategies that vary from the 'contextual related content' generated by software codes, to 'content adaptation' based on geographical location, to 'automatic filters' designed to privilege stories by popularity, to more complex systems that recommend content based on a user's profile from records of behaviour and registration data (Thurman, 2011).

These filter types have the potential to disrupt or displace professional news judgement while offering an enhanced service but they also raise important new questions about the role of the journalist as gatekeeper. We have referred a number of times in this book to the role of the prod-user in co creating journalistic texts. However, news accommodation systems introduce a new variable to the process.

The news editors interviewed in Thurman's study were largely positive about giving their users some degree of filtered control within the walled gardens of their own branded sites; but, these were:

> ... tempered by feelings that personalisation should be limited in scope, simple to set up, and not replace the status quo. Concerns centred around personalisation's impact on journalists' professional identities and the value journalists add; and readers' demand for, and ability to make use of personalised news. (Thurman, 2011)

Editorial control or dictating 'what is news' and what prominence each story should be given is central to the professional identity of news workers and their role as gatekeepers. The quote above suggests that there is a desire to control or slow down user-customisation. These are predictable responses to any challenge disrupting established practices and provide a good example of the 'accelerator and brake' theory of technological adoption cited earlier.

User demand can also act as a brake on the process through conservative adoption. Thurman reported anecdotal evidence from his interviewees that the uptake of personalisation was still relatively low and suggested in his conclusions that audiences place great value on editorial decisions made on their behalf, displaying an aversion to making choices and an inability to know their own mind well enough to predict their content preferences (Thurman, 2011).

A pioneering newspaper publisher in Berlin launched *Niiu* in 2009 using digital printing and syndication deals to give readers a personalised daily newspaper delivered to their door. It was made up of content from various print and online sources such as geo-tagged weather reports, cherry-picked sections from a range of national and international papers such as *Die Zeit* and *The New York Times* alongside RSS feeds, favourite blogs, crosswords and cartoons.

The marketing proposition assumed people still preferred the printed word for its convenience and user-friendliness and that they would pay a premium for this luxury if it was personalised. The publishers claimed that there was no time lag and even the adverts could be targeted and personally addressed to Mr Jones or Mrs Smith. *Niiu* achieved a circulation of 5,000 readers within the first six months of launch and the producers were surprised to see their customer demographics skewed to the younger reader with 42% between the ages of 19 and 29. The expectation had been that mostly older readers habituated into a lifetime of newspaper readership would dominate their customer database; yet, it was the younger reader more acculturated to exercising choice and reader-agency fuelling sales suggesting the value associated with news customisation was age-related. Although, no conclusions can be reached from just one case study, it would be interesting to further test the hypothesis that 'The Daily Me' is more a young person's product and it's the older generation that are asking for the continuity of stable brands and conventional delivery systems.

Demand-led News

> News, we are warned, will be transformed further into a discourse of personalisation, dramatisation, simplification and polarisation. (Fenton, 2009: 9)

When news was first introduced on television, there was considerable concern around the dumbing-down of content (see Chapter 1). *Amusing Ourselves to Death*, the title of Neil Postman's landmark book on the role television's introduction played in American society is a personal lamentation on the tragic loss of what Postman calls the 'Age of Typography' and the ascendancy of the 'Age of Television'. In it he describes the problems associated with attempting to convey complex messages through the television screen and how those messages are necessarily changed creating an irreversible shift in the content and meaning of public discourse. He contends that:

since the two media (print and television) are so vastly different they cannot accommodate the same ideas. As the influence of print wanes, the content of politics, religion, education and anything else that comprises public business must change and be recast in terms that are most suitable to television. (Postman, 1987: 8)

Although questions still remain about the role television plays in shaping our culture, research has indicated that our diet of news hasn't necessarily become poorer, but certainly more varied with extremes at either end of the quality spectrum (McNair, 1999). As television discourses became more embedded its epistemology became more invisible and attention turned to how society should properly administer the freedoms associated with the next 'new' technology.

It could be argued that the addition of television news to the media ecology wasn't systemically disruptive in the way journalism online had the potential to be. It was a repackaging of radio with pictures added; but it still functioned within limited bandwidth with producer control over when and how the product was to be delivered and what it looked like. It used metrics in the form of audience ratings, but, very much confined itself to a one way communication model. However, the leap to digital production on the web ensured that temporality, mobility and interactivity all disrupted news work processes.

The popularity of social sites such as YouTube, Facebook and MySpace and their increasingly important role in the construction and dissemination of news have been implicated in blurring the boundaries between news and non-news spaces allowing serious content to morph into entertainment and lifestyle. The concern is that, unchecked, news customisation will narrow people's fields of interest in such a spectacular way that it will undermine the very function of news within a democratic public sphere. The primary mission of public service news has always been to expose listeners and viewers to things they wouldn't normally encounter, and it's argued that, 'a market dominated by countless versions of "Daily Me" would make self-government less workable [and] create a high degree of social fragmentation' (Sunstein, 2001: 192).

In a speech predicting the way television news will be delivered in the not-too-distant future, the Vice President of CNBC envisaged a multiple choice rather than linear television news bulletin. When cross examined about the effect of crowd-powered dynamics given that, with two million users on YouTube, the top metrics are for, 'a baby biting his brother's finger; Susan Boyle and a sneezing panda', she expressed confidence in her organisation's ability to navigate between the pull of public appetite for triviality and the push of editorial stewardship. She said they would have to apply strict editorial controls, otherwise CNBC would lose its editorial integrity and it wouldn't be able to charge for its content (Stelzner, 2010).

Here Stelzner reminds us of an important reality, the fact that with the exception of public service news, most journalism must function as a commodity to be bought and sold in the marketplace and it must survive as a provider of popular information and maintain both economic and professional integrity. However, it's unsurprising that journalism's remediation online encourages a degree of moral panic now that journalists and editors are no longer as effectively shielded from consumer-metrics.

As commercial competition intensifies, there remains the possibility that news agendas will narrow and the trend towards the merger of news, entertainment and opinion – tabloidisation – will accelerate. In his detailed examination of how news might change within the digital landscape, Currah looks at the dangers of news publishers, 'morphing into "digital windsocks", shaped by the direction of the prevailing clickstream'. He worries about how, 'lacking a clear roadmap, news publishers are more likely to follow the trails of the clickstream in the pursuit of digital success' (Currah, 2009: 85). News workers claimed to be quite aware of these dangers, understanding the important division between editorial and commercial imperatives. One publisher insisted:

> We do not break down revenues by story. We are editorially pure in that sense. I am a custodian of journalism; there is no commercial pressure to dilute standards. … to place stories just for advertising potential. (Currah, 2009: 86)

Despite this assertion, the clarity that comes from precise metrics showing what stories are popular and which ones are not might be too compelling to ignore and on the face of it, the comment above seems a little naive. As we discussed in Chapter 1, advertising pressure is often indirect and the 'editor' may be acting as only one isolated institutional actor without regard to or direct knowledge of other parts of the organisation. The level of professional autonomy within a newsroom should act as a 'brake' to counteract commercial forces; yet, conditions in newsrooms across the world have seen journalists' workloads increase and layoffs and buyouts a common reality. Currah reported that some of his industry interviewees from both quality and tabloid papers had started to link reporters' salaries to the clickstream data, making journalists wealthier the more they cater to popularist tastes.

This trend towards infotainment is not new. Television news has often been accused of trivialising the line-up to attract viewers. Yet, the pressure for commercial operators to fashion bulletins to make them appetising to the biggest possible audience is still evident, especially as the market for news grows more crowded and competitive. Mark Wood, CEO of ITN News, conceded:

> We are certainly doing a lot more coverage of show biz and entertainment … The huge risk is with demand-led news is that people will just look at a fraction of what is actually going on in the world; the tiny segment that interests them … the whole world can be collapsing around you but you wouldn't know. (Currah, 2009: 89)

Another trend Currah notes is the weighting of news in favour of comment and opinion (2009: 129). There has been a rise in the popularity of 'star commentators' with personality who are given the freedom to give opinions on the news. This new army of commentators or 'the commentariat' (Lloyd and Hobsbawm, 2008) has enormous social and democratic clout. There are moments when the star-turn such as that enjoyed by the BBC's Robert Peston after exposing the vulnerability of the UK's banking system in 2007, mix the important with the popular – but the two aren't always natural bedfellows.

A series of big scoops about the financial crisis have thrown the BBC's Robert Peston into the limelight, with the result that he now enjoys star status, an enviable clickstream record (with over 650,000 hits per day to his blog) and hence significant influence in the reporting of economic policy and related financial developments. In this fashion, the highest paid stars are quickly emerging as gatekeepers between the news and the public (Currah, 2009: 131).

A news agenda full of comment has the potential to drive out investigation. The ability to analyse complex problems and investigate the minutiae of corporate activities and government claims takes time and resources. Entertainment news is cheaper and safer. How to pay for this kind of quality is a concern across all Western democratic states.[1]

Hyper-individualisation

We've been examining what makes for a well-functioning system of free expression, and to show how, 'consumer sovereignty', in a world of limitless options, could undermine that system. A well-functioning system might be said to encourage the kind of public sphere that recognises common experiences, in which people hear messages that challenge their prior convictions, and in which citizens can present their views to a broad audience (Sunstein, 2001). Yet, there are clear countervailing forces that are more inclined to break audiences down into consumer groups based, in the last analysis, on their profitability. However, whilst technology is characteristically co-opted to the needs of particular political and economic interests, the degree to which 'good' or 'bad' outcomes are achieved depends on the flexibility and openness of a given technology. The role of regulation, coupled with the complex cultural histories of each individual nation are important factors in this process.

An important debate in the UK through the 1990s and into the 21st century centred on how democracy might be transformed with 'consumers in charge' (see O'Malley and Jones, 2009). There was tension between those who valued the top-down universal address afforded by broadcasting versus those who felt we should be more comfortable allowing consumers to make up their own minds about what was good for them. Those who attempted to engage in discussions of what broadcasting can constructively contribute to society risked regressing into the 'dangerous territory of paternalism'. It became far less acceptable over this time to put across a picture of the viewer as vulnerable and requiring protection or as Richard Collins described, 'requiring tutelage by platonic guardians running the system' (ibid: 192).

Alan Peacock, Chair of the influential Peacock Committee[2], took the view that, 'the fostering of qualities which forge a nation's character and influence and which are generally respected, such as enterprise, inventiveness, tolerance, and justice, is hardly the function of a broadcasting system, rather it is the function of an educational system in the widest sense' (Peacock, 2005: 52). Put another way, the Peacock Committee considered that broadcasting didn't deserve to occupy a special place outside the domain of the market, preferring a bookstore model, with its diverse product range satisfying both high and low brow taste and popular and elitist themes, and where consumer choice drove the production of the books displayed. The view of the consumer as sovereign, holding broadcasters to account through their purchasing decisions, made sense within the framework of Peacock's goal of a full broadcasting market.

Under the influence of the Peacock Report, those concerned with regulating British media were heavily invested in a future where user-instigated activity might drive demand. The suggestion was that news consumers should be treated like responsible adults free to choose for themselves what news they needed or wanted to consume (see Jones, 2009: 187–206). A critical discourse analysis of the 2000 Communications White Paper detailed a semantic shift in the government's conception of people from citizens to consumers very evident in the years leading up to the creation of Ofcom (the UK Communications Regulator) in 2003. Dawes found that the citizen was being constructed in increasingly individualistic terms shifting to the private realm and away from collective experience. He also noted that the balance of agency was shifted with the citizen constructed as passive and the consumer as active. The consumer acting in his or her own interest thus replaced the democratic concept of the public sphere. In this way, consumerism was located in terms of public rights within a framework of private citizenship. This rhetorical shift reframed the government's understanding of citizenship within consumerist terms and paved the way for an economic model of broadcast regulation reconstructing social values and public interests in economic terms (Dawes, 2007). Hence a shift towards individualism and consumerism was already embedded in the policy rhetoric of UK regulators, even before the complexities of internet-enabled communications were introduced.

In the past, the paradigm of a healthy civic commons, where debate amongst all members of society could be fostered, rested on the old fashioned concept of a national conversation stimulated by a mass, top down address. Alternative and radical media existed to challenge this homogeneity; but typically the majority experienced the same limited range of broadcast communication at more or less the same time. In the UK, with its strong PSB history, debate was commonly supported through the output of public service broadcasters such as the BBC. Weakening the universal address had the potential to jeopardise this process, which would be further compromised if citizens became too narrowly defined as consumers within the new communications environment, for, as James Curran writes, 'People who are informed and active participants in civil society are a much more formidable and less biddable force than those who are only "active" at the level of consumption' (2002: 238).

We've established that in a media ecology defined by fluidity and unlimited choice, citizen's interactions are seemingly impossible to control through old fashioned gatekeeping models such as top-down national broadcasting. For example, the UK's Electoral Commission was able to mount a very successful campaign on Facebook during the 2010 General Election targeted at young voters to get them to register their vote. A broadcast news bulletin couldn't have achieved such targeted success and this provided a useful illustration of how the national conversation must adapt to take account of news customisation trends.

Coleman (2005) and Scannell (2005) both ponder the realities of a fragmented and disjointed civic audience and the impact on the future of public service communications. Scannell is pessimistic, linking the decline of broadcasting with the demise of the BBC and aligning digital, narrowcast media with Peacockian free market concepts of individualistic consumer address and personalisation of experience (Scannell, 2004). Coleman also talks of the need to be addressed as a 'citizen' rather than 'mere consumers or free-floating egos' and acknowledges the deep pessimism surrounding the demise of a universal discourse of citizenship where, 'the fragmentation of the media audience (…) is regarded as a metaphor for the tribal disintegration of the public' (Coleman, 2004: 89).

The mass reach that broadcasting traditionally offered, often described as the glue that cements society, was gradually losing its cohesive qualities. The fear was that, once that reach is fragmented into many consumerist spheres a comprehensive public sphere might be undermined. In an unprecedented era of choice, the concept of a single broadcaster empowered to be 'the glue' that binds the nation together, seems a very outdated notion. The concept of choice is at the centre of this debate. Does endless choice encouraging citizens to gravitate to channels reflecting their own worldviews necessarily bring about the collapse of the public sphere, or is this simply another attempt at scaremongering in response to new technology whose impact has not necessarily been fully catalogued?

Born recognised this tension in her 2006 attempt to rethink the nature and scope of public service broadcasting and to 'justify its existence anew' (Born, 2006: 102). She argued strongly for a need to counteract the prevailing forces of consumer-driven news production, believing that it needed to be supported by a mass broadcasting system (the one-to-many model) that should be at the heart of the space for exhibiting and experiencing diversity (Born, 2006: 114). She underpins this point by quoting Stuart Hall, 'the quality of life for black or ethnic minorities depends on the whole society knowing more about the black experience' (Hall, 1993: 36). Hence, one of the important features of mass broadcasting is its ability to ensure that as many people as possible will encounter materials on important issues, whether or not they have specifically chosen the encounter. News customisation risks polarising people's views with like-minded people driven increasingly far apart, simply because most of their discussions are with one another.

As with all such remediation debates, there is anxiety over what is to come. The next generation of news audiences will be invited to negotiate the full range of options open to them. They will be given unprecedented choice and the hope is that this choice will enrich rather than impoverish. The fear is that choice will magnify the worst excesses of consumer-driven news and yet, that was also the fear when television came onto our media landscape.

Raymond Williams (1974) reminds us that we shouldn't allow ourselves to be lulled into a belief that new technologies have a special power to shape and transform society. Yet, the introduction of a new communications medium can engender debate about how society should best organise itself and in doing so, suggests new possibilities and creates new communication paradigms.

The moral panics associated with news customisation and the rise of factual-entertainment within the news diet of citizens, are predictable reactions to media in transition. There is commonly a period of experimentation and chaos that can have productive or destructive outcomes before things settle or normalise. The hope is, as McNair predicts, that, 'the online environment will generate its own methods of quality control', accepting the danger that, 'existing boundaries between professional and amateur, between platforms, between sub-genres of journalism, between the journalisms of information and entertainment – already dissolving, will be eroded further' (McNair, 2009: 349):

> It's easy to see how, by giving people the power to become their own news editors, they might sink down their own insulated 'cultural boltholes'. But, as one critic writes, we have always been our own editors and how one personalises news is simply a question of 'new methods, not new habits'.

Every time we consume media, we make choices, consciously or not. When we skip articles, choose one newspaper over another, switch television channels, or tune in to a radio station we decide what we want to consume. The internet has simply provided tools to make the selection process broader, easier and better structured (Hauser, 2009).

'The Daily Me' could be interpreted as a useful way of improving accountability between 'the people formerly known as the audience' and 'the people formerly known as the journalists'. If news agendas become more transparent and through the story selection process news values more subject to scrutiny, this might be seen as a solution to the democratic deficit in news production. The disruption of power relations enabled through computer code has the potential to cut across hierarchical communication routines, although we must acknowledge that the gatekeeping role isn't being eradicated but merely displaced as the code-writers become the new aristocracy. They may understand the complexity of their algorithms, but few others do (see Jones and Martin, 2010). This suggests researchers must quickly turn to understanding the complexity of programming in order to develop a better understanding of emergent patterns of gatekeeping.

On the negative side of the balance sheet it is clear that technology is not always liberating and often news work exists within constraining, 'journalistic iron cages wherein technology is enshrined in news practice that foregrounds rationalisation and marketisation at the expense of ideal democratic objectives' (Fenton, 2009: 15). Yet, solutions may present themselves that counterbalance the potential deleterious effects of news customisation.

Currah puts some faith in the need for news organisations to ignore the rush to generate clicks in favour of connecting with the public through the reputation that comes with their identities or through, 'the prism of existing editorial and brand values'. He argues that advertisers are increasingly demanding 'engaged not transitory eyeballs' and that a more viable strategy might be, 'for news publishers to identify and follow "editorial isolines" as they navigate the trails of the clickstream. In practice, that would entail a strategic focus on certain kinds of coverage and hence, certain audiences, whilst sidelining others' (Currah, 2009: 89).

If being true to your brand ensures a more robust business model then it is conceivable that there will continue to be many popular 'quality' places to go for news and the concern that news seekers will only consume a diet of entertainment and trivia might be premature. There are ways that news consumers, even those who choose to customise their diet, can build in serendipity into the algorithms but there is disagreement amongst news editors as to whether this will actually happen:

> Serendipity was a 'pleasure', according to FT.com's James Montgomery, who worried that 'really good' articles might not be discovered if they lay outside the readers' 'personalised preferences'. Only Almar Latour (Managing Editor of the Wall Street Journal) disagreed, saying that 'you can build things so that you allow people to personalise for serendipity'. (Thurman, 2011)

BBC columnist Bill Thompson agreed with Latour, suggesting that there are ways to build in imperfection because web communication is unpredictable and the filters, no matter how sophisticated, 'let my friends' interests and activities percolate through and ensure that I am kept aware of things that are important but which I am not especially interested in. In that sense they replicate the serendipity that comes from reading newspapers, but in a more nuanced way' (Currah, 2009: 151).

Why should news editors do all the work for the news consumer? Their decisions will always play an important role in informing readers, but the very act of setting up a 'Daily Me' suggests an active audience wanting to take some control over its diet, possibly more engaged than the average consumer.

Finally, we must recognise that despite the potential for change, the normative functions of the newsroom will typically reassert themselves. We may find that journalism doesn't change as much as we fear (or hope) and it's only the devices from which we consume content, and revenue streams that are changing. Current digital remediation might be seen as a, 'supercharged version of that which came before' but still maintain the 'operational closure of the professional journalistic system' (Deuze, 2006: 72).

Endnotes

1   A decennial study of US journalists from 1982–2002 and in a 2007 follow-up study shows a decrease in the ability to get important subjects covered in the news. This decrease was most pronounced among those working for daily newspapers, but also evident for television journalists (Weaver, 2009: 396).
2   The 1996 Peacock Committee's Report on Financing the BBC was seen to have had a far-reaching impact on the development of communication policy in the UK moving away from paternalistic control of broadcasting to a system based on consumer sovereignty within a broadcasting market.

8

Mobile Journalism – From Desktop to Pocket

We've drawn on examples of how internet technologies have been used to create a new digital space for journalism, documenting changes to news work, funding models and the structures that underpin news as it made its transition online. This chapter looks at what happens when news goes mobile, and how this environment is changing people's relationship with the news they encounter on the move. Adoption of new media technologies is never straightforward and it is useful to identify specific technological trends to help understand the consequences of digital remediation such as the shift from our desktop to our laptop to our pocket.

Remediation

Media in transition is notoriously difficult to catalogue and the move to mobile consumption of digital media is in the very early stages of development.[1] Yet, there is no better time to document this transition than when the process of remediation is in its infancy. The potential for enhanced localness, customisation and mobility are all developments connected to the remediation of news. Each technology presents radical new possibilities that might serve to enhance the quality and democratic potential of news discourses and at the same time each presents potentially significant threats. Despite initial fears, it is not easy today to imagine a world without the internet, and previous to that, a world without television or radio.

Bolter and Grusin define 'remediation' as a process whereby each new medium promises to reform its predecessors by offering a more immediate or authentic experience. The promise of reform inevitably leads the user to compare the pros and cons of old and new media becoming acutely aware of the possibilities and limitations of both. Technologies don't eliminate one another, they enhance or subtly change one another taking their place side-by-side in the new media ecology (Bolter and Grusin, 1999). This chapter on mobile journalism provides a useful illustration of this concept.

'Portable, Perpetual, Personalised and Participatory'[2]

In the US at the end of the noughties, a quarter of adults accessed news every day on their phones and PDAs – personal digital assistants (Pew Research Centre, 2010b). In the UK data from Nielson showed an accelerated use in smart phone users accessing the internet with 13.5 million frequent users, doubling from 2008 to 2010 (Ofcom, 2010). Internet enabled phones accounted for almost all mobile devices sold and by 2015, research suggests, more of us will be accessing the internet from our mobile devices than our desktop computers (Morgan Stanley, 2010).

In a multi-tasking world where no one medium struggles to get anyone's full attention, bite-size news spoon-fed through controlled gateways or mobile applications proved increasingly popular. News seekers, it seemed, valued the accessibility and speed offered through their palmtop devices. In 2010 in just one day, Britons typically spent seven hours watching TV, surfing the net and using their mobile phones. However, because a lot of this time was spent using more than one console – mobile and TV, laptop and TV – the average person actually spent nearly nine hours consuming media of one form or another (Ofcom, 2010).

This multi-console use guaranteed that consumers increasingly flirted with or grazed through their digital media. Research showed that when people accessed a web news site they spent an average of just three minutes surfing the content (Pew, 2010b) and the average user read only 20% of the text on each electronic computer page (Perez, 2008). On a small mobile screen this time was reduced even further and contrasted sharply with the way people continued to read their printed newspapers. These took an average of 60 minutes on Saturday and 40 minutes on weekdays to read (Brooks, 2007).

Open vs. Closed and the Value of 'Instant'

Mobile users were characterised by the US Pew Research Centre as information seekers wanting to consume media on their own terms, and were typically white, male and averaging 34 years old (Pew Research Centre, 2010b). Hence, the goal was to produce content that was fast, flexible and user-friendly to serve this demographic and this led to the increased popularity of controlled 'back-end' applications on mobile devices where users forwent the general purpose browsing experience. A kind of 'dumbed down' browser was created to optimise the mobile functionality and Apple's iPod and iPad were two popular products that recognised and quickly capitalised on this. These platforms used applications ('apps') that were based on closed, proprietary networks and represented a major departure from the open browser systems prevalent from 1990–2009. They were easier to navigate and 'less about the searching and more about the getting' than the traditional HTTP web protocols (Anderson, 2010b). This shift sparked a debate about whether the web was now largely redundant in the face of this newer and easier-to-use technology.

A front page feature in *Wired* magazine, 'The web is dead: long live the internet,' suggested that the previous free-wheeling nature of the web was coming to an end.

> Over the past few years, one of the most important shifts in the digital world has been the move from the wide-open Web to semi closed platforms that use the internet for transport but not the browser for display. It's driven primarily by the rise of the iPhone model of mobile computing, and it's a world Google can't crawl, one where HTML doesn't rule. And it's the world that consumers are increasingly choosing. (Anderson, 2010b)

This provocative article was designed to spark a debate over the future of our media consumption and by inference, how we want to pay for it. Closed, back-end systems are much easier to monetise than open, front-end systems:

> Because the screens are smaller, such mobile traffic tends to be driven by specialty software, mostly apps, designed for a single purpose. For the sake of the optimised experience on mobile devices, users forgo the general-purpose browser. They use the Net, but not the Web. Fast beats flexible. (Anderson, 2010b)

A Second Chance

As discussed in Chapter 3, marketers found that monetising news amidst the free-flowing chaos of the web was challenging to the point of bankruptcy. It was clear that new financial models were needed, ones that leveraged the power of the internet and where content was able to reassert its primacy over the technology that underpinned its access. A second chance to claw back what had been lost through the web came in the form of 'news-in-your-pocket':

> It's not much of a revolution yet, but what is increasingly apparent is that mobile devices have the potential to offer the journalism business that rare and beautiful thing: a second chance – another shot at monetizing digital content and ensuring profitability that was missed during the advent of Web 1.0. (Brainard, 2010)

Brainard's argument is built on the premise that readers would discover news on the move has a value worth paying for because it offers an attractive 'curated' and 'effortless' experience and the average consumer isn't interested in working to discover the information she needs for herself. He suggested that the attraction of a less chaotic user interface facilitated through mobile gateways called 'news apps' was worth paying for:

> Think of surfing the Web as wandering through a museum warehouse, piled with every dusty knickknack it ever collected, and using mobile readers as visiting its galleries, where experts have lovingly gathered highlights. (Brainard, 2010)

True to the spirit of remediation, this new medium borrowed features from both its web and television news forbears. It took on qualities similar to 24 hour television news with its pre-packaged bulletin, supportive framework and linear qualities, easy to digest and readily available and at the same time, adopted something from its web counterparts offering a limited but important degree of interactivity yet more reliable, quick and easy to use. Add to this the mobility function and the end result is reassuring and perfect for the grazing and multi-tasking habits allied with mobile news access.

News businesses didn't have an effective way of securing payment from the internet customer. This was because when people began paying the ISPs rather than the producer, content and access were effectively disaggregated. The mobile applications force customers to line up behind closed gateways allowing news producers to bill directly for their mobile news content. Yet there were problems with that approach:

> What publishers must realize is that the golden egg of the 'revolution' is not that e-readers offer a second chance to monetize digital content on mobile devices alone, but rather digital content on all platforms. Web sites must be pulled into the equation. (ibid.)

Hence, you can't close one door without closing all doors to free content. The paradigm shift needed for news consumers to accept that they might have to pay for news in their pocket and on the generative medium of the web was problematic. Research suggested that only 7% of online users could be convinced to pay for their favourite online news site (Pew Research Centre, 2010b). Yet, one major international news tycoon, Robert Murdoch, was willing to take the chance that this might be enough to justify erecting paywalls. Excited by the promise of 40 million iPads in circulation by 2012, he moved to create a 'tablet-centric' subscription product for PDAs with dedicated content produced for that platform. The gamble was that with an aggressive push to introduce readers to mobile consumption combined with a standing charge for readers online, he could arrange his product line exclusively behind paywalls:

It's going to be a success. Subscriber levels are strong. We are witnessing the start of a new business model for the internet. The argument that information wants to be free is only said by those who want it for free. (Murdoch, 2010)

Murdoch was unsurprisingly bullish about the prospects of converting his readers to a pay-as-you-read model. It was effectively an attempt to introduce artificial scarcity through the web. He hoped that if this business speculation paid off others might be willing to follow his lead despite the fact that as we saw in Chapter 3 there was plenty of evidence suggesting that news consumers were ill-disposed to paying for web news and very willing to switch to free sources should paywalls be erected.

The Triumph of Curation?

As the first decade of the 21st century ended, the web interactivity which brought with it the erosion of barriers between news maker and news user, were widely seen to herald a more democratic or pluralistic period in journalism. All this risked being swept away in a tidal wave of pre-configured apps.

The natural path of industrialisation, 'invention, propagation, adoption and control' (Anderson, 2010b) was on the verge of being realised. Since the web could not be effectively monetised through openness, perhaps 'closedness' was where the value might be captured and the curated experience might render the flexibility and freedom of the Web a thing of the past. If internet use were to default to the closed option of proprietary gateways, historians may well document that era of a low-barrier-to-entry web, where small and large players compete side-by-side in an open news ecology, as an adolescent use of this medium. The 'generative age' of the web where everyone is free to create, might be subsumed by the triumph of curation and closed networks as it matured.

Yet, remediation is a game played out in many stages. Social adoption of technology, as we saw in Chapter 7, is never a straight curve – more of a zigzag. The web may have lost its dominance, but, its next evolution, HTML5, offers flexibility along with an app-like interface so it looks, feels and functions exactly like an app:

If a standard Web browser can act like an app, offering the sort of clean interface and seamless interactivity that iPad users want, perhaps users will resist the trend to the paid, closed, and proprietary. But the business forces lining up behind closed plat-forms are big and getting bigger. This is seen by many as the battle for the soul of the digital frontier. (Anderson, 2010b)

This chapter began by saying that trends are easy to spot, but their long term impacts are less so. It could be in a few years time that the provocative headline, 'The web is dead: long live the internet' might well be replaced with, 'The web might be a bit less important to more people in about 5 or 10 years' (Schofield, 2010) or, 'The web isn't dead; it's just continuing to evolve' (Ingram, 2010) although these alternative headlines aren't quite as punchy.

The question for news providers is how they might be able to claw back some of what they lost, when they decided to sell their crown jewels to the future through the web.

The Social Circulation of News

We've looked at how institutions and consumers are adapting to this new mobile technology but there are other significant forces at work connected to the world-wide adoption of PDAs that are fundamentally changing news work while also promoting citizen agency and democratic voice.

While corporations are learning to listen, filter and harvest social news to great advantage by using Twitter and other social news channels such as YouTube, MySpace and Facebook, citizens are also learning how to harness the power of social news flows, very often to create news reports that challenge those of the mainstream

Technological forces are often synonymous with political and cultural change and the dramatic rise in mobile phone use across both the Northern and Southern hemispheres has significant potential to disrupt the political process by playing an important role in the maturation of democracies.

Madrid Bombings

One of the first times where mobile technology was used to effectively galvanise political pressure was just after the Madrid train bombings in 2004. The Conservative government under Jose Maria Anzar was widely blamed for carrying out a deliberate deception by attempting to pin responsibility for the train bombings on Eta Basque separatists. This deception led directly to his defeat days later in national elections when his party was replaced by the Socialists. The impression that the government was withholding information about the attack incensed voters who, empowered with mobile phones, sent SMS text messages which in turn sparked unprecedented flash demonstrations on Election Day eve. There was a big spike in mobile phone use at the time as peer–peer communications spread virally across the country alerting voters to the conspiracy. This helped galvanise public opposition against the incumbent government. It was in the pre-Twitter days, but none the less symptomatic of the power of social news flows and voter mobilisation.

This was one early example of how social news was used to provide a powerful counterflow of information which became informally networked. This type of information flow is characterised by its unpredictability, classlessness and non-hierarchical nature and since 2004 Twitter has become particularly symbolic of this type of news.

Iranian Elections 2009

The 2009 Iranian elections provided the backdrop for another dramatic example of the use of mobile technology harnessed in the cause of democracy. In Iran demonstrations were staged shortly after the announcement that incumbent Ahmadinejad had won a landslide victory as Iranian political reformists protested that the result was illegitimate.

Neda Agha-Soltan, a 26-year-old whom her relatives said was not political, became an instant symbol of the anti-government movement. Her shooting stirred outrage worldwide because a video filmed on a mobile phone made history when it was circulated widely throughout Iran and the rest of the world. The video shows her death at the hands of the Iranian militia in vivid and horrific detail. After its release, it spread virally across the web and news organisations around the world took note. Hundreds of thousands of viewers saw the young woman's death prompting international protests. The video became a rallying point for the reformist opposition in Iran despite the fact that the Iranian government had blocked many websites including Facebook and jammed satellite television signals. Iranians used anti-filtering software to download the images and some uploaded the footage to their mobile phones and used Bluetooth technology to share it.

The news of Neda's death was received differently across the generations in Iran. Telma Parsa, an Iranian student blogger wrote:

> My brother and I often forget that the state-run TV is almost the only way our parents, like many Iranians of their generation, get information. The state knows this very well. […] As for the current protests, the state-run TV refers to the demonstrators as 'mobs.' Broken shops and burned cars are the only parts of the protests the regime TV is prepared to air. Interviews show people in the street complaining that 'mobs' have ruined their businesses and students who cannot study because of the noise the 'mobs' make. What is never even implied in the TV is that hundreds of thousands of Iranians in major cities are marching peacefully in the streets to show their lack of trust in the state-announced election results. Nor will the clip of Neda's murder ever make the airwaves. (Parsa, 2009)

He went on to describe how his mother was not touched by the video of Neda because it was not compatible with her essential presumptions. 'She cannot believe, for instance, that a Basij member could kill an innocent girl. To my mother, Basij members are the embodiment of everything admirable'. The role of social news in breaking down the state monopoly of broadcasting will have a significant effect on the flow of information within totalitarian states, but this impact will always be muted by the generational response. In addition, the battle will be fought between state and citizen for control of information flow. Software providers for mobile phones such as Nokia Siemens were accused of assisting the Iranian government by selling technology to help monitor communications across the mobile networks including calls, text messaging, instant messages and web traffic.

In defence they argued that these intercept systems were standard and that no government, Western or otherwise, would permit networks to be built without this functionality. Indeed, the UK, the US and around the Western world, government agencies cooperate on eavesdropping, phone tapping, spying and surveillance of political movements on the grounds of what they call 'public order'. In the case of Iran, a spokesman for the company said that while the government can monitor how Iranians use their phones, 'The amount of information that is coming out of Iran from ordinary users because they have connectivity that they would not have had before is of a net benefit to them' (MacKey, 2009).

This provides another example of the zigzag adoption of new technology. The open systems which have been synonymous with web use since its inception are often inconvenient and troublesome for governments and corporations alike. Nokia Siemens may be correct in its 'net benefit' assumption, suggesting that the adoption of the mobile technology they supplied to Iran has ensured at least the beginnings of a level playing field between the users of social media and those that would prefer inconvenient truths stay hidden.

As PDAs become more prevalent in all continents, the hope is that technology will become a powerful agent for change:

> It is now possible for Africans to send articles and images (still and moving) about events taking place in their countries without using a computer and without a traditional internet connection. Under those circumstances the bigger the number of people expressing their opinions through technology, the stronger becomes democracy. (Goggin, 2010: 106)

One progressive example of this technology used to harness cultural and political change is 'Ushahidi', which means 'testimony' in Swahili. It's a citizen-run website initially developed to map reports of violence in Kenya after the post-election fallout at the beginning of 2008. It has since been instrumental in building tools for, 'democratising information, increasing transparency and lowering the barriers for individuals to share their stories'. It does this through citizen reports which are then tabulated through open source software for information collection, visualisation and interactive mapping. Its aim is to use technology to circumvent or disrupt conventional information flows (see http://www.ushahidi.com/).

In this way, use of networked technologies specifically RSS have meant that news gathering can also become news production, or news distribution through the social circulation of news. 'It's now easy to film some raw material on your mobile phone using Qik. It's published on Qik, with an update on Twitter too. The video feed is embedded on your blog or news site, and once again RSS distributes it anywhere you or someone else wants' (Goggin, 2010: 108).

Such principles are notable in a variety of alternative journalism projects in Europe and North America, such as Indymedia, which are constantly adapting to new technological potential, providing new forms of access to those who are otherwise excluded from or misrepresented in corporate media.

However, the reality may simply be that the technology will serve whatever master has most power and financial clout. Certainly extensive use of Twitter in countries with authoritarian regimes might be perilous as governments learn how to exploit it to gather intelligence to use against dissidents. In fact, as Twitter use becomes more common, governments are likely to exploit its use to gather open-source intelligence and identify dissent at very early stages. Certainly in the 2010 student protests in the UK it was clear that the police and security services were monitoring websites, blogs and Facebook pages to counteract protests and to identify, arrest and harass the protest leaders. Of course, those same technologies were used to organise the protests, to expose police brutality and policing techniques that breached human rights provisions, and to criticise the corporate media's focus on violence and disruption.

Another counter-prevailing force to the development of social news through PDAs is the state's control over the carrier networks. For example, scholars have documented the Chinese government's strategy to adopt aggressive commercialisation without any moves to independence in their communication strategies. This trend is referred to as 'Guo Jin Min Tui' – state advances, private sector retreats (Xin Xin, 2010). China's IT infrastructure has developed in a unique way over the last 12 years – 800 million Chinese now have mobile phones (50% of the population) and many of these subscriptions are being purchased in rural China, up until recently a hinterland for communications technology with very little internet penetration. Advertising revenue from the mobile phone far exceeds all other media, making China a very distinctive telecommunications market.

Africa and China are both good examples of how important the mobile phone has become in establishing networks of communication but their effectiveness as a tool for promoting citizen agency and democratic voice remains to be proven. In countries where the use of desktop computing is still relatively rare, mobile devices are useful in bypassing the need for an internet connection, yet their use as a force for political change is, as we've discussed, potentially restricted.

Identifying specific technological trends such as the shift of news from desktop to pocket helps us understand the consequences of digital remediation; yet we've seen in this chapter how the adoption of new media technologies is rarely straightforward and that the social uses governments, citizens and corporations put technology to is fundamental to their adoption and development.

Although the move to journalism online precipitated a huge shift in news culture in the 1990s and 2000s, history may recognise the sudden, meteoric rise in ownership of mobile devices around the world at the end of the noughties as more significant. Undoubtedly, as Bolter and Grusin identified in their work on remediation (Bolter and Grusin, 2000), the future of digital news will reside in its claims to immediacy, interactivity, accessibility and instantaneity.

Endnotes

1   Mobile consumption of analogue media began as motor vehicles were equipped in the 1960s with radios and audio cassette machines. This had a significant effect on the way news was programmed and scripted on the radio which lasts to this day.
2   Pew Research Center, 2010b

Media Law and the Challenges of the Internet

The digital world clearly affords opportunities for new forms of journalism to flourish. In some respects, there is a sense that journalism is less constrained on the internet because it is cheap to distribute material via the internet, because it is unlicensed and difficult to censor, because it transcends borders, and because it is almost unlimited in its size and scope. The proliferation of blogs, online magazines, collaborative projects and user-generated content is a clear indication that journalism has become a less restricted practice, open to all with available means, though there are clear tensions between conflicting forms of use.

However, journalism is not restricted primarily because of the technologies through which it is mediated, but, of course, because of the policy choices made by governments. Whilst there are ever more opportunities to participate in journalism, and whilst there are fewer obstacles to publish, the state retains its right to legislate over citizens, organisations, practices and technologies. The question we consider here is how journalism encounters law in the online environment.

Globalisation, the Internet and Law

Digital journalism does not exist in a vacuum. As we have seen it is in part structured by the economic environment in which it takes place. Here we consider how law also mediates journalism. It is the state that draws up legislation, rules and regulations affecting journalism, media organisations and technologies. For example, the development of journalistic culture was in part a result of the state assuring rights and responsibilities for writers through the development of constitutions, policies and laws relating to speech, media and communication. Indeed, states regulate the formation of media organisations as companies and allocate rights and responsibilities to them as media organisations and as companies. Finally, states play a significant role in the development and deployment of media technologies.

However, many scholars argue that processes of globalisation and technological development have threatened the capacity of the state to continue to assert its traditional forms of legal authority. Such developments include the internationalisation of the economy, the resulting growth of international and regional blocs (Ohmae, 1995, 1999; Lechner and Boli, 2004), and the growth of cross border environmental, economic and technological risks have stymied that capacity of the state to manage its territory (Beck, 1992; Giddens, 1999; Held and McGrew, 2007). Others have pointed to the role of virtuality, international mobility, diaspora populations, and the decline of national publics in reconstituting the relationship between the legal subject and the state (Archibugi and Held, 1995; Sassen, 1996; Hardt and Negri, 2000). In relation to journalism, scholars have suggested that traditional news organisations have failed to adapt to this new reality, instead remaining largely within parochial, nationally based paradigms (Gavin, 2002; Pfetsch et al., 2008).

A classic statement of the perceived role of the internet in this restructuring came from cyber-libertarian John Perry Barlow. His (1996) very influential, 'Declaration of Independence of Cyberspace', claimed that governments 'have no sovereignty where we gather', that:

> We did not invite [governments to the internet]. You do not know us, nor do you know our world. Do not think that you can build it, as though it were a public construction project. You cannot. It is an act of nature and it grows itself through our collective actions … Your legal concepts of property, expression, identity, movement, and context do not apply to us. They are based on matter, there is no matter here.

Ten years later Dean et al. (2006) argued that the internet and the networked society it created is bringing about the end of the liberal democratic state, which is unable to function in such an environment. Perhaps its inability to control digital journalism is evidence of this.

Besides these normative arguments against government interference, other writers have argued that the 'nature' of internet technologies makes it impossible to regulate users. For example, John Gilmore famously suggested that the technological structure of the internet makes it impossible to censor because, 'the internet treats censorship as damage and routes around it'.

These considerations on globalisation and technology have encouraged the idea that a weakened state cannot effectively regulate amorphous, deterritorialised technologies like the internet, or its users. Indeed, in the case of conservative states like Iran or illiberal states like China, there has been a good deal of celebration of the difficulties those states face in regulating the internet. But these tend to be based on a misunderstanding of the nature of political power vested in the nation state. Some scholars (e.g. Barbrook and Cameron, 1995) suggested they were based on a particular 'Californian ideology', which marks the internet to the present day, and reflects a delusion about the relation between political economy and the state in much of the rhetoric about the internet, animated by hyper-individualism, property rights and neo-liberal economics.

Whilst Perry Barlow's claims may have rhetorical appeal, the internet was in fact built as a 'public construction project' and states do have sovereignty over it. The US Department of Defense oversaw the early development of the internet before the Department of Commerce took over control in the early 1990s. In each state governments have encouraged, managed and regulated the development and use of the internet and associated technologies. Regulation, or the lack of it, is always an ultimate decision of a state, and this explains why the development, availability and use of the internet differs from state to state (Abbate, 2000; Barney, 2001; Salter, 2011).

Nevertheless, for many international journalistic organisations and for many human rights organisations, liberal conceptions of the state, of technology and of free speech are used to judge internet regulation. States, on this account, have no right to regulate. The technology itself is framed in terms of political liberalism. For example, each year Reporters Without Frontiers publishes a list of 'enemies of the internet', as if the internet contains within it innate liberal rights.

However, as we shall see, state power remains strong, constraints on journalistic practices are applicable and actionable even in the most liberal of states, and with the growth of international of law-making institutions and international cooperation, the promise of the internet to free journalism may not be what it seems.

Journalism and Intellectual Property

Alongside the development of the internet and digitalisation, the intensification of 'intellectual property rights' or IPR has led to significant restrictions on the collection and dissemination of data. We saw in Chapter 2 how Dan Schiller pointed to the role of IPR regulation under the auspices of international organisations. Understanding the ideas of IPR is crucial for journalists wishing to negotiate the online environment.

Intellectual property rights include more commonly known terms such as copyright, trademark and patent. The rights themselves generally consist in being recognised as the author, designer or inventor of a thing. The thing itself can include written work or other artistic endeavours, a process, medicines and foodstuff, design, discovery or a physical artefact.

The most important legal framework for IPR is the World Trade Organisation's (WTO) Agreement on Trade-Related Aspects of Intellectual Property Rights

(TRIPS). The TRIPS forces members of the WTO to adopt what is essentially an Anglo-American approach to the result of intellectual labour, often to the detriment of poor countries. Its main provisions appear in Box 9.1 below.

Box 9.1 Main provisions of the TRIPs

Main provisions of the TRIPS:

Copyright extended to 50 years after the death of the author

Copyright on film and photography fixed at 50 years in total

Copyright becomes automatic rather than a result of application

Computer programs receive the same protection as literary works under copyright law

Fair use restrictions on copyright claims and public interest exceptions to patent claims to be weakened

Patents claims can extend to all fields of technology

Each state signatory to TRIPS must ensure that it implements laws on IPR that do not favour its own citizens or prejudice foreign companies.

The online journalist is here faced with a number of critical issues – some obvious, others less so. There is a tendency to see artefacts on the internet as existing in a 'free' public domain. Indeed, whereas previous copyright policies governed a media environment where people produced, exchanged and consumed physical artefacts (a book, a CD or a newspaper), digitalisation makes reproduction and distribution easier and cheaper, though costs are not zero. Indeed, the price of a book, CD or newspaper never did reflect merely the cost of production and distribution. Rather other economic mechanisms – supply, demand, profitability, unit cost and so on – would set prices.

Therefore it is perhaps unsurprising that as reproduction and distribution is made easier copyright control becomes deeper and more wide-ranging. The height of this deepening of control was the US's 1998 Digital Millennium Copyright Act (DMCA), which effectively ended copyright's status as a limited right. The extensive copyright introduced in the DMCA meant not only that copyrighted material was to be further protected, but also that applications that can circumvent protection would be illegal. As Lawrence Lessig put it, this law affords producers, 'the power to control how... [content]... is played, where, on what machines, by whom, how often, with what advertising' (Lessig, 2000). Perhaps the most important element of the DMCA is its jurisdiction. As we will find with a number of legal provisions, it also applies outside the home state.

Of course intellectual property existed long before TRIPs and the DMCA – its origins lay in the 19th century. However, it is a choice of governments whether to protect intellectual property, whether to treat information as a commodity alongside bangles, badges and plastic toys. Indeed if the job of a journalist is to facilitate the free-flow of information in order to inform a democratic public, then it may appear that intellectual property gets in the way. Similarly, intellectual property seems to contravene some human rights provisions. For example, the Universal Declaration on Human Rights includes the right to freedom of opinion and expression including the right to, 'seek, receive and impart information and ideas through any media and regardless of frontiers' (Article 19).

The fight against the particular Anglo-American formulation of intellectual property reached its height in the 1970s with the 'non-aligned' movement (generally newly independent, decolonised, states neither associated with the Soviet bloc nor the capitalist bloc during the Cold War). These newly independent states sought to protect their independence against the domination of more 'developed' nations. They considered control over indigenous forms of information and communication to be a crucially important component of independence. These concerns were expressed most coherently in the United Nations Economic, Scientific and Cultural Organisation's (UNESCO) 'MacBride Report'. The MacBride report recommended the establishment of a 'New World Information and Communication Order', founded upon principles of media democratisation, media pluralism and egalitarian access to media platforms and information they contain or distribute. This necessarily challenged the traditional conception of intellectual property.

The US fought vigorously against the UNESCO proposals, collectively known as the New World Information and Communication Order (NWICO) in the 1970s and 1980s. As Dan Schiller (2007) points out if the US had lost that fight, then, 'the result would be to divert and potentially block attempts by the United States ... to recast information into a general foundation for profit-seeking market expansion'. As the US became 'increasingly cognizant of the need to combat stagnation', it sought to defeat the NWICO movement, succeeded in so doing, and thus secured an international basis for information to take the commodity form (Schiller, 2007: 38–9). Although the World Summit on the Information Society is in many respects a more radical movement against intellectual property and commodification than was the NWICO (Mastrini and de Charras, 2005), the TRIPs and DMCA are clearly the pinnacle of the US's hegemony in this area.

For some scholars, the TRIPs and DMCA seem to contradict the technological potential of the digital age (Lessig, 1999). Such scholars consider these legal provisions to threaten the potential for the internet to be used to co-create and distribute cultural products in new and innovative ways, instead imposing 'normal' market relations of artificial scarcity and monopolisation (Berry and Moss, 2008).

However scarcity is almost always 'artificially' constructed, as is 'property', through legal relations. It should, therefore, not be surprising that corporations work with governments to impose property relations and market relations on their products. Nevertheless, Berry, Moss and Lessig are right to point to the potential that is threatened, and to the implications of this threat. Their most significant point is that 'old' legal provisions are being imposed on new conditions, thereby threatening innovation and change. As we have seen, corporations have been struggling to establish acceptable online journalism business models for many years in many respects because they have failed to recognise potential, instead embracing outdated conservative models of investment and profit.

The legal framework that corporations push for has indeed already threatened the technological potential of the web for online journalism. For instance, hyperlinking enabled relatively unproblematic social relations on the web. But this simple relation became qualified as economic colonisation advanced.

The use of hyperlinks has been met with legal challenges on numerous occasions, and almost always in relation to the protection of commercial interests. One of the first cases involving news organisations saw two online newspapers in the UK's Shetland Isles, *Shetland Times* and *Shetland News* taken to court. In early 1996, *The Times* applied to the Scottish High Court for an injunction against the managing director of the *Shetland News*. The reason for *The Times'* request was that the *News* was organised on the basis of deeplinking to articles in *The Times*, thus bypassing *The Times'* front page and most importantly the advertising carried therein. *The Times'* case was based on an accusation of copyright infringement on the part of *Shetland News*, under the UK's Copyright Designs and Patents Act, 1988. Although the motivation was loss of advertising revenue, the legal charge was that by deep-linking to content without any indication of the origins of the material, *The Times'* copyrights were infringed.

In July 2002, the Danish Newspaper Publishers Association set something of a precedent by winning a case to ban others linking to any page other than its home page (*Wired*, 2002a). A similar case in Germany was brought to court on the basis of the European Union's Database Directive, wherein the selection and arrangement of content in a database, in this case a website, is protected from access; the court found against the site making the link (*Wired*, 2002b). With the increase in the quantity and proportion of commodified content, and its concentration in the hands of a few companies, the threat is that hyperlinking may well become reduced outside the realm of commercial relations. Indeed, the World Wide Web Consortium (the governing body for the web) has been looking at ways to commodify links for a number of years.

The European Union's Database Directive also became a point of reference in a somewhat bizarre legal case in the UK. It may well be counter-intuitive, but sporting fixture lists are not necessarily classed as public information. Rather fixture lists are recognised as intellectual property. Indeed, in 2004 the company that provides the fixture information for English football's Premier League, Football DataCo, took legal action to prevent newspapers publishing their fixture lists without paying for a licence. Football DataCo had made its claim on the basis of the Database Directive, claiming that the fixture list existed in a database and should therefore be protected as commercial information. Football DataCo then used intellectual property laws to enable it to charge outlets to publish the fixture lists. It has since sold the exclusive republication rights to the Press Association, which resells to news organisations. However, a controversy broke out when, in addition to the Press Association's republication charges of £9,000 for national newspapers and £22,500 for news websites per season, it sought to claim a percentage of newspapers' advertising revenue.

'Framing' is another of the immanent properties of the web, another integral piece of HTML code that can help journalists display information. It refers to a method of displaying a web page within another, based on the HTML 'frame' tag. This method of displaying information can be used to either remove the content from its context, say by displaying a newspaper article without the surrounding website, or can allow access to several sources from a central location. For example, a website might use frames to display a number of links to documents and charts, which load into the right hand frame. Framing can prove very useful for journalists attempting to provide politically relevant information to citizens or indeed to critically contrast information, news and opinion from a range of sources. All of these are what we might consider to be acceptable, or in fact necessary, activities in a public sphere.

Such activities also met with protest from economic interests, because framing supposedly confuses ownership over content and reduces the ability of the framed site to control access. As an illustration of this contestation, in 1997 *The Washington Post*, Times Mirror, Time Warner, CNN, Dow Jones and Reuters New Media took legal action against a news aggregator, TotalNews, for framing their websites. TotalNews had linked to these sites by using frames to provide a wide-ranging and comparative news service. However, this was seen as contrary to the commercial interests of the news services it linked to. The case was settled out of court whereby TotalNews agreed only to frame sites that had given express permission and the plaintiffs agreed to issue 'linking licences' to TotalNews as long as they did not use frames (for a summary, see CNET, 1997).

Whilst this case involved commercial organisations as both plaintiffs and defendant, it usefully illustrates how intellectual property claims can challenge the potential of the online environment – in this case to protect the overall commodity form, not least so that 'branding' stays intact and that adverts can be seen. The implications are particularly serious, for example, for the act of providing evidence in through a link. In 2006 the news industry began to take serious note of changes to the distribution of information, when the World Association of Newspapers initiated court proceedings against news aggregators, demanding they pay for linking to and framing content of its members (*Financial Times*, 2006). This position was typified in the view of then *The Daily Telegraph* editor, Will Lewis:

> Our ability to protect content is under consistent attack from those such as Google and Yahoo! who wish to access it for free. These companies are seeking to build a business model on the back of our own investment without recognition. All media companies need to be on guard for this. Success in the digital age, as we have seen in our own company, is going to require massive investment ... [this needs] effective legal protection for our content, in such a way that allows us to invest for the future. (cited in Greenslade, 2007)

Despite some legal victories on intellectual property rights, it is not clear that legal protection is the preferred future for the news industry. Nevertheless, attempts to prevent the free circulation of information persist. For example, legal measures were instigated in 2009 by two leading US industry players, Associated Press and *The Wall Street Journal* to determine whether news aggregation was indeed theft and whether the copyright holder could legitimately claim money back in recognition that traditional news gathering operations created value along the supply chain. They wanted to exercise some control over the practice and profit of 'news scraping'. Their key targets were Google, Yahoo and other aggregators such as the Drudge Report. William Singleton, CEO of MediaNews, said, 'We can no longer stand by and watch others walk off with our work under misguided legal theories' (Osnos, 2009). Taking aim at the way these new conglomerates spread news across the internet, The Associated Press said that websites using the work of news organisations must obtain permission and share revenue with them, and that it would take legal action against those that did not (Perez-Pena, 2009).

As we have seen, some news organisations have prevented their content from being aggregated by news aggregators such as Google. For instance Rupert Murdoch's News Corporation invoked copyright laws to prevent Google from publishing or even providing access to its news content, and in 2010 implemented 'paywalls' around its websites to ensure that all users pay for access. In a speech on the subject, Murdoch said, 'we are going to stop people like Google or Microsoft or whoever from taking stories for nothing ... there is a law of copyright and they recognise it' (*The Guardian*, 2010). Indeed, whenever one accesses a news website, one is assumed to have 'agreed' to its intellectual property claims, such as the one in Box 9.2 on page 123.

Box 9.2 The BBC's Intellectual Property Claim, from BBC Online's Legal Disclaimer

The BBC's Intellectual Property Claim;

'All copyright, trade marks, design rights, patents and other intellectual property rights (registered and unregistered) in and on bbc.co.uk and all content (including all applications) located on the site shall remain vested in the BBC or its licensors (which includes other users). You may not copy, reproduce, republish, disassemble, decompile, reverse engineer, download, post, broadcast, transmit, make available to the public, or otherwise use bbc.co.uk content in any way except for your own personal, non-commercial use. You also agree not to adapt, alter or create a derivative work from any bbc.co.uk content except for your own personal, non-commercial use. Any other use of bbc.co.uk content requires the prior written permission of the BBC.'

At the same time, however, many new media analysts (such as Lessig, 1999; Berry and Moss, 2008) continue to argue that digitalisation necessarily challenges old conceptions of property rights and the old means of distributing, using and exchanging information. We see here that intellectual property claims can significantly affect the ability of journalists to facilitate the free flow of information. Many forms of information that a budding online journalist may consider to be in the 'public domain' are not in fact there. However, alongside the legal codification of commercial constraints on the free flow of information, we find legal provisions for political constraints too. We consider these constraints in the next section.

Let Me Past, I'm a Journalist!

Much of the debate about what constitutes journalism (see Chapter 1) can be understood through the concept of recognition. One may simply answer the question, 'What is journalism?' with the answer, 'It is what journalists do'. But as we saw with the case of blogging, it is increasingly unclear who journalists are.

It is rare in any country for journalists to be officially recognised, licensed or registered by the government. However, in many countries there are voluntary systems of registration through associations, trade unions and through media organisations.

Many countries have journalist associations that issue press cards to journalists. In the UK the National Press Card, overseen by the Press Card Authority, is issued through one of 16 'gatekeepers', which are made up of the major national news organisations and journalistic and news associations. In turn most of those require persons wishing to register as journalists to earn their income from journalism. The Commission de la Carte d'Identite des Journalistes Professionnels issues a similar card in France. Importantly, as with the UK's National Press Card police forces in most liberal democratic states often help manage press accreditation, usually on the basis of the applicant working for a traditional news organisation.

In a similar vein, public and private institutions tend to offer special access to persons recognised as working for news organisations. In India the Press Information Bureau of the Government of India allows access to journalists with proven experience. In the US, the Standing Committee of Correspondents approves press passes for the White House if the applicant's, 'principal business is the daily dissemination of original news and opinion of interest to a broad segment of the public' and is not part of the federal government. Of crucial importance, White House accreditation requires that the applicant passes background checks by the US Secret Service. In the UK, journalists do not join the Parliamentary Press Gallery as independent journalists but as representatives of the news organisations that sponsor their applications.

Most institutions, organisations and events will require those wishing to engage them in a journalistic capacity to be formally recognised as such. For example, United Nations conventions, G8 meetings, football matches, trade shows and the like all allocate passes to journalists. However, of crucial importance is the fact that this also allows them to refuse entry to those who don't achieve accreditation.

Help Me, I'm a Journalist!

Journalists may seek recognition in order to receive protections that enable them to do their work. Journalists may need to travel to restricted areas, to interview controversial people, to investigate sensitive documents or to infiltrate criminal organisations. As such, they may be working on the fringes of the law, or may need to gather sensitive information of public importance. To carry out such work they are often afforded protections in the form of what are commonly referred to as 'shield laws'.

Shield laws restrict the state's capacity to interfere with the work of journalists. In the UK there are such provisions to protect journalists, as section 10 of the 1981 Contempt of Court Act, which recognises the journalist's right to protect a source but allows an exception if, 'disclosure is necessary in the interests of justice, national security or in the prevention of disorder or crime'. Of course this latter exception is not absolute; judges will be expected, for example, to weigh these interests against the public interest. There are also provisions in the 1984 Police and Criminal Evidence (PACE) Act to protect journalistic material, which is defined as, 'material acquired or created for the purposes of journalism'.

In the US, various states have implemented shield laws to protect journalists from government intrusion. For example, California has shield laws that apply to the, 'publisher, editor, reporter, or other person connected with or employed upon a newspaper, magazine, or other periodical publication, or by a press association or wire service, or any person who has been so connected or employed'.

Shield laws are, however, rarely if ever absolute. Indeed there have been a number of cases in which reasons of state have overridden the rights of journalists, often in the form of contempt of court provisions. One of the most high profile cases of contempt occurred in the US, when *The Washington Post* journalist Judith Miller was imprisoned for refusing to reveal the Bush White House source who exposed a CIA operative whose husband was opposed to the Bush administration's invasion of Iraq in 2003. In a similar vein in 2007 two journalists for the Australian daily, the *Herald Sun*, Michael Harvey and Gerard McManus, were convicted under contempt rules for failing to reveal their sources for a story on a government clamp down on war veteran entitlements.

So, accreditation tends to associate journalists with news organisations. Similarly shield laws, where they exist, tend to extend to those who work for news organisations. On occasion the recipients of such protections are less well defined, as in the case of the PACE Act. In the case of the PACE provisions news organisations and journalist associations initially requested special protections from the state. However, Robertson and Nicol (1992: 207) explain the crucial legal issues at the heart of the problem of recognition:

> many of their members subsequently changed their minds when it became apparent that the special treatment awarded them in the Act would necessarily involve the courts in defining 'journalism' and in operating a special regime that would accord to practitioners favoured treatment by comparison with ordinary citizens. The special status offered by the Act infringes the principle that journalism is not a profession, but an exercise by occupation of the citizen's right to freedom of expression.

In the US there has been a similar debate over the status of journalists. Although individual states have had shield laws for many years, established constitutional principles have prevented legislation at the federal level, due to the 1972 Branzburg versus Hayes judgement. In this case three journalists who had in different investigations gathered information on drug use and on the Black Panthers political party were subpoenaed to appear in court and divulge information. They refused to appear on the basis of journalistic privilege and took the case to the Supreme Court. The Court ruled that to afford journalists special privileges would contravene the First Amendment of the US constitution – the right to freedom of the press. The reason for this is that it would have allowed federal government to decide who was and who was not a journalist.

He is Not a Journalist, He's a Very Naughty Blogger!

Given that accreditation, access and protection tend to associate journalists with persons generating income from journalism or being affiliated to a news organisation, it is unsurprising that new forms and practices of journalism would be hard to fit with existing provisions.

For example, ought a person who is employed as a journalist with the *Financial Times* and a person who sporadically updates a blog of her personal observations of general political matters both be granted access to a meeting of the World Bank?

For a long time journalists' associations, media organisations and institutions did regard the blogger as a lesser journalist. However, the tide is slowly turning. The UK's National Union of Journalists admitted its first blog-only member in 2007. Although this may have seemed a turning point in terms of recognition, the blogger in question was admitted because he was a full-time, paid, professional blogger working freelance for a mainstream media company.

In the USA, in 2009, the New York Police Department was sued by three online journalists, including a blogger, who were denied press credentials by the Department. They won the case, and as their lawyer explained:

> This step recognises that bloggers are twenty-first-century journalists … It's an important first step, but only a first step, because we still need to address the constitutional problem of who gets press credentials in New York City. The Police Department should not be in the business of determining who's a journalist. (*The New York Times*, 2009b)

In 2005 the White House issued accreditation to its first blogger, though it took until 2010 for the UK Parliament to begin to consider allowing bloggers to get passes for the House of Commons Lobby.

Whilst there are some indications that online journalists working for non-traditional projects are being recognised, this is taking place only within the existing systems of recognition. There is also evidence of countervailing pressures that are retarding radical change.

Journalistic privilege was tested to the limit in 2005 when a US blogger and video activist, Josh Wolf, uploaded footage of a demonstration that turned into a riot to Bay Area Indymedia and to his own blog. He published his edited footage, but police suspected the unedited footage would reveal the identities of persons implicated in alleged criminal activities. The District Court subpoenaed him to reveal his footage and to testify before a Grand Jury. However, Wolf refused, claiming journalistic privilege, though the prosecution (and some journalists) argued that he did not qualify as a protected journalist. Tony Burman (2007), former editor-in-chief of the Canadian Broadcast Corporation, referred to Wolf as a, 'symbol of the internet age', precisely because his case showed how blurred the definition of a journalist had become.

The controversy over privilege arose because (like so many celebrated dissidents in Burma, Thailand and Tibet) Wolf is a blogger and an activist, and as such did not fit within California's definition of a journalist. However, for his part, Wolf, 'considers himself a journalist in the same tradition as independent pamphleteers like Thomas Paine' (2007), himself a target of legal repression in the 18th century.

In contrast, say, with Perrin (see Chapter 6), Wolf defined himself as a journalist, but not as a conventional one. Though he was unable to convince the Court that he could claim legitimacy as a journalist, Wolf consistently refused to cooperate with the subpoena. As a consequence of this he was sent to prison for contempt and stayed there for seven and a half months, the longest a journalist had been imprisoned in the US.

In a less 'political' case, in 2010 California police raided the home of Jason Chen, the editor of the technology news website Gizmodo, and seized computing equipment. The reason given for the raid was that Gizmodo had received 'stolen goods' in the form of a pre-release of a new version of the Apple iPhone. Lawyers for Gizmodo's parent company, Gawker Media, argued that the police had violated California's shield laws and therefore Chen's rights as a journalist.

Perhaps most disturbingly, in 2010 a New Jersey court ruled that its shield laws did not apply to bloggers claiming to be journalists. The judges hearing the case said, 'Simply put, new media should not be confused with news media' (Law.com, 2010).

The 2009 Free Flow of Information Act, which sought to provide a federal shield law in the US, loosened the definition of a journalist to persons who are not necessarily affiliated to a news organisation. However, it did require that to gain recognition, the subject of the shield would have to make their living from journalism.

A more radical solution than trying to gain recognition from existing institutions is the potential of forming new accreditation bodies to provide bloggers and other non-traditional journalists with accreditation. However, as an indication of the conservative leaning of many journalists, the proposal was met with disdain from traditional organisations. In 2010 the global citizen journalism site, Demotix, began to issue its own press cards. Whilst this might be regarded as an innovative, forward looking move that seemed to finally recognise the new realities facing journalism, the response of the UK Press Card Authority was one of dismissal, with its chairman seeking to 'alert' the police to the existence of this unofficial card (*Press Gazette*, 2010). Similarly, Wikinews has begun to issue its own accredited press cards, the value of which remains to be seen.

Publishers, Pressure and Libel

Libel laws remain a significant constraint on journalists and are particularly strong in the UK. Indeed, it was only from 1843 that truth could be used as a defence in English courts, but still to this day the onus is usually on the defendant to prove her allegations to be true. Of crucial importance for online journalists, English law allows for prosecution on the grounds of libel regardless of the original place of publication. This means that if an article published on a Singapore web server slandering a businessman from Colombia is accessible in London, the businessman can sue the publication in London on the basis of English libel law.

One of the most important recent legal precedents in respect of English libel law was the moderation of the truth defence by the 2001 'Reynolds judgment', which resulted from a case brought by the former Irish PM Albert Reynolds against *The Times*. In this case, *The Times* had made allegations against Reynolds that turned out to be incorrect. However, the judge ruled that they were published in good faith and in the public interest, and that the public interest overrode the truth as a defence. In summing up the case of Reynolds vs. Times Newspapers Lord Nicholls outlined ten factors to consider in libel cases, including public importance, urgency and overall tone. Nicholls assigned great importance to the perceived public interest in publishing stories that may not be wholly true. To this end, the Reynolds judgement extended journalistic privilege, wherein Lord Nicholls referred to, 'the need, in the public interest, for a particular recipient to receive frank and uninhibited communication of particular information from a particular source'. As we shall see, although 'the public interest' defence can trump many of the restrictions on journalists, its meaning is ambiguous and ideologically loaded. If 'public interest' is the public interest that the state recognises, restrictions can be circumvented. However, if the concept of 'public interest' that the journalist works with differs from that which the state accepts, then problems arise. Importantly, Nicholls also ruled the truth defence is unnecessary only if the accused has been invited to comment.

Of crucial import, in 2006 a court hearing a libel case against *The Times* judged that the Reynolds privilege is limited. In this instance, the newspaper had reported on the investigation into an allegedly corrupt police officer, naming the police officer and details of his alleged wrong doings. An official police investigation later cleared the officer. The problem faced in this case related not to *The Times* newspaper, but to its web archive. The original article was ruled as protected under the Reynolds privilege. However, the archived version online was protected only to the point at which the officer was cleared of wrongdoing. Thereafter the allegations should have been withdrawn or modified on the archive.

Nick Armstrong (2008) argues that although the current legal consensus is that the internet should be dealt with on a par with existing media there are strong reasons to reject that settlement. For him the important point of libel law is that the wrong is done not when the defamatory utterance takes place or when it is written, but from the time it is published. As he explains:

> the libel occurs, where the material is received, i.e. read by the third party. Hence in an internet context, the wrong takes place where the material is accessed – not where the statement is typed, or where it is uploaded to a server.

So when a defamatory statement is transmitted on an ISP's servers, the ISP 'publishes' the statement wherever it is accessed anywhere in the world.... Furthermore, each time the statement is 'published', i.e. each and every time it is accessed, a separate and distinct cause of action is generated. And the right to sue runs for a year (the 'limitation period') from each separate publication. So whereas a newspaper will normally be safe from action a year after a particular day's issue hits the streets, a website is permanently at risk as long as the material remains on its site – because each hit will be a new publication.

Although this legal principle may seem modern, it actually dates back to 1849 when a wealthy German aristocrat, the Duke of Brunswick, sued the *Weekly Dispatch* for defamation. The original publication was 17 years before the case was raised, but the Duke's lawyers obtained another copy from the publisher, which the court understood as republication. This 150 year old ruling now forms part of the very foundation of defamation law as applied to the internet.

Another key principle in understanding the specificity of internet libel relates to the case of Godfrey versus Demon Internet (2001). Lawrence Godfrey was a physicist who was defamed on a Usenet message board. Godfrey informed the 'publisher', Demon Internet, whose computers hosted the discussion group, of the inaccuracy and harm of the postings, but Demon did not remove them.

Godfrey subsequently took Demon to court for publishing defamatory comments, and the case was to set a legal precedent that has impacted on online publication ever since. The 1996 Defamation Act had provided a defence of those accused of publishing defamatory comments. The so-called 'Section One' defence stipulated that a defendant would be protected if they could show they were not the author, took care in relation to its publication, or did not know that they were contributing to the publication of a defamatory statement.

In this instance, Demon was unable to claim ignorance, as Godfrey himself informed them of the defamation. Therefore, the court found in favour of Godfrey. The consequence of this, as Armstrong points out, is that, 'as the ISP will not usually be in a position to test the veracity of the publication, it is normally advisable for it to err on the side of caution regardless of whether the author of the material insists on the truth of his/ her statements'.

He makes the further point that if the title of an article or web page makes it obvious, 'that there is a high risk of defamatory material being posted ... the ISP should have been proactive in removing web pages or blogs of this sort in order to prevent the libel occurring in the first place, rather than waiting until companies actually complain'. If not damages awarded could run into the tens or hundreds of thousands of pounds, even if the material is available for only a few hours.

Libel and the Economic Impulse

The key issue confronting digital journalists is the economics of libel. For a major newspaper, publishing a controversial, possibly defamatory story is often an economic issue. The publisher will often calculate the risk of a libel payout against the projected economic benefit from publishing a story. So, for example, a tabloid will regard the publication of a story about a well-known pop-singer's private life as a surefire way to attract readers. The economic pay off in the short and long term may be huge. The pay out in libel costs will be weighed against this income generated.

On this account, newspaper publishers, for instance, have a normative responsibility to ensure the truth is published. However, given the possibility of gaining sales from erroneous but scurrilous reports, there is also an economic motivation to publish possibly libellous copy. The costs of losing a libel case may be weighed against the buzz surrounding the paper and extra sales that result from it. This dynamic changes online. Compared to the profits made by a newspaper publisher from a single issue of a newspaper, the profits made by an ISP from hosting a blog are tiny – for example, a relatively popular blog will, by itself, generate almost no revenue whatsoever and may even cause losses as an individual blog. Accordingly, whilst a newspaper publisher may be prepared to spend hundreds of thousands of pounds to defend the publication of an article because of its profitability, an ISP sees no such compulsion.

Accordingly, law firms have adopted an aggressive strategy toward bloggers and news websites. In the early 21st century they began to issue 'take down' or 'cease and desist' notices on behalf of clients who perceive articles to be defamatory. The take down notice informs the publisher that the article is defamatory, and that legal action will be initiated unless the publisher removes the article immediately. Much of the time the notices are generic and are not addressed to an individual. For example, one such notice, addressed to no individual reads, 'If you are a person who was responsible for the publication and/or distribution of the ... XXXX'.

Often these notices are sent directly to the hosting company, the 'publisher'. When this happens the most likely outcome, as Armstrong points out, it that the host will be 'proactive in removing web pages or blogs', they err on the side of legal caution. They have no financial or significant reputational interest in protecting material, and certainly would not seek to contest a claim in an expensive court case. As a result, there is a tendency for ISPs to remove material at the slightest provocation with little or no consultation with the author, regardless of its veracity. The implications of this for the principle of free speech are enormous.

In fact European policy in the form of European Communities Directive 2000/31/EC encourages web hosting companies to take sites down by granting immunity to web hosting companies if they remove potentially libellous material when asked.

The Problem of Jurisdiction

Perhaps the most pernicious element of libel law is the practice of 'libel tourism', wherein litigants can choose a jurisdiction in which to prosecute a case. Libel tourism has a long history. For example, as far back as 1996 the Russian oligarch, Boris Berezovsky, sued *Forbes* magazine over an article entitled 'Godfather of the Kremlin', in which he was accused of being corrupt. Although *Forbes* was at the time distributed mainly in the USA, Berezovsky chose to prosecute the case in London, where libel laws are much stricter. He was able to do this simply because the article was available (though not widely circulated) in the UK. The practice of libel tourism continues to the present day, and has seen newspapers sued, books pulped and websites deleted from the internet. More recently Berezovsky successfully sued the Russian television station, RTR Planeta (broadcast in England via satellite) in London.

In an early case involving the internet, in 2004 boxing promoter Don King successfully petitioned to sue Lennox Lewis' US lawyer in London for comments made on US boxing news websites fightnews.com and boxingtalk.com.

In Indonesia in 2007 three Supreme Court judges reversed an earlier decision on an article in *Time* magazine that suggested the Indonesian dictator and his family had amassed a fortune illegally. The reversal saw £52 million in damages awarded against *Time* magazine. Fortunately for *Time* magazine a third and final hearing went in its favour.

France is another site for libel tourism. Although there the damages awarded are lower and trials can take much longer than in the UK, the big appeal is that French law can compel the publisher to publish a timely and complete retraction alongside of the plaintiff's reply. For these reason the publishers of *The Daily Telegraph*, the Barclay Brothers, sought redress against *The Times* in France.

This phenomenon is significantly compounded on the internet, due to the fact that as soon as a web page is accessed in a country it is thereby 'published' there. In Germany in 2010 German citizen, Boris Fuchsmann, sued *The New York Times* after it published a story in which Fuchsmann was referred to as a criminal. The lower German courts determined that the story was in a section that was not aimed at German readers. However, the German Federal Court overturned the earlier decisions basing its decision on the fact that there are around 15,000 German citizens who were registered to use *The New York Times* website.

Whilst in the case of *The New York Times* the court determined that the size of the readership justified the case going ahead, in Ireland, a state in which libel damages are generally regarded as excessive, a blogger was taken to court for defamation in a case that had legal minds abuzz. The blog in question, ardmayle.blogspot.com, made untrue allegations about a senior Irish civil servant and his partner. The case was settled out of court with the author agreeing to award the civil servant 100,000 Euro.

As solicitor and law blogger McIntyre (2010) reported, the surprising feature of this case related to the fact that the blog was 'very low profile'. Google registered no links to the blog whatsoever, it had been viewed only once a day since it was started. It is therefore difficult to explain why the damages were so high if they are supposed to take into account the extent of publication.

Of perhaps greatest concern in terms of libel tourism is Singapore. Singapore is an authoritarian state, which has extended its grip to the internet – for example, internet cafes may be held responsible for material uploaded or read in them – and has very strong libel laws. Consequently its political leaders have won libel cases against Bloomberg's website, *The Far Eastern Economic Review* (owned by Dow Jones), *The Wall Street Journal*, and the *International Herald Tribune*. Individual bloggers have also fallen victim to Singapore's strict rules on defamation. For example, US blogger Gopalan Nair was arrested and tried for insulting a judge. Another blogger, Jiahao Chen, this time a Singaporean living in the US was forced to close his blog and apologised when a Singaporean government agency merely threatened legal action.

Whereas a magazine, newspaper or television channel has to be physically distributed to a specific country, a web publisher has little control over where copy is read, potentially making it subject to all jurisdictions around the world. Thus libel tourism combined with the effectiveness of take down notices provides intense threats to the ability of journalists to publish controversial material online. However, although the law on this matter seems rather firm, there are instances of online publications fighting back, as we will see in the next section.

Case Study: Libel and Indymedia

We have seen in Chapter 4 how Indymedia facilitates anonymous participation and subjective journalism. The citizens who participate in IMCs are often irreverent and have little interest in neutralising facts, so libel actions are a constant threat. Indeed, IMCs receive sporadic complaints from legal representatives of institutions and individuals who claim to have been defamed. These legal complaints are circulated and discussed on the IMC 'Legal' email list.

On 13 and 21 September 2007, IMC UK received letters from Schillings law firm on behalf of the Uzbek billionaire Alisher Usmanov, demanding the removal of an article written by the former British diplomat Craig Murray. Murray had accused Usmanov of being a 'heroin trafficker', a 'thug' and a 'criminal'. Murray had made the accusations already in a book, and then on his blog. However, the latter was also served with a notice from Schillings. When Murray's ISP took down his blog, the article in question was reproduced on blogs around the world, many of which were also served with notices from Schillings, and most of which complied. The article was then posted to IMC UK, bringing legal attention to Indymedia.

Unlike mainstream organisations, IMCs do not have legal teams, but instead depend on volunteers, who might have some knowledge of law, to make decisions via the legal email list. The legal list was notified of the letter online some time after it was received via the main email address. IMC participants tend to make judgements on legal complaints on a case-by-case basis, often using political rather than legal reasoning. When an article is clearly and intentionally harmful, participants take them down on notification. However, with more politically charged articles, they tend to be aware of the journalistic duty to publish information in the public interest, even when it is controversial. In this instance, discussions about how to deal with the Schillings request were long and drawn out, with participants split between those who wanted to keep and those who wanted to modify the original article.

The problem for lawyers is that IMC UK participants are more like avatars, insofar as most participants use secure pseudonyms. Further, participation is fluid with people coming and going, and there is no formal hierarchy of office, so there is no recognised managing editor or suchlike. This initially led some participants to consider themselves secure from legal threats – however, it was suggested by some on the list that although most participants could not be identified (IMCs tend not to log IP addresses, thus providing anonymity), an aggressive lawyer might realise that someone with a real identity must sign agreements with the web server company, domain name registrars and so on. Such persons may be considered liable.

As the discussions progressed over many weeks, participants contacted the original author to try to find out whether the publisher of the original book had its legal department verify the claims made in it. There was no response. Participants then discussed whether they believed the claims made by Murray to be true. Although no-one was able to decide conclusively, some participants declared themselves prepared to go to court. However, without verification of the claims, no truth-defence could be made in court, so some participants argued against the idea. Another aspect of the truth defence could have been claimed, based on the 'Reynolds Judgement'. Whereas IMC UK might have won a court case on the basis of most of the factors, the fact that there was no attempt to include the (potential) claimant's position would have invalidated the defence.

While this was going on, a participant noted that an MEP had repeated Murray's claims in the European parliament. Some participants proposed that IMC UK could keep the article up and claim qualified statutory privilege. However, the claim was based on a misunderstanding. In the sense intended by some of the participants, privilege was understood as the right to report comments made in parliament (in this case the European Parliament). However, privileges extends only to the words directly reported in context and does not then extend to the rest of an article.

Although there was some consideration that it would be unlikely that a court would award significant damages to Usmanov, on the basis that he was a billionaire and IMC UK is not-for-profit with no significant assets, most participants agreed to a proposal to rewrite the article. It was proposed and accepted (amidst some resistance from the more 'radical' participants) that the article should be rewritten as an article about an attack on IMC UK by Usmanov and his lawyers, that it should be put on the front page (the original was hardly visible) and that, to explain why Usmanov had called upon his lawyers, some of the original claims would have to be repeated as allegations.

Shillings did not contact IMC UK again with regards to the Usmanov case, though libel notices from others have continued. From a political point of view IMC UK mounted an important defence of their right to publish. Perhaps the strength of UK libel law is also its weakness. As lawyers are confident that a simple letter is enough to scare an ISP into action, in many cases it seems that they fail to pursue cases.

However, IMCs ought not be overconfident. Although they tend not to gather data on participants in their sites, the law in the UK can compel website owners to share information on users with the police.

Not Just News

Indymedia, like so many news websites, is not just a vehicle for distributing journalistic copy. In the first instance, and unlike most news sites, it allows anybody to post news articles, and perhaps more importantly, allows readers to comment. Features such as comments and chat rooms allow for a much greater range of voices to be heard than the carefully managed vox pops of radio and television and the letters section of newspapers. The liberal-democratic benefits of this are significant. However, at the same time the website owner may be legally liable for objectionable material therein.

The legal basis for this responsibility was confirmed in a 2007 case in the British High Court. The Chairman, Directors and Chief Executive of Sheffield Wednesday Football Club took the owner of owlstalk.co.uk to court to uncover the identities of persons who posted comments to a discussion board. The comments were taken to be highly defamatory of the plaintiffs and the court ordered that the website owner must reveal the identities of the most abusive of the participants. The website may have been liable not only for court costs and related legal costs of the club, but also for damages. The club decided to withdraw the case in the end, but the legal precedent stood. Indeed, as Nick Armstrong (2008) wrote in the *New Law Journal*:

> websites and web pages which on the surface seem neutral may be sitting on a time bomb if internet users are posting harmful or hurtful material. Obvious examples are the rapidly expanding areas of social networking sites – MySpace

and Facebook being the obvious ones – and self-publishing blog facilities such as Google's 'blogger'.

In the US in July 2010 Gaston County court ruled that the online newspaper, the Gaston Gazette would not have to reveal the identity of a person who posted a comment after a news article due to First Amendment protection and state shield laws.

The Cost of Libel

The cost of libel cases against significant national and international publications can be huge. For example, the *Daily Mail's* 2008 tussle with Sheldon Adelson, one of the richest people in the world resulted in a £4 million legal bill for the *Mail*. Such awards are substantial in the first instance because of the cost of taking libel cases to court, which is why defamation is often referred to as a rich man's law. For instance, the pornography and news publisher Richard Desmond reported that the cost for taking a journalist to court for alleged defamation in a book was £1.2 million.

Such expensive battles are not uncommon in British courts, but the formula for damages is complex. Robertson and Nicol (2002: 143–4) explain that a basic sum is awarded based on the gravity of the libel. The amount awarded should then be influenced by whether the publisher publicly apologises and corrects the error in a timely fashion, the honesty of the mistake, the pre-existing flaws in the reputation of the claimant. Further consideration will be given to the extent of circulation of the libellous statement, the prominence of the defamatory remarks and their repetition elsewhere. As noted above, on the internet the circulation and repetition of libellous remarks may be far greater than with, say, a limited circulation magazine.

Some online publications have, however, been subject to quite substantial damages claims. In July 2010 dadsplace.co.uk had to pay out a record £100,000 in damages to a man continuously defamed on the website.

The irreverent online football magazine, Football365.com (which is now owned by BSkyB) saw its freewheeling style slowed when a football manager successfully sued for defamation. The interesting aspect in this case is that the manager, Martin O'Neill had two complaints, neither of which were caused by original journalism on the part of Football365. The most substantive complaint related to the website republishing a false article that *The Mirror* had published and corrected previously. The subsidiary complaint related to comments made on the website's specific section for reader comments. Thus two non-original comments made about someone in a notoriously opinionated and comical online magazine resulted in unspecified but 'substantial' damages being paid out.

Beside damages, courts may award injunctions against the further publication of libellous or otherwise sensitive material. Normally, if a claimant has been successful in a libel case, apology, correction and withdrawal of the offending article accompanies the award of damages. However, to ensure that the article no longer offends a court may demand republication is forbidden through an injunction, or as it is commonly referred to in the US, a 'cease and desist' notice. This will be returned to later in this chapter.

Unsuspecting Cases

Facebook and Twitter form a significant part of the modern journalists' toolkit, providing enhanced means of distribution and feedback between journalists and audiences. However, they are also subject to legal constraints.

For example, in 2009 the singer Courtney Love was subject to court action by a fashion designer that she had severely criticised on her Twitter page, thus initiating the first Twitter libel case. Later that year celebrity nutritionist Sanford Siegal, filed a libel case in the US against the TV personality Kim Kardashian because of comments made on her Twitter page.

In 2009 a US schoolboy filed a case against Facebook for allowing the publication of defamatory remarks about him by his classmates. The court determined that the page was a private forum that had attracted only 6 members, so the case was thrown out. In contrast in the UK two years earlier a businessman was awarded £22,000 after discovering a former friend had set up a fake profile with his name, attributing false and offensive interests and the like to him. In 2010 a man posted manipulated images of a former friend 'involved' in indecent acts with children to his Facebook page. In this instance, though, as hundreds of people were able to view the images along with defamatory comments, the damages were deemed to be £11,000.

In 2010 even Amazon book reviews came under scrutiny when an academic historian sued another over comments published on the site. Nearly a decade earlier Northern Irish MP David Trimble successfully sued Amazon UK for selling a book that had defamed him, having already sued the publisher of the book in question.

Injunctions and Resistance

Serious infringements of the law – or even potential injunctions – may result in a court imposing an injunction on copy to prevent it circulating any further. An injunction may be awarded in the case of libel, breach of privacy, state security, confidentiality or in relation to court reporting.

Although injunctions can be severe and firm, their use may on occasion be criticised by journalists. Some injunctions are straightforward and uncontroversial, such as if someone has been clearly defamed, or if a child's identity needs to be protected. Other injunctions may be seen as unreasonable. This concern often results in extended media coverage being given to the case in hand.

One famous example of this involved former secret service officer Peter Wright's book, *Spy Catcher*. Wright exposed many secrets of British intelligence institutions, including domestic subversion and foreign assassination plans. The government sought to ban the book, largely based on national security and official secrets provisions. *The Guardian* and *The Observer* sought to report some of Wright's key claims but were served with injunctions. The problem the British government faced at the time was that the ban only covered England and Wales, so the book could be bought in Scotland. Wright fled to Australia, where the book was also freely available. The absurdity of the situation consisted in the fact that the secrets of the British Secret Service were known across the world, where the book was freely available but not, initially, in England and Wales. This absurdity was compounded by the fact that many commentators considered the book to be largely uninteresting, with government ban promoting the book far beyond desert.

Injunctions are usually awarded after publication, so as not to interfere with the legal norms surrounding the concept of prior restraint – that is the norm that journalists are held to account for what they publish, not what they might publish in the future. There are occasions on which injunctions may be sought prior to publication, especially when the claimant's privacy (protected under human rights law) may be at stake. If an injunction is not made before publication, then the breach of privacy is irreversible

In a case from 2008, the Formula One racing boss, Max Mosley sought an injunction to prevent the publication of a video and stills of a sexual experience he was involved in. The *News of the World* had obtained the video, written an article about it and published both on its website. Amber Melville-Brown (2008) explained that although the court found that the *News of the World* had unquestionably breached the human rights (right to privacy) of Mosley, there was little the court could do to prevent further breaches. The internet ensured that once the information is out there, it stays out there, regardless of any injunction against the original publisher. As the judge stated, 'the material is so widely accessible that an order in the terms sought would make very little practical difference … the granting of an order against this respondent at the present juncture would merely be a futile gesture'.

The judge was in some respects correct. But the problem was not just that the video had already been published. Just as in the *Spycatcher* case, the very act of taking the case to court exposed the story to much greater publicity than there would have been otherwise.

Interestingly it seems the spread of the video has been somewhat prevented by a legal request to Google UK not to link to the video. Thus a search for the video on

Google.co.uk leads users to a results page with a note at the bottom that reads, 'In response to a legal request submitted to Google, we have removed 1 result(s) from this page. If you wish, you may read more about the request at ChillingEffects.org'. The ChillingEffects.org website is a repository for cease and desist notices and explains the particular case. On this occasion it seems that the request was made on copyright grounds (under the US's Digital Millennium Copyright Act), presumably by the *News of the World*, which indicates the limits of News Corporation's commitment to freedom of information. Nevertheless, ChillingEffects.org offers the option of searching across national domains, so whereas there are restrictions on Google.co.uk, the offending material can be found elsewhere.

Injunctions are used not only in cases affecting individuals, but also in more general areas of law. For example, the Dutch government sought injunctions against the US news agency Associated Press to prevent the circulation of unauthorised photographs of its Royal Family. US lawyers have applied for injunctions in the UK to prevent the publication of pictures of US golfer, Tiger Woods. Domestic government injunctions in the US are very rare as they are generally thought to contravene free speech provisions in the constitution.

Perhaps one of the most significant injunctions of recent times involved two British men who had, when they were children, murdered a toddler. Having served their sentences for the murder, they were given new identities. Given the strong feelings of members of the public toward the men, the British government decided that their identities should be kept secret forever, and that this injunction should be applicable worldwide. Although legal experts consider a worldwide injunction as almost impossible to uphold due to the nature of international media, especially with the internet, the British government has in fact already prevented unspecified foreign magazines from publishing their identities.

Together with libel measures, 'court restrictions' often form the core of journalists' awareness of law. Contravention of restrictions of courts can land journalists in significant trouble, with large fines to pay. Again, though, the ability of courts to impose such rules is difficult. For instance, in 2005 Canadian courts had imposed a publication ban on testimonies to a corruption inquiry that may have led to trial. However a US blogger posted the testimonies. As a consequence of the interest attracted by the US blogger, and akin to the Mosley case above, the judge who imposed the ban was forced to withdraw it as impractical.

Moderating Libel?

The sense of frustration journalists and news organisations felt at the stringency of libel laws around the world have led to many calls for reform. In the UK both the Labour government of Gordon Brown and the subsequent Conservative administration under David Cameron committed themselves to reforming libel law, especially shoring up the public interest defence, preventing multiple publication cases and most notably restricting libel tourism.

The Irish government reformed its libel laws in 2010, but as the *Irish Times* (2010) put it, it was a missed opportunity: 'For example, it fails to account for ISPs or to rebalance the burden of proof from the defendant to the plaintiff. The centrepiece defence of fair and reasonable publication is unworkably narrow'.

In the US one of the most infamous cases of libel tourism has resulted in significant legal change. In 2003 Bonus Books published Rachel Ehrenfeld's book *Funding Evil: How Terrorism is Financed and How to Stop it*. In the book, Ehrenfeld accused Saudi businessman Khalid bin Mahfouz of funding what she referred to as terrorist groups. Bin Mahfouz strenuously denied the allegations and successfully sued her in an English court, even though the book was not published in England. Ehrenfeld countersued on the basis that bin Mahfouz had violated her constitutional rights on the basis of laws that were inapplicable in the USA. She lost the case.

The important aspect of Ehrenfeld's case is that it led to a change in the law. The first step was the 2008 Libel Terrorism Protection Act in New York State. The Act sought to protect US citizens who were being subjected to libel cases abroad, stating that New York courts could rule a finding of a foreign court unenforceable if it did not weigh the libel claim against US-style provisions for free speech. In 2010 the US Federal government passed a similar law, the Securing the Protection of our Enduring and Established Constitutional Heritage Act, which provided the same protections. The new law would effectively prevent libel tourism against US citizens. Iceland passed a similar law – known as the Icelandic Modern Media Initiative – in 2010, which contained a range of other protections to create an 'off-shore' haven for journalism.

Conflict, Journalism and Jurisdiction

Although defamation law receives a great deal of attention from journalists and news organisations, there are many other aspects of law that illustrate the complications of applying law in a medium with porous borders.

Each state has particular laws that regulate media and communication. Whilst most countries have signed up to the United Nations' International Bill of Rights, the adherence to the rights guaranteed therein varies between states. Often the political, social and religious culture of a given state will mark the development of media laws. The strategic position of the state will dominate developments; it is very unusual, for instance, for a state to guarantee media freedom when its existence is at risk.

Accordingly, one of the key aspects of state security relates to this exception – the rules of conduct when a state faces significant threats. Thus, many states that face subversion from within and without, such as Iran and Cuba, have extensive media regulation. However, it is not just such states whose journalists are required to act in accordance with security guidelines. All liberal democracies provide for media freedom, but expect media to adhere to guidelines and norms that prevent civil and international disturbance.

In the UK, for example, the government and the news industry operates a 'Defence Advisory Notice' (DA Notice) system, which operates to, 'prevent inadvertent public disclosure of information that would compromise UK military and intelligence operations and methods, or put at risk the safety of those involved in such operations, or lead to attacks that would damage the critical national infrastructure and/or endanger lives' (Defence, Press and Broadcasting Advisory Committee, 2010a). Standing notices cover a broad range of security activities, ranging from the location of offices and personnel, to covert domestic operations and military planning (see Defence, Press and Broadcasting Advisory Committee, 2010c).

The DA Notice system is a form of voluntary censorship in which editors agree the sensitivity of information with the government and therefore do not publish certain material. As the Committee puts it, most editors, 'do not want to publish something which really would be damaging to operations or to lives, and if therefore they are persuaded that some detail would do damage, they usually do not publish such detail'. Although the government has no official sanction within the DA Notice system, it can, 'initiate police and/or legal action, including seeking a court injunction to stop something being published' (Defence, Press and Broadcasting Advisory Committee, 2010b).

Digital journalism can disrupt the DA Notice system, not least because it has depended on the organisational arrangements of media that have facilitated the system hitherto. These arrangements are described by Fitzgerald and Bloch (1983) as a, 'cosy relationship between Whitehall and the national media manifested by the panoply of lobbies and private briefings, of which D Notices are but a partial formal expression'. However, as we have seen, digital journalism allows for a much broader range of journalists and journalistic practices than ever before, so governments can no longer rely on cosy relationships with unknown persons.

Additionally, and perhaps most importantly, the porous borders that are possible online mean that is it increasingly difficult to ensure control within a territory. Thus, whilst the government may convince editors of national newspapers to censor certain information for reasons of operational security, they will not find it so easy to censor independent bloggers residing abroad, even with an injunction. Furthermore, the competitive nature of journalism (and as we have seen the logic of injunction) means that once it is in the public domain, news organisations will scramble to report on it, thus rendering agreements and injunctions inutile.

Controls on journalists are particularly strong during conflicts. In most instances, journalists and the authorities in a particular jurisdiction share a similar worldview and similar concerns, so there is no need for the state to use repressive tactics. Rather, the norms and laws that restrict journalistic practice in conflict situations are understood to be commonsensical.

In recent conflicts, such as in Iraq and Afghanistan, military media managers have sought to use soft power to control journalists. Rather than impose strict curtailments on the movement of journalists, media managers use the danger of warzones to encourage journalists to 'embed' into military units. The process of embedding means that journalists tend to see the conflict from the perspective of the soldiers with whom they were embedded. The success of this soft power has been trumpeted by the US Department of Defense. As a result, coalition troops were, 'portrayed by embedded journalists as fierce, efficient warriors as well as compassionate individuals' and the necessary cooperation involved, 'fostered improved relationships between the media and the military' (Rodriguez, 2004).

In addition to the subtle control of journalists, as Bamford (2005) explains, the US government in particular formed the Information Operations Task Force (IOTF). The IOTF was charged with selling the invasion of Iraq to journalists and members of the public around the world by, 'developing and delivering specific messages to the local population, combatants, front-line states, the media and the international community', by producing and scripting television news segments, 'built around themes and story lines supportive of US policy objectives'. At the same time the office would find ways to, '"punish" those who convey the "wrong message"'. One senior officer told CNN that the plan would, 'formalize government deception, dishonesty and misinformation'.

The IOTF contracted the public relations firm, The Rendon Group, which was charged with engaging in 'military deception' online. The main reason a private contractor was used was that it could do things that official government agencies would be constitutionally forbidden from doing. Bamford goes on:

> The company was contracted to monitor internet chat rooms in both English and Arabic – and 'participate in these chat rooms when/if tasked'. Rendon would also create a website 'with regular news summaries and feature articles. Targeted at the global public, in English and at least four (4) additional languages'.

The problem for the US government in pursuing such a course of action was that the federal government is forbidden from propagandising to its own citizens. As Dearth (2002) explains:

In the Digital Age, the distinctions that we like to make in democratic societies between what is civil and military, what is domestic and foreign, make little sense – certainly less than they once did. Digits do not recognize political borders, and they wreck havoc with pristine philosophical distinctions. In an increasingly global Information Space, we must remember to take care that we do not pollute our own information environment in pursuit of the corruption of someone else's.

Slipping Through the Security Net

While liberal democracies tend not to use repressive techniques on journalists during conflicts, this does not mean they are completely free. Indeed, the greatest challenge to states during conflicts is when their success may be threatened during the information war.

In this sense, the internet has afforded an unrivalled opportunity for people to communicate, report and distribute information, bypassing traditional routes. This makes it ever more difficult for states to control.

During the war in Sri Lanka, the Tamil diaspora was adept at utilising the internet to publish information about the conflict around the world. This was particularly important given the degree of control that the Sri Lankan government had imposed on reporting the conflict. Journalists in many other conflict zones, such as Colombia or Israel, in which journalists are unable to or face difficulties in collecting and publishing information, have come to depend on the internet as a means of distribution.

Despite the level of media control exerted in Iraq during the US-led invasion of Iraq, the invasion and subsequent war saw the emergence of the war blogger journalist, such as CNN's Kevin Sites. This meant that the new methods of soft power exercised by the US–UK coalition were confronted by new forms of power on the part of citizens and journalists. A number of Iraqis were blogging in English from inside Iraq, presenting a view of the war that was different from both that of the Iraqi government and of the Coalition. Baghdad Girl, Baghdad Burning, and most notably Where's Raed? (the 'Baghdad Blogger') generated large followings in the English speaking world and presented the opportunity to write from a warzone completely bypassing military or government authorities. Though subject to strong controls, military bloggers published footage from their helmet cameras that showed the war from the perspective of the individual (US) soldier.

The internet also afforded opportunities for non-state actors whose voices would normally be excluded from all official reporting. Voices of Iraq, and Iraq Occupation and Resistance Report, for example, gave the perspectives of those regarded by the US government as 'illegal combatants' and 'terrorists' and who would thereby be excluded from news discourses.

Similarly the invasions of Iraq and Afghanistan saw a massive amount of information released via autonomous websites that may otherwise have never been seen. For example, Iraq Body Count (IBC) was set up to record the otherwise ignored number of deaths that could be attributed to the invasion. Although the figures used by IBC were criticised as being low (dependent as they were on reported deaths), the tag line of the site (a quote from a US general saying 'We don't do body counts') indicates its significance. icasualities.org did the same for coalition deaths, which are also censored.

With the spread of English-language websites more generally a plethora of information was forthcoming, which was not subject to vetting by invading states. Besides the data emanating from information sites like IBC, from military opponents and from the anti-war movement, the internet has been used to distribute a mass of video material that would never have been allowed onto television, whether by legal or political restraint. Perhaps the most significant instance of 'counterinformation' being released online was that of Wikileaks.

From 2007 Wikileaks – a 'wiki' website that publishes leaked government and corporate documents, making them publicly available – released thousands of leaked government documents from around the world, from evidence of government corruption in Kenya, illegal activities of the Swiss bank Julius Baer, and US government instructions for mistreating detainees at the Guantanamo Bay prison to the British National Party member list, toxic waste dumping in Africa and classified video footage of a US helicopter shooting civilians – including journalists – in Iraq.

Wikileaks does not actively publish the leaks, but allows whistleblowers to release information anonymously and securely. However, it does verify documents before they are finally released on the website. The site has become a crucial part of the journalists' toolkit. The spokesperson for Wikileaks, Julian Assange, describes the project as, 'creating a space behind us that permits a form of journalism which lives up to the name that journalism has always tried to establish for itself. We are creating that space because we are taking on the criticism that comes from robust exposure of powerful groups' (*The Observer*, 2010).

When it was first formed in 2007, Wikileaks was welcomed by Western media organisations. It was celebrated as a new set of armaments against state secrecy. *The Washington Post* (15 Jan 2007), for example, told its readers, 'You're a government worker in China, and you've just gotten a memo showing the true face of the regime. Without any independent media around, how do you share what you have without landing in jail or worse?' *The Post*'s excitement seemed to have been prompted by the idea that Wikileaks, 'targets regimes in Asia, sub-Saharan Africa and the Middle East... It's significant that their emphasis seems to be on relatively closed societies rather than the US or Europe, that have a rather robust media sector'.

The Post's position was typical of Western media organisations – Wikileaks was to be welcomed as long as its targets were acceptable. However, its value began to be questioned when its independence started to expose the political alignment of news organisations. Although the independence of Western news organisations is celebrated by Western news organisations, critics have often pointed to their adherence to the worldview of the home state. And indeed, as Wikileaks began to expose the wrongdoing of Western powers in Iraq (through its publication of the US 'War Diaries' in October 2010, and in Afghanistan before that), the tone began to change.

One of the most significant moments in the War Diaries saga was the open letter sent to Wikileaks by the supposedly independent Reporters Without Borders (RWB). Although RWB describes itself as a press freedom organisation, it saw fit to reprimand Wikileaks for the, 'incredible irresponsibility you showed when posting your article (on the Afghan War Diaries)'. The gist of RWB's letter was that the leaked documents posed an unacceptable threat to the US military and its collaborators in Afghanistan.

In response to the threat Wikileaks poses to governments, persons working for it have come under surveillance and have complained of harassment. In 2009 German police raided the home of the registrant of the German domain name after the site released the Australian government's 'blacklist' of censored websites. Governments have sought to increase sanctions against those who leak documents.

The strength of concern over Wikileaks can be seen in the report, 'Wikileaks. org – An Online Reference to Foreign Intelligence Services, Insurgents, or Terrorist Groups?', published under the auspices of the US Department of Defense Intelligence Analysis Program. The report was drafted to, 'assesses the counterintelligence threat posed to the US Army by the Wikileaks.org website.' Its findings make for interesting reading. The concern over Wikileaks is clear from the outset, for it, 'represents a potential force protection, counterintelligence, operational security (OPSEC), and information security (INFOSEC) threat to the US Army'.

One of the clear objectives of the DoD, as of other military and civilian intelligence organisations around the world, is to find ways to mitigate the threat of Wikileaks. In the US, the document reports that the inclination is toward, 'The identification, exposure, termination of employment, criminal prosecution, legal action against current or former insiders, leakers, or whistleblowers could potentially damage or destroy this centre of gravity and deter others considering similar actions from using the Wikileaks.org website'.

Crucially, the document identified a broad range of surreptitious threats to Wikileaks. 'Efforts by some domestic and foreign personnel to discredit the Wikileaks.org website include allegations that it allows uncorroborated information to be posted, serves as an instrument of propaganda, and is a front organisation for the Central Intelligence Agency (CIA)' (Department of Defense, 2008).

In December 2010 Wikileaks released another tranche of US Government documents, this time a release of US embassy cables from around the world. Despite the promise of the internet and related policies of free speech, Wikileaks had already been under attack but faced further threats. The site was initially hosted in the US, but because of the greater provisions for freedom of expression and greater protection for journalistic freedom, it was moved to Sweden in 2007. However, with the embassy cable leaks, the fight against Wikileaks took on a new dimension. Its main spokesperson faced rape changes, which seemed to many to be suspiciously timed, and whistleblowers were arrested. Bradley Manning, a 22-year-old US soldier behind the War Diaries leak for instance, was arrested and held without charge in a military prison, where he faced appalling conditions, including 23 hours a day in a small cell, which he spent in complete isolation. Manning faces 50 years in prison if he is found guilty.

Further to this, the Wikileaks case exposed the overlapping interests of the state and corporations, which so many media critics have drawn attention to. Wikileaks faced the withdrawal of payment and donation-facilitated services from PayPal, Visa and Mastercard, Amazon withdrew its hosting service, and even Apple withdrew an app that mediated Wikileaks. However, as testament to the difficulties involved in censoring the internet, and to the value of support from serious news organisations (in this case *The Guardian* stood beside Wikileaks from the outset), Wikileaks has weathered the storm, though a number of its workers and partners have had their lives ruined.

Beside the high-profile sites such as Wikileaks, much of the most realistic imagery of wars over the past decade has been carried by video sharing websites, including YouTube and former 'gore sites' such as rotten.com and ogrish.com, which gained fame in the world of journalism by carrying video and photographic footage of various atrocities in Iraq and around the world without concern for national interests and state security.

Ogrish had come to attention for releasing footage of dead and dying people without seeking permission from family members. In violation of privacy and other media laws in most countries, Ogrish held on to the notion that it was providing an insight into aspects of everyday life that are sanitised by corporate news media. Since gaining such notoriety, ogrish.com has reinvented itself as a clearinghouse for raw video footage. In transforming into Liveleak.com it has gone some way to shaking off its old image, yet it still points to an ambiguity in media regulation and law – not just the problem of jurisdiction, but also the problem of regulatory paradigms on a multimedia platform.

Before moving to consider some of the regulatory issues relating to digital journalism, it is worth noting important legal tools that are especially important in an online environment, of which journalists and editors may not have as much awareness of as more specific restrictions on reporting.

Since 2001 most states around the world intensified repression of subversive materials. In the US and UK so called anti-terrorist legislation, such as the US PATRIOT Act and the 2006 UK Terrorism Act, has restricted access to public information, increased surveillance, broadened definitions of terrorism (and of what constitutes support for terrorists), and has imposed strong sanctions on anyone who might be considered to be 'aiding terrorism'. To aid this security drive both the US and the UK (and many other states around the world) have made it much easier for law enforcement officials to gain access to information, including from journalists, and often require ISPs to collect and store the data generated by the use of the internet.

After 2001, the US imposed some of the most significant restrictions on information gathering of any liberal democratic state. We have seen how commercial laws have restricted access to and distribution of material, but further restrictions have been imposed at a public level. For example, as Sandra Braman points out in 2001 US President Bush succeeded in assigning himself the right to veto the transfer of presidential records to the US National Archives (Braman, 2006: 151), reclassifying information that had been declassified under the Clinton administration (Braman, 2006: 206), and slowing down the declassificiation of documents that have passed the 25-year rule (Braman, 2006: 207). The impact of the Homeland Security Act and the PATRIOT Act on freedom of information has led to whole government departments being exempted from Freedom of Information legislation. The extent of these changes is deeply disturbing, whether in specific cases (such as information being withdrawn from the websites of the US Geological Survey, the Environmental Protection Agency and the Internal Revenue Service), or in more general terms (such as the provision to exempt agencies that willingly submit information to the Department of Homeland Security from freedom of information requests) (Braman, 2006: 207). Thus the ability of journalists to collect government information from physical sites or online sources is severely curtailed.

The PATRIOT Act also curtailed protection for journalists and other persons gathering information, effectively removing the need for reasonable cause for a police search. As journalists in the US are not constitutionally protected with a Federal shield law, and as the PATRIOT Act has cross-border scope, its implications for journalists are crucial. The US Electronic Privacy and Information Centre points out that the Act allows security services to have general search warrants (that is, which don't specify an individual or a site to search), that persons (and establishments) can be searched without being informed, that no search is necessary to spy on a person's internet activities, and that a person need not be made aware of the evidence used against them (Braman, 2006: 135).

Sometimes such laws may be used directly against journalists. The ubiquity of media production equipment can enable many more people to take part in reporting the news. As Eamonn McCabe (2005) notes:

In this digital age, we are now all photographers and there are no rules or right ways of doing things any more. Often the amateur is the first on the scene of a huge tragedy or big news story. Mobile phones, for instance, were the first to record the mayhem of the tube bombs in London and I am sure some of the best photographs of Elton John's wedding were taken by well-wishers in the crowd, who got a lot closer than the professional news photographers.

However, in the UK there have been a number of cases of police officers using the Terrorism Act to prevent people (including journalists) taking photographs in public, on occasion detaining them and confiscating equipment. Free speech campaign group, Article 19 (2006), has continuously expressed 'grave concerns' over the impact of UK terrorism legislation on freedom of expression, specifically citing concerns over 'the broad definition of terrorism', 'the use of anti-terror laws to stifle legitimate social and political protest', and 'prohibitions' on the 'encouragement', 'other inducement' or 'glorification' of terrorism. In its submission to the International Commission of Jurists' panel on Terrorism, Counter-Terrorism and Human Rights, Article 19 expressed concern that, 'together as well as individually, these vaguely phrased prohibitions criminalise the legitimate exercise of freedom of expression and have a real chilling effect on debate on matters of public interest' (2006: 1). For Article 19, the vague terms used in the Act, such as 'encouragement', 'inducement', 'indirect encouragement or other inducement', 'glorification' and 'justification' may prevent public discussions that attempt to understand the motivation of violent actors, and may criminalise criticisms, 'of the liberal western way of life' (2006: 7). They remind us that, 'freedom of expression protects not only views that are favourably received; but precisely those that are controversial, shocking or offensive. The press and others have a right to air such views; and the public as a whole has a right to hear them' (2006: 7).

From the UK to Australia, injunctions have been used in many court cases against suspected 'terrorists'. In 2005 alone, Australian courts issued 1,000 'suppression orders' attempting to prevent pertinent information getting into the public sphere (*The Australian*, 2006). The Australian Government introduced a particularly draconian Anti-Terrorism Act in 2005, to which journalists are subject, whether online or not. Like the UK's Libel Act, the scope of the Australian terrorism legislation expanded beyond its borders, making it particularly important for online journalists. The Act reintroduced many outdated legal measures, including sedition. Under the Act, a person may be guilty of 'seditious intent' by bringing the Sovereign into hatred or contempt, by urging disaffection against the Constitution, the Government or Parliament. The law also forbids anyone to attempt to change the law by anything other than lawful means or to promote hostility that would threaten the peace of Australia.

The Act goes on to outline actions that may count as outright sedition. These include the afore mentioned seditious intentions as well as urging persons to engage in conduct to assist a country or organisation at war with Australia whether or not a state of war has been declared!

The scope of the Act is dramatic, not least because it is applicable extra-territorially, which means that, for an example, an Afghan journalist who objects to the invasion of his country is subject to the law should they vocally oppose the occupation of Afghanistan. The impact of the ability to report on conflicts is clear.

When a state faces significant threats from journalists, the situation can be far worse than that of Australia, and points to circumstances that can result from overzealous 'security' measures. Sri Lanka's 30-year civil war (which ended in 2009), between ethnic Tamils (whose combatants were called the Tamil Tigers) in the north and east and the Sri Lankan state, saw more journalists killed than in any other conflict. Between 2006 and 2009 14 media workers were killed, most of them being Tamil journalists shot in the street by unidentified gunmen – Tamil activists tended to accuse the government-backed Sri Lankan army. For its part, the Sri Lankan government implemented strong 'anti-terrorist' legislation, ostensibly to aid its effort against the Tamil guerrillas. However, the legislation, especially the Prevention of Terrorism Act, has been frequently used to gag journalists trying to cover the Tamil experience of the conflict. In one such example, Tamil journalist Jayaprakash Sittampalam Tissainayagam was arrested and detained while trying to cover the impact of the conflict on Tamil civilians for, 'aiding and abetting a terrorist organisation' (Amnesty, 2009).

In the case of Sri Lanka, even the collection of information is a struggle for journalists. The dissemination can be even more challenging, with Tamil newspapers being targeted by the army. The response of Tamils was to move media operations out of Sri Lanka and thereby avoid direct repression. For instance, the Tamil Television Network was moved to Paris, France for this purpose. However, after the global crackdown on political and media freedom from 2001, the Tamil Tigers were classified as a terrorist group, and entities that were regarded as generally supportive of them began to be targeted by police and state authorities. Accordingly, after the Sri Lankan government made representations to the French government the Network was closed down.

It has proven far more difficult for states to close down Tamil online news services. The main Tamil news website, Tamilnet continued to function throughout the war as it was based in the United States. However, the Sri Lankan government ordered Sri Lankan ISPs to ban access to it (as the German government had done to Ogrish), thereby preventing its news from circulating in that country. Furthermore, in a clear indication of the limits to the 'virtuality' of online journalism, its editor, Dharmalingam Sivaram, was abducted and killed in Sri Lanka in 2005.

Despite their problems, internet technologies do offer a safer way for journalists to communicate, and this must not be underestimated. As Nigerian blogger Ayobami Ojebode (2008) explains:

Online journalism has been considered the safest form of journalism, the least susceptible to state clampdown. It has negotiated for itself a clear space in the public sphere for citizens' engagement of government, its actions and policies. This form of journalism is understandably attractive to Nigerians given the experiences of orthodox journalists in the hands of the Generals Ibrahim Babangida and Sani Abacha – Nigerian military dictators who hounded and pounded journalists for nearly fourteen years.

However, on occasion a state may choose to exercise even tighter control over the capacity of a perceived enemy to communication. For example, in another indication of the limits to virtuality, the Palestinian delegation complained to the 2003 World Summit on the Information Society that the Israeli army had, 'continual control over the Palestinian frequency spectrum', refused to allow, 'linking the occupied areas of Jerusalem to the Palestinian network', prevented direct access of the Palestinian 970 country code to the international network, denied the fibre-optic linking of Palestine to the outside world, confiscated telecoms equipment, systematically destroyed the Palestinian infrastructure by demolishing, 'communication towers … public and private radio and television station transmitters … [and] communication and electricity poles and towers' (WSIS, 2003).

Hatred and Fear Across Borders

It is not just in armed conflict that journalists may be restricted. Indeed, legislation in various countries prevents journalists from writing about crimes in particular ways. In the UK, the 2006 Racial and Religions Hatred Act makes it an offence to incite 'hatred' of a person on the basis of race or religion, though it does specify that the writer or utterer intends to incite hatred.

More pertinently for the online journalists, many states have strong laws against holocaust denial and anti-Semitism. Spain, France, Switzerland, Austria and a number of other European states have made both holocaust denial (and sometimes denial of genocide more generally) and anti-Semitism (and sometimes racism more generally) criminal offences. This includes, as in Austria's National Socialism Prohibition Law, holocaust denial:

> in print or in broadcast or in some other medium, or otherwise publicly in any manner accessible to a large number of people, if he denies the National Social genocide or the National Socialist crimes against humanity, or seeks to minimize them in a coarse manner or consents thereto to justify them.

German law on holocaust denial makes it a crime regardless of where the denial is first published, in provisions similar to UK libel law. The jurisdictional extension was implemented partially to prevent holocaust deniers in Germany who move publication sites abroad from escaping German jurisdiction. It became more pertinent a matter since the spread of the internet – with a new law to address this being implemented in 1997. For example, Ernst Zündel ran his Zündelsite website from Canada, though it was physically located in the US. Zündel had published material in the US and on his website, but never specifically in his homeland, Germany. However, when deported back to Germany, he was arrested and convicted. Similar cases have been tried in Germany and Australia. For example, Frederick Toben, organiser of the Adelaide Institute, published anti-Semitic and holocaust denial material on the Institute's website and was subsequently convicted in Germany and Australia, even though Toben argued that his material had not been published in Germany. The German court, however, insisted that the material could be accessed there, so its laws held.

In 2010 *The Times* published a photo of an unveiled Iranian woman, who was then facing a death sentence for adultery, on its website. As the website is available globally, the photo was viewed in Iran, and although the woman's son claimed it had been incorrectly attributed and *The Times* corrected the mistake, the woman still faced punishment.

The issue here returns us to the question of jurisdiction with such an international medium. Whether regarding libel, terrorism or incitement, legal measures are being applied to the online environment, with sometimes problematic consequences for digital journalists.

Falling Foul: Controversies, Raids and Subpoenas

Most journalists will hardly notice the existence of the state whilst carrying out their work, in some respects because, as many scholars have argued, journalists tend to adopt official discourses and to interface with the state. This fact becomes most evident in oppositional and alternative journalism projects. Although Iran or China may spring to mind when we consider state clampdowns on online oppositional media, as seen with 'terrorism' legislation, there are plenty of examples of liberal states restricting oppositional journalism.

Although there are still questions about the ability of states to control the internet, online journalists are legal subjects whether they like it or not, and their tools are similarly subject to laws as other material items. Thus, as we have seen, the internet does not entirely transcend jurisdictional control. It may not be as easy to control as licensed media, but control can be exerted over all material items. In 2004 IMC UK witnessed the realities of state power.

On Thursday 7 October 2004, the Indymedia UK website went offline. Few of the participants were aware of how and why this happened – the site just disappeared. It was not, however, just IMC UK that went down. Another 21 IMC sites (which were hosted on the same server) also went down. The problem for

IMC UK was that its site was hosted on the servers of a US hosting company, which had been requested to comply with a subpoena from the Federal Bureau of Investigations.

In 2003 and 2004 an Italian magistrate was investigating a number of 'terrorist' acts committed in Italy and elsewhere in Europe, in particular the attempted bombing of Romano Prodi, responsibility for which was supposedly admitted on an Indymedia website. However, the magistrate found that the site was not hosted in Italy, but in the US – exploiting supposed 'borderlessness' to receive greater constitutional protection. Therefore in April 2004 she requested that the United States Judicial Authority obtain log files from Indymedia's web hosting company, Rackspace. The magistrate had requested that the US authorities subpoena Indymedia Global for IP logs. However, although Rackspace is a US company, the servers in question were physically located in the UK. This meant that the FBI could not directly comply with the request. Instead it had to make the request to the UK authorities. The important point about these requests is that they were made under the Mutual Legal Assistance Treaty – an agreement between states to cooperate on legal investigations across borders without necessarily having formal laws in common. This enabled cross-border cooperation, using a treaty to distribute police powers across jurisdictions. The seized servers were eventually returned, but new legal norms had been established, which Privacy International referred to as, 'international cooperation gone awry'.

IP log subpoenas are often issued due to the anonymity of online activity, especially with open media projects such as Indymedia. In 2005 police in Bristol, UK sought access to the Bristol Indymedia IP log to identify the person who had written a story about a 'direct action' they had initiated – in this case materials were thrown at a train carrying cars from the port through the city of Bristol in a protest about climate change. However, in keeping with other IMCs, Bristol IMC preserves the anonymity of participants by deleting IP logs and was thus unable to reveal the logs. However, in June 2005 the police raided Bristol IMC, seizing its web server under the PACE Act, and arrested a participant for incitement to criminal damage. Indymedia claimed journalistic privilege, having informed the police in the first place that there were no IP logs, and were joined in their campaign by Liberty, the National Union of Journalists (NUJ) and so on. The police ended up having to issue an apology and pay compensation.

The claim to 'journalistic material' used the same PACE Act under which it was seized. Although the argument was well supported by other organisations that sympathised with Bristol IMC, such as the NUJ, it was somewhat misplaced. In the first instance, journalistic privilege is not protected in the same way as, say, lawyer's privilege. Journalistic privilege (in this instance to protect a source) is significantly qualified. Although journalistic material is protected under the PACE Act, that protection can be easily overturned by a judge or even by the invocation of special procedures. Furthermore, as outlined above, the protection of journalistic material is subject to other issues – especially the 'public interest'. It is clear that a judge would see the action as criminal damage, and its reporting as the glorification of vandalism, and therefore there is no public interest defence.

In the USA, Indymedia which was also targeted by state subpoenas. In 2009 the Indiana District Court commanded that US Indymedia hand over all data on IP traffic to and from the site on 25 June 2008. The subpoena demanded not just the raw IP data but detailed user information including telephone records, credit card numbers, social security numbers, drivers' licence numbers, student identification numbers and so on. The subpoena also gagged Indymedia, preventing them from publicising the fact they had received it. US Indymedia immediately began to campaign against the subpoena, only to find that it had been incorrectly issued and was thereby invalid.

In 2007 the editors of the *Phoenix New Times* news website were served with a subpoena to reveal data on anyone who had used the site over a period of four years. The subpoena demanded information on pages read by each visitor as well as reporters' notes stretching back three years. The editors claimed that the subpoena was issued by the Arizona court as retaliation for articles they had published which were critical of the country Sheriff, though the court claimed it was due to the website having published the Sheriff's home address. As with the Indymedia subpoena, this one included a gag forbidding reporting on it. However, the editors did publish a report exposing the subpoena and were subsequently jailed (*The Arizona Republic*, 2007). The charges and the subpoena were subsequently dropped.

Similar subpoenas to identify commentators and bloggers have been issued in Memphis (against the blog, MPD Enforcer 2.0), in New York (against the online newspaper, *The Chester Chronicle*) and in many other states.

Box 9.3 Bloggers Under Pressure

Greece 2006: blogger, Antonis Tsipropoulos, has his home raided and is arrested by police because his news aggregation site linked to a satirical web page in the US.

Egypt 2007: blogger, Abdel Karim Suleiman, is jailed for four years for insulting Islam and insulting the president.

Saudi Arabia 2008: blogger, Fouad al-Farhan, has his home raided and is arrested and detained for investigating the arrest of dissident academics.

Malaysia 2008: blogger, Raja Petra Kamarudin, detained for sedition, insulting Islam and inciting racial tension relating to his exposés of abuse of power. He fled to the UK in 2010 from where he runs his site.

UK 2008: blogger, Gavin Brent, arrested and fined for writing 'grossly offensive and menacing messages' relating to his treatment by the police on his blog.

Nigeria 2008: blogger, Jonathan Elendu, arrested for 'acts of sedition', which related to his involvement in exposing wrongdoing within government circles.

US 2009: blogger, Jeff Pataky, has his home raided and equipment confiscated on the basis of 'harassment' as Pataky's blog was highly critical of the local police.

Multimedia and the Regulatory Paradigm Explosion

Online video content has in much of the world presented enormous challenges to policy makers and regulators. Much of Europe, for instance, makes quality requirements of broadcasters. This usually takes the form of public service broadcasting (PSB) requirements. However, as Ithiel de Sola Pool (1983) argued decades ago in the US, the technical arguments for PSB – that in a medium of spectrum scarcity such as broadcast analogue television PSB is needed – dry up when there is spectrum abundance.

Nevertheless, most states treat the moving image as a special media category and impose conditions on the broadcast of such images. However as the regulations relate to the medium 'broadcast' rather than the content, once this content moves to the internet, there is not a clear regulatory convention within which it can be framed.

Although in 2006 the European Commission sought to extend its Television Without Frontiers (TWF) directive to the internet, and thereby regulate online video, the proposals were rejected in the replacement TWF directive, the Audiovisual Media Services Directive. The replacement, however, only applies to commercial, 'television-like' services.

In Canada discussions took place in 2009 to consider the erosion of Canadian culture that is said to accompany the fact that the majority of online content accessed by Canadians does not originate from Canada. A coalition of interested groups proposed to impose a levy on ISPs to fund content production. In the US, the National Hispanic Media Coalition, comprised of more than 25 organisations, requested the US Federal Communications Committee (FCC) to investigate hate speech and misinformation online. They suggested that their main concern was that:

The internet gives the illusion that news sources have increased, but in fact there are fewer journalists employed now than before. Moreover, on the internet, speakers can hide in the cloak of anonymity, emboldened to say things that they may not say in the public eye. Even worse, sometimes anonymous internet speakers hold their information out as news, leaving the public with the difficult job of discerning fact from fiction. (National Hispanic Media Coalition, 2010)

Whilst it is unlikely that the FCC would intervene presently, the petition does indicate concerns about the quality of online journalism.

When in Taiwan a Hong Kong media magnate was denied a television broadcast licence for his Next TV news channel due to what the Taiwanese National Communications Commission (NCC) referred to as the 'graphic content' of its other operations the tycoon simply moved his operations online. The NCC responded that it would monitor Next TV with the view to introducing regulations (*Taipei Times*, 2010).

In China the government introduced regulations for online video and audio content in 2007. The regulations pertain to production and editing of publicly accessible content through the internet and mobile phone networks. Online audio and video service providers are required to apply for licenses, for which they may qualify if they are majority state-owned, 'a comprehensive program censoring system, legal program resources, legal funding sources, and "standardized technology"' (Marbridge Consulting, 2007). Many other countries simply block web case and online video sites if they are likely to distribute 'controversial' material.

Although there have been discussions in some liberal states about regulating webcasts and online videos, they have seemed impracticable to policy makers. However, attempts to protect intellectual 'property' have been heard by policy makers and companies. Indeed, this is what the revised TWF directive attends to. In 2008 the media corporation owned by the Italian Prime Minister, Silvio Berlusconi, launched procedings against YouTube for copyright infringement. Subsequently, in 2010, his government proposed strict legislation to protect commercial content from being distributed in violation of copyright law via YouTube and similar services. The proposal would make ISPs and video service providers responsible for monitoring and removing material. Google, the company behind YouTube, questioned the need for legal action, as it already forbids copyrighted content from being uploaded. Nevertheless, other media giants such as Viacom, the French broadcaster TF1 and a number of music publishers have taken action against YouTube or sought agreements over revenue sharing.

Afterward – The End of News?

> News is a form of culture invented by a particular class at a particular point of history – in this case the middle class largely in the eighteenth century ... (it) does not represent a universal taste or necessarily legitimate form of knowledge ... but an invention in historical time, like most other human inventions, will dissolve when the class that sponsors it and its possibility of having significance for us evaporates. (Carey, 1989: 17)

Carey wrote this long before news journalism's first major encounter with the internet. He articulates a perennial idea which transcends the technological and situates news as a form of culture sponsored, as it has been for centuries, by a controlling class.

The question remains whether the normative values of the 19th and 20th century newsrooms will reassert themselves and established power relations continue or if the changes identified in this book will mark a significant turning point. Yet, if the migration of journalism online tells us anything, it's that news can no longer be reduced to a narrow corporate-centric information genre produced by major media corporations.

With the major restructuring of the relationship between the public and the media, traditional news organisations face enormous competition in informing the public. Self-evidently hypertext-based journalism is becoming the central form of production and distribution of news, challenging old notions of separate mediated identities and endowing readers with agency, production and distribution capacity – introducing a new 'class of sponsors' and bringing a new 'significance'. Twitter is particularly symbolic of these changes with its accessibility and distributive mechanisms showing strong counter-flow possibilities. Attempts to embrace these polyvocal, fragmented, two-way discourses have the potential to offer us alternatives (some radical) to traditional journalistic narratives.

A number of scholars have suggested that the internet can be used to reform democracy by increasing participation in the process of making decisions, by facilitating the social circulation of news and by challenging political institutions to listen, filter and harvest this news flow more effectively. News is now entrenched in social media spaces and the observations of non-journalists are increasing their circulation and these voices require the services of curators, weeders and archivists. Journalists are responding by rethinking their professional role so they might find ways to add value in the facilitation of social dialogue as gatherers and sharers of information.

Changes to News Work

As a result of these changes a new set of essential craft skills is emerging for all those working in journalism – 'professional' or otherwise.

It's not sufficient simply to be able to write, the next-generation journalist will need to be able to find and download data, use statistical software, be comfortable with advanced web-scraping strategies to analyse social news flows, and have the basic technical skills to facilitate their work. Certainly numerical literacy has never been more important to journalism and tomorrow's journalists cannot afford to be without a good maths qualification. Tim Berners Lee, the inventor of the web, stressed the importance of data-literacy in a speech reported by *The Guardian* newspaper in 2010. He suggested that the days of getting stories by chatting to people in bars are mostly behind us. He believes that the future of journalism lies in being just a little bit nerdy:

> In his [Berners-Lee] view, it lies with journalists who know their CSV from their RDF, can throw together some quick MySQL queries for a PHP or Python output ... and discover the story lurking in datasets released by governments, local authorities, agencies, or any combination of them – even across national borders. (Arthur, 2010)

Digital datasets are becoming increasingly important to investigative reporting and skills in data evaluation will be able to provide the kind of news that people value. Spotting trends that no one else has noticed to uncover corruption or waste or simply identifying information to help consumers make choices about what products and services to buy, will all depend on finding the way around the journalist's new digital tool box.

The inclusion of a broader range of news workers, and the fact that many are now unpaid, raises new challenges about how to sustain such work. We identified such challenges, and the problems they raise, throughout this book. Taken from a managerial perspective, we have shown how the opportunities afforded by new technologies have been missed. Executives, interested primarily in providing often short-term financial gains to investors, missed key opportunities by attempting to move the old paper and television cash-cows online, or by considering new technologies merely as opportunities for cost-cutting. Professional journalists have, naturally, been concerned about the very real issues of jobs, pay and conditions of employment.

The question that journalists and editors have addressed adequately and systematically is how to interact with the dearth of information and unpaid news workers. The notion that there's an oversupply of information, of digital cameras, of websites, blogs, and people willing to communicate using them, does no more to invalidate the practice of journalism than the availability of running shoes, gyms and joggers invalidates professional runners. Indeed, there should be a qualitative difference between professional and amateur journalists.

The question that must now be asked is, what do journalists add to reporting, analysis and commentary as journalists? On this analysis we may suggest that professional journalists can and should uphold the standards associated with excellence. When there are so many sources of reporting, it is the standards that allow us to distinguish those forms of reporting that have the ability to attract audiences and therefore investment. So rather than executives viewing the digital world as one in which professional journalism can be done as cheaply as amateur journalism, perhaps it is instead an opportunity for investment in quality, so that journalists retain many of their key skills but also add new skills, which take money and resources to harness effectively. The future for journalism is to integrate all that the digital and online worlds have to offer, to improve and renew journalism for generations to come.

References

Abbate, J. (2000) *Inventing the Internet*. Cambridge, MA: MIT Press.

Adam, G. Stuart (1993) *Notes Towards a Definition of Journalism: Understanding an Old Craft as an Art Form*. St Petersburg, FL: The Poynter Institute for Media Studies.

Aldridge, M. and Evetts, J. (2003) 'Rethinking the concept of professionalism: the case of journalism', *The British Journal of Sociology*, 54(4): 547–64.

Alexia.com (2010) *Drudge Report – Site Report* [Online]. Available at: http://www.alexa.com/siteinfo/drudgereport.com# (accessed September 2010).

Allan, S. (2004) *News Culture*, 2nd edn. Maidenhead: Open University Press.

Allan, S. (2006) *Online News*. Maidenhead: Open University Press.

Amnesty International (2009) *Sri Lankan Journalist's Year of Detention for Reporting on the War* [Online]. Available at: http://www.amnesty.org/en/news-and-updates/news/sri-lankan-journalists-year-detention-reporting-war-20090305 (accessed December 2009).

Anderson, C. (2009a) 'Some industries are more free than others', *Financial Times*, 2 July. Also available online at: http://blogs.ft.com/gapperblog/2009/07/some-industries-are-more-free-than-others/. (accessed August 2010).

Anderson, C. (2009b) *Free: The Future of a Radical Price*. New York: Hyperion.

Anderson, C. (2009c) *Interview with Chris Anderson* [Online]. Available on Amazon website at: http://www.amazon.com/Free-Future-Radical-Chris-Anderson/dp/1401322905. (accessed August 2010).

Anderson, C (2010) 'The web is dead? Long live the Internet', *Wired Magazine* [Online]. Available at: http://www.wired.com/magazine/2010/08/ff_webrip/all/1 (accessed August 2010).

Andrews, R. (2009) 'Pay-to-read – cash cow or red herring?', *The Guardian*, 10 August. Available at: http://www.guardian.co.uk/media/2009/aug/10/newspapers-paid-content-charging-paywalls. (accessed August 2010)

Archibugi, D. and Held, D. (1995) *Cosmopolitan Democracy: An Agenda for a New World Order*. London: Polity.

Armstrong, N. (2008) 'Blog and be damned?', *The New Law Journal*, 158(7312).

Arthur, C. (2010) 'Analysing data is the future for journalists, says Tim Berners-Lee', *The Guardian*, 22 November.

Article 19 (2006) *The Impact of UK Anti-Terror Laws on Freedom of Expression*. Submission to ICJ Panel of Eminent Jurists on Terrorism, Counter-Terrorism and Human Rights, London.

Atton, C. (2008) *Alternative Media*. London: Sage.

Avilés, J., León, B., Sanders, K. and Harrison, J. (2004) 'Journalists at digital television newsrooms in Britain and Spain: Workflow and multi-skilling in a competitive environment', *Journalism Studies*, 5(1): 87–100.

Bad Idea Magazine (2010) *Interview: Paul Bradshaw, of UK Crowdsourced Journalism Project Help Me Investigate*[Online].Available at:http://www.badidea.co.uk/2010/01/interview-paul-bradshaw-of-uk-crowdsourced-journalism-project-help-me-investigate/ (accessed June 2010).

Bagdikian, B. (2000) *The Media Monopoly*. Boston: Beacon Press.

Bamford, J. (2005) 'The man who sold the war', *Rolling Stone Magazine*, 12 January.

Barber, L. (2010) *Why Journalism Matters* [Online]. Available at: http://www.pressgazette.co.uk/story.asp?storycode=43985 (accessed July 2009).

Barbrook, R. and Cameron, A. (1995) *The Californian Ideology* [Online]. Available at: http://www.hrc.wmin.ac.uk/theory-californianideology-main.html (accessed January 2005).

Barker, G. (2008) quoting Amon G. Carter, publisher, The Fort Worth Star-Telegram in 'Then and Now', Online Journalism Symposium speech, University of Texas.

Barlow, J. P. 'A Declaration of the Independence of Cyberspace'. Available at: http://www.islandone.org/Politics/DeclarationOfIndependance.html, (accessed May 2009).

Barnett, R. (2008) Speech at the Society of Editors Conference. [Online]. Available at: http://www.societyofeditors.co.uk/ (accessed December 2008).

Barnett, S. (2009) *Journalism, Democracy and the Public Interest: Rethinking Media Pluralism for the Digital Age*, Reuters Institute for the Study of Journalism, Working Paper. [Online]. Available at: http://reutersinstitute.politics.ox.ac.uk/fileadmin/documents/Publications/The_rise_of_social_media_and_its_impact_on_mainstream_journalism.pdf (accessed March 2010).

Barnett, S. (2010) 'Minding the regional news gap', *British Journalism Review*, 21(1).

Barnett, S. and Seymour, E. (1999) 'A Shrinking Iceberg Travelling South: Changing Trends in British Television: a Case Study of Drama and Current Affairs', London: Campaign for Quality Television.

Barney, D. (2001) *Promethius Wired Chicago*. Chicago: University of Chicago Press.

Bärthlein, T. (2008) '*Malaysiakini.com: Flagship of Free Media' Deutsche Welle* [Online]. Available at: http://dwelle.de/southasia/SoutheastAsia/1.234145.1.html (accessed May 2009).

BBC Creative Future (2006) [Online]. Available at: http://www.bbc.co.uk/pressoffice/pressreleases/stories/2006/04_april/25/creative_detail.shtml (accessed March 2009).

BBC (2010) *BBC Strategy Review* [Online]. Available at: http://www.bbc.co.uk/bbctrust/assets/files/pdf/review_report_research/strategic_review/strategy_review.pdf/ (accessed August 2010).

Beck, U. (1992) *Risk Society: Towards a New Modernity*. London: Sage.

Benkler, Y. (2006) *The Wealth of Networks: How Social Production Transforms Markets and Freedom*. London: Yale University Press. Available online at: http://www.benkler.org/Benkler_Wealth_Of_Networks.pdf (accessed July 2010).

Benson, R. (2009) 'Futures of the News: International Considerations and Further Reflections', in Fenton, N. (ed) *New Media, Old News*. London: Sage. p. 198.

Berry, D. M. and Moss, G. (eds) (2008) *Libre Culture*. Canada: Pygmalion Books.

Billington, P. (2010) quoted in *Web Journalism*, Tunney, S, Monaghan, G (eds.) Sussex University Press. Chapter 6 p. 114.

Boczkowski, P. J. (2004) 'The processes of adopting multimedia and interactivity in three online newsrooms', *Journal of Communication*, 54(2): 197–213.

Boczkowski, P. and de Santos, M. (2007) 'When more media equals less news: Patterns of content homogenization in Argentina's leading print and online newspapers', *Political Communication*, 24: 167–90.

Bolter, J. D. and Grusin, R. (1999) *Remediation: Understanding New Media*. Cambridge, MA: MIT Press.

Born, G. (2006) 'Digitising democracy', *The Political Quarterly*, 76(1): 102–23.

Bourdieu, P. (1983) *The Field of Cultural Production*. Cambridge: Polity Press.

Bradshaw, B. (2009) 'Royal Television society biennial convention' speech [Online]. Available at: http://blogs.journalism.co.uk/editors/2009/09/17/ben-bradshaws-speech-in-full-bbc-has-probably-reached-limits-of-reasonable-expansion/ (accessed September 2009).

Brainard, C. (2010) 'A second chance', *Columbia Journalism Review*, July/August. Available online at: http://www.cjr.org/cover_story/a_second_chance.php? (accessed May 2010).

Braman, S. (2006) *Change of State: Information, Policy, and Power*. Cambridge, MA: MIT Press.

Braverman, H. (1974). *Labour and monopoly capital: The degradation of work in the twentieth century*. New York & London: Monthly Review Press.

Brennan, B. (2009) 'The future of journalism', *Journalism*, 10(3): 300–2.

Bromley, M. (1996) 'How Multiskilling Will Change the Journalist's Craft', *Press Gazette*, 22 March, p. 16.

Bromley, M. (1997) 'The End of Journalism? Changes in Workplace Practices In the Press and Broadcasting in the 1990s', in M. Bromley and T. O' Malley (eds), *A Journalism Reader*. London: Routledge. pp. 330–50.

Brook, S. (2007) 'Newspaper reading habits revealed', *The Guardian*, 26 October. Available online at: http://www.guardian.co.uk/media/2007/oct/26/sundaytimes.pressandpublishing (accessed August 2010).

Brown, K. and Cavazos, R. (2003) *Empirical Aspects of Advertiser Preference and Program Content of Network Television*. Federal Communications Commission Working Papers.

Bruns, A. (2005) *Gatewatching: Collaborative Online News Production*. New York: Peter Lang.

Bruns, A. (2008) *Gatewatching, Not Gatekeeping: Collaborative Online News* [Online]. Available at: http://snurb.info/files/Gatewatching,%20Not%20Gatekeeping.pdf (accessed May 2009).

Burman, T. (2007) *Jailed Journalist a Symbol of Internet Age* [Online]. Available at: http://www.cbc.ca/news/about/burman/letters/2007/03/jailed_journalist_a_symbol_of_1.html (accessed September 2009).

Cameron, D. (2010) *Big Society Speech* [Online]. Available at: http://www.number10.gov.uk/news/speeches-and-transcripts/2010/07/big-society-speech-53572 (accessed August 2010).

Carey, J. (1989) *Communications as Culture: Essays on Media and Society*. Boston: Unwin Hyman.

Carnegie Trust (2010) *Making Good Society: Commission of Enquiry into the Future of Civil Society in the UK and Ireland* [Online]. Available at: http://democracy.carnegieuktrust.org.uk/files/Makinggoodsociety.pdf. (accessed October 2010).

Carter, S. (2009) *Digital Britain* [Online]. Available at: http://www.culture.gov.uk/images/publications/digitalbritain-finalreport-jun09.pdf (accessed November 2009).

Chalaby, J. (1996) 'A comparison of the development of French and Anglo-American journalism, 1830s–1920s', *European Journal of Communication*, 11(3): 303–26.

Chandran, P. (2009) *Are we Trying Hard Enough?* Paper given at the International Symposium for Online Journalism, University of Texas. [Online]. Available at: http://online.journalism.utexas.edu/program.php?year=2009 (accessed May 2010).

Chapman, J. (2005) *Comparative media history: An introduction: 1789 to the present.* Cambridge: Polity.

Chomsky, D. (1999) '"An interested reader": Measuring ownership control at *The New York Times*', *Critical Studies in Media Communication*, 23(1): 1–18.

CNET (1997) *Total News, Publishers Settle Suit* [Online]. Available at: http://news.cnet.com/2100-1023-200295.html (accessed December 2010).

CNN Money (2003) *The Secrets of Drudge Inc. How to Set up a Round-the-Clock News Site on a Shoestring, Bring in $3,500 a Day, and Still Have Time to Lounge on the Beach* [Online]. Available at: http://money.cnn.com/magazines/business2/business2_archive/2003/04/01/339822/index.htm (accessed June 2008).

Cohen, E. (2002) 'Online journalism as market-driven journalism', *Journal of Broadcasting and Electronic Media*, 46(4): 532–48.

Coleman, S. (2004) 'From service to commons: Re-inventing a space for public communication', in J. Cowling and D. Tambini (eds), *From Public Service Broadcasting to Public Service Communications*. London: IPPR. pp. 89–99.

Coleman, S. (2005) 'New Mediation and direct representation: Reconceptualising representation in a digital age', *New Media and Society*, 7(2): 177–98.

Coleman, S., Anthony, S. and Morrison, D. (2009) *Public Trust in the News: A Constructivist Study of the Social Life of the News*. Reuters Institute for the Study of Journalism, University of Oxford. [Online]. Available at: http://reutersinstitute.politics.ox.ac.uk/ (accessed December 2009).

Collins, R. (2009) 'Paradigm found: The Peacock Report and the genisis of a new model UK broadcasting policy', in T. O'Malley and J. Jones (eds.) *The Peacock Committee and Uk Broadcasting Policy*, London: Palgrave.

Colombia Journalism Review (2010) *Magazines and Their Web Sites March 2010.* [Online]. Available at: http://www.cjr.org/behind_the_news/magazines_and_their_web_sites.php (accessed April 2011).

Cooper, S. (2006) *Watching the Watchdog: Bloggers as the Fifth Estate*. Spokane, WA: Marquette Books.

Cottle, S. (1999) 'From BBC Newsroom to BBC Newscentre: On Changing Technology and Journalist Practices' *Convergence* 5(3): 22–43.

Craig, R. (2004) 'Business, advertising, and the social control of news', *Journal of Communication Inquiry*, 28(3): 233–52.

Currah, A. (2009) *What's Happening to our News?* Reuters Institute for the Study of Journalism [Online]. Available at: http://reutersinstitute.politics.ox.ac.uk/fileadmin/documents/Publications/What_s_Happening_to_Our_News.pdf (accessed March 2010).

Curran, J. (1991) 'Rethinking the media as a public sphere' in P. Dahlgren and C. Sparks (eds), *Communication and Citizenship, Journalism and the Public Sphere in the New Media Age*. London: Routledge.

Curran, J. (2002) *Media and Power*. London: Routledge.

Curran, J. (2010) *Local Journalism and Democracy. Transcript from Putting the Crisis in Local Journalism on the Political Agenda*. Goldsmiths University: London. [Online]. Available at: http://www.gold.ac.uk/global-media-democracy/events/localjournalismcrisis/james-curran/ (accessed July 2010).

Curran, J. and Seaton, J. (2003) *Power without Responsibility*. London: Routledge.

Dacre, P. (2010) *UK Editor's Code* [Online]. Available at: http://www.editorscode.org.uk/downloads/reports/webLH_Report_2009.html (accessed 30 July 2010).

Dahlberg, L. (2005) 'The Corporate Colonization of Online Attention and the Marginalization of Critical Communication?' *Journal of Communication Inquiry* 29 (2):1–21.

David, A. (2009) 'Politics, Journalism and new Media: Virtual Iron Cages in the New Culture of Capitalism' in N. Fenton (ed), *New Media, Old News*. London: Sage. pp. 121–137.

Davies, N. (2008) *Flat Earth News*. London: Chatto and Windus.

Dawes, S. (2007) *Reducing the Difference between Citizens and Consumers: A Critical Discourse Analysis of the Communications White Paper 2000*. Paper presented at the MeCCSA Graduate Conference, University of the West of England.

Dean, J., Anderson, J. W. and Lovink, G. (eds) (2006) *Reformatting Politics: Information Technology and Global Civil Society*. London: Routledge.

Dearth, D. (2002) 'Shaping the information space', *Journal of Information Warfare*, 1(3): 1–15.

Defence, Press and Broadcasting Advisory Committee (2010a) *Notes* [Online]. Available at: http://www.dnotice.org.uk/ (accessed July 2010).

Defence, Press and Broadcasting Advisory Committee (2010b) *Frequently Asked Questions* [Online]. Available at: http://www.dnotice.org.uk/faqs.htm (accessed July 2010).

Defence, Press and Broadcasting Advisory Committee (2010c) *Standing DA Notices* [Online]. Available at: http://www.dnotice.org.uk/danotices5.htm (accessed July 2010).

Demos (2004) *The Pro-Am Revolution*. London: Demos.

Department of Defense (2008) *Wikileaks.org – An Online Reference to Foreign Intelligence Services, Insurgents, or Terrorist Groups?* [Online]. Available at: http://file.wikileaks.org/file/us-intel-wikileaks.pdf (accessed August 2010).

de Sola Pool, I. (1983) *Technologies of Freedom*. Cambridge, MA: Belknap Press.

Deuze, M. (2005) 'What is journalism? Professional identity and ideology of journalists reconsidered', *Journalism: Theory, Practice, Criticism*, 6(4): 442–4.

Deuze, M. (2006) 'Principal components of digital culture', *The Information Society*, 22(2): 63–75.

Deuze, M. (2007) *Media Work*. Cambridge: Polity.

Dickinson, R. and Bigi, H. (2009) 'The Swiss video journalist: Issues of agency and autonomy in news production', *Journalism*, 10(4): 509–26.

Digital Britain Report (2009) London: Department for Business Innovation and Skills, DCMS, June [Online]. Available at: http://webarchive.nationalarchives.gov.uk and http://www.culture.gov.uk/images/publications/digitalbritain-finalreport-jun09.pdf (accessed June 2009).

Domingo, D. (2006) *Inventing Online Journalism: Development of the Internet as a News Medium in Four Catalan Newsrooms*. PhD dissertation, Universitat Autònoma de Barcelona.

Domingo, D. (2008) 'Interactivity in the daily routines of online newsrooms: Dealing with an uncomfortable myth', *Journal of Computer-Mediated Communication*, 13(3): 680–704.

Downing, J. (2001) *Radical Media, Rebellious Communication and Social Movements*. London: Sage.

Dupagne, M. and Garrison, B. (2006) 'The meaning and influence of convergence', *Journalism Studies*, 7(2): 237–55.

Eckman, A. and Lindof, T. (2003) 'Negotiating the gray lines: An ethnographic case study of organizational conflict between advertorials and news', *Journalism Studies*, 4(1): 65–77.

Ehrenfeld, R. (2003) *Funding Evil: How Terrorism is Financed and How to Stop it*. Los Angeles, CA: Bonus Books.

Enders Analysis (2010) [Online]. Available at: http://www.endersanalysis.com/publications. aspx?q=IFNC (accessed March 2010).

Engel, M. (2009) 'Local papers: an obituary', *British Journalism Review*, 20: 55–62.

Eurostate (2008) 'Internet usage in 2008 – Households and Individuals', Brussels: European Commission.

Evans, B. (2010) *Paywalls and the Size of Newspapers*, Enders Analysis [Online]. Available at: http://www.endersanalysis.com/publications.aspx (accessed August 2010).

FactCheck.org (2010) *About Us* [Online]. Available at: http://newstrust.net/about (accessed August 2010).

Fenez, M. and van der Donk, M. (2009) *Moving into Multiple Business Models – Outlook for Newspaper Publishing in the Digital Age*, Price Waterhouse Coopers [Online]. Available at: http://www.pwc.com/images/em/newspaperoutlook2009.pdf (accessed March 2010).

Fenton, N. (2009) *New Media Old News*. London: Sage.

Financial Times (2006) 'Search Engines Challenged on "Theft"' [Online]. Available at: http://www.ft.com/cms/s/d0e8cf3e-928d-11da-977b-0000779e2340.html (accessed February, 2006).

Fitzgerald, P. and Bloch, J. (1983) 'Encounter with a D notice', *Index on Censorship*, 12(6): 34–8.

Franken, A. (2003) *Lies and the Lying Liars Who Tell Them*. New York: E. P. Dutton.

Franklin, B. (1997) *Newszak and News Media*. London: Hodder Arnold.

Gavin, N. (2002) 'British journalists in the spotlight, Europe and media research', *Journalism*, 2(3): 299–314.

Ghandi, M. (circa 1910) Extracted from P. B. Sanchay, *Mahatma Ghandi and Journalism*, The Hoot [Online]. Available at: http://www.thehoot.org/web/home/searchdetail. php?sid=1780&bg=1 (accessed December 2009).

Giddens, A. (1999) *Runaway World: How Globalization Is Reshaping Our Lives*. London: Profile Books.

Gillmor, D. (2004) *We the Media*. Sebastopol, CA: O'Reilly.

Gillmor, D. (2006) *From Dan: A Letter to the Bayosphere Community*, Bayosphere [Online]. Available at: http://bayosphere.com/blog/dan_gillmor/20060124 (accessed November 2006).

Gitlin, T. (2009) Conference paper, Journalism in Crisis Conference, University of Westminster, 18 May.

Glasgow Media Group (1976) *Bad News*. London: Routledge & Kegan Paul.

Goggin, G. (2011) 'The intimate turn of mobile news' in G. Meikle and G. Redden (eds), *News Online: Transformations and Continuities*, Palgrave.

Goldhaber, M. (1997) 'The attention economy and the net', *First Monday Journal*, 2(4–7 April). [Online]. Available at: http://firstmonday.org/htbin/cgiwrap/bin/ojs/index.php/fm/issue/view/79 (accessed January 2009).

Greenslade, R. (2005) 'So what will we be wrapping our fish and chips in?', *The Daily Telegraph*, 6 December: B8–9.

Greenslade, R. (2007) *Telegraph 'Needs to Protect Content from Google'* [Online]. Available at: http://www.journalism.co.uk/news/telegraph-needs-to-protect-content-from-google-/s2/a53277/ (accessed December 2010).

Grossman, L. (2006) Time's Person of the Year: You [Online]. Available at: http://www.time.com/time/magazine/article/0,9171,1569514,00.html (accessed April 2009)

Habermas, J. (1989) *The Structural Transformation of the Public Sphere* (trans. T. Burger and F. Lawrence). London: Polity Press.

Hall, S. (1993) 'Which public, whose service?', in W. Stevenson (ed.), *All Our Futures: The Changing Role and Purpose of the BBC*. London: BFFI. pp. 36–47.

Hall, S. et al. (1978) *Policing the Crisis: Mugging, the State and Law and Order*. London: Macmillan.

Hallin, D.C. (2009) 'Not the end of Journalism History', *Journalism*, 10(3): 332–334.

Hallin, D. and Papathanassopoulos, S. (2002) 'Political clientelism and the media: Southern Europe and Latin America in comparative perspective', *Media, Culture & Society*, 24(2): 175–95.

Hamlyn, R., Mindel, A., McGinigal, S. (2009) Digital Britain: Attitudes to supporting non-BBC regional news from the TV licence fee, DCMS. [Online] Available at: www.culture.gov.uk/.../TNS-BMRB_DBsupportregionalnews_finalreport.doc (accessed September 2010).

Hardt, H. (1990) 'Newsworkers, Technology and Journalism History', *Critical Studies in Mass Communicaiton*, 7(4): 346–365.

Hardt, M. and Negri, A. (2000) *Empire*. Cambridge, MA: Harvard University Press.

Hauser, E. (2009) 'The daily me is neither new or bad', *The Huffington Post*, 1 April. [Online]. Available at: http://www.huffingtonpost.com/eduardo-hauser/the-daily-me-is-neither-n_b_181922.html (accessed May 2010).

Held, D. and McGrew, A. (2007) *Globalisation Theory: Approaches and Controversies*. London: Polity.

Hemmingway, E. (2008) *Into the Newsroom. Exploring the Digital Production of Regional Television News*. London: Routledge.

Herman, E. and Chomsky, N. (1994) *Manufacturing Consent: The Political Economy of the Mass Media*. London: Vintage.

Herman, E. and McChesney, R. (1997) *The Global Media: The New Missionaries of Corporate Capitalism*. New York: Continuum.

Hermida, A. (2009a) 'The blogging BBC: Journalism blogs at "the world's most trusted news organization"', *Journalism Practice*, 3(3): 1–17.

Hermida, A. (2009b) 'Let's talk: How blogging is shaping the BBC's relationship with the public' in S. Tunney and G. Monaghan (eds), *Web Journalism*. Sussex: Sussex University Press. pp 306–16.

Hermida, A. and Thurman, N. (2007) Comments please: How the British news media are struggling with user-generated content [Online]. Available at: http://online.journalism. utexas.edu/2007/papers/Hermida.pdf (accessed December 2007).

Hirschorn, M. (2009) 'Last stand: Why *The Economist* is thriving while *Time* and *Newsweek* fade', *The Atlantic*, July/August: 48–55.

Hitwise (2008) *Yahoo!, Google and MSN: News Services Compared* [Online]. Available at: http://weblogs.hitwise.com/robin-goad/2008/10/yahoo_google_and_msn_news_services_ comparison.html (accessed May 2009).

Hitwise (2009a) *Online News Aggregators – Friend or Foe?* [Online]. Available at: http:// weblogs.hitwise.com/heather-dougherty/2009/04/online_news_aggregators_friend. html (accessed May 2009).

Hitwise (2009b) *Celeb and Entertainment Searches Dominate Google News* [Online]. Available at: http://weblogs.hitwise.com/robin-goad/2009/03/celeb_and_entertainment_searches_ google_news_uk.html. (accessed August 2010)

Hitwise (2010) 'Facebook Largest News Reader?' [Online]. Available at: http://weblogs.hit-wise.com/us-heather-hopkins/2010/02/facebook_largest_news_reader_1.html (accessed December 2010).

HMSO (2005) The Review of the BBC's Royal Charter – Volume One Report. [Online] Available at: http://www.publications.parliament.uk/pa/ld200506/ldselect/ ldbbc/50/50i.pdf (accessed April 2007).

Home Office (1986) *Report of the Committee on Financing the BBC*. London: HMSO, Cmnd. 9824.

Horrocks, P. (2006) *The Future of News*. London: BBC. [Online]. Available at: http:// www.bbc.co.uk/blogs/theeditors/2006/11/the_future_of_news.html (accessed December 2008).

Horrocks, P. (2008) *The Value of Citizen Journalism*. London: BBC. [Online]. Available at: http://www.bbc.co.uk/blogs/theeditors/2008/01/value_of_citizen_journalism.html (accessed 9 January 2008).

Howe, J. (2006) 'Gannett to Crowdsource News', *Wired* [Online]. Available at: http://www. wired.com/software/webservices/news/2006/11/72067 (accessed September 2008).

Hunt, J. (2010) *No Public Subsidy for Outdated Regional News* [Online]. Available at: http:// www.conservatives.com/News/Speeches/2010/01/Jeremy_Hunt_No_public_subsidy_ for_outdated_regional_news.aspx (accessed August 2010).

Hyde, M. (2010) 'Naomi Campbell, blood diamonds and the media freeing frenzy', *The Guardian*, 5 August. [Online]. Available at: http://www.guardian.co.uk/lifeand style/lostinshowbiz/2010/aug/05/naomi-campbell-liberia-blood-diamonds (accessed August 2010).

IFJ (2005) *Media Power in Europe: The Big Picture of Ownership*. Brussels: IFJ.

Ihlwan, M. (2009) 'Korea's OhmyNews seeks a fresh business model', *Bloomberg Business Week*, July [Online]. Available at: http://www.businessweek.com/globalbiz/content/ jul2009/gb20090714_537389.htm (accessed July 2009).

IMC UK (2002) *Principles of Unity* [Online]. Available at: http://docs.indymedia.org/view/Global/PrinciplesOfUnity (accessed December 2002).

IMC UK (2003) *About Us* [Online]. Available at: http://www.indymedia.org.uk/en/static/about_us.html (accessed December 2003).

IMC UK (2004) *The IMC – A New Model*. Indymedia in association with Hedonist Books.

IMC UK (2010) *Mission Statement* [Online]. Available at: http://uk.indymedia.org/ms.php3 (accessed December 2010).

Ingram, M. (2010) *The Web isn't Dead: It's Just Continuing to Evolve* [Online]. Available at: http://gigaom.com/2010/08/17/the-web-isnt-dead-its-just-continuing-to-evolve/ (accessed August 2010).

Irish Times (2010) 'Defamation Act a welcome but imperfect reform for libel cases', *Irish Times* [Online]. Available at: http://www.irishtimes.com/newspaper/ireland/2010/0118/1224262561743.html (accessed January 2010).

Isaacson, W. (2009) 'How to save your newspaper', *Time*, 5 February.

Jackson, M. (1997) quoted in Salter, L. 'Structure and forms of use: A contribution to understanding the role of the Internet in deliberative democracy.', *Information Communication & Society*, 7 (2): 185–206 (p. 200).

Jarvis, J. (2006) 'It takes guts to hand your crown jewels to the future', *The Guardian*, 19 June. [Online]. Available at: http://media.guardian.co.uk/print/0,329507958-105337,00.thml (accessed August 2006).

Jarvis, J. (2009a) 'Rupert Murdoch's move to charge for content opens doors for competitors', *The Guardian*, 6 August. [Online]. Available at: http://www.guardian.co.uk/media/2009/aug/06/rupert-murdoch-charging-for-content (accessed September 2009).

Jarvis, J. (2009b) *To Newspaper Moguls: You Blew It* [Online]. Available at: http://www.huffingtonpost.com/jeff-jarvis/to-newspaper-moguls-you-b_b_184309.html (accessed January 2010).

Jarvis, J. (2009c) 'Jeff Jarvis on tough love', *Washington Post*, 19 April. [Online]. Available at: http://www.washingtonpost.com/wp-dyn/content/article/2009/04/17/AR2009041702662_2.html (accessed April 2009).

Johnson, S. and Starr, P. (2009) 'Will the coming age of news be better than the old?', *Prospect Magazine*, May: 26–30.

Jones, J. (2009) 'PSB 2.0 – UK broadcasting policy after Peacock', in T. O'Malley and J. Jones (eds), *The Peacock Committee and UK Broadcasting Policy*. London: Palgrave.

Jones, J. and Martin, R. (2010) 'Crypto-hierarchy and its discontents: Indymedia UK', in C. Rodriguez, D. Kidd and S. Stein (eds), *Making Our Media, Global Initiatives Toward a Democratic Public Sphere: Vol. 1*. New Jersey: Hampton Press.

Jones, J. and Royston, M. (2007) 'Crypto-hierarchy and its Discontents. Indymedia UK' in C. Rodriguez, D. Kidd and L. Stein (eds), *Making Our Media: Global Initiatives Toward a Democratic Public Sphere Vol. One*. Cresskill, NJ: Hampton Press.

Jones, L. (2006) 'Don't be deluded: A blog does not make a journalist', *Press Gazette*, July.

Journalisted.com (2010) *About Journalisted* [Online]. Available at: http://journalisted.com/about (accessed August 2010).

Jury, L (2005) 'TV Plays Safe with Soaps and Neglects Innovation', *The Independent,* January 17 p. 7.

Keane, J. (1991) *Media and Democracy.* London: Polity.

Keen, A. (2007) 'Digital Narcissism', *Globe and Mail,* 7 June p.10.

Keen, A. (2008) 'Arianna Huffington (Portrait)', *Prospect Magazine,* August: 50–3.

Kierkegaard, S. (1967) *Søren Kierkegaard's Journals and Papers* (edited by H.V. Hong and E.H. Hong). Indiana: Indiana University Press.

Kiley, S. (2001) 'War of words', *Evening Standard,* 5 September.

Kim, D. and Johnson, T (2009) 'A shift in media credibility: Comparing internet and traditional news sources in South Korea', *International Communication Gazette,* 71(4): 283–302.

Kovach, B. (2005) 'A New Journalism for Democracy in a New Age' Speech given in Madrid, Spain, February 1, 2005 [Online]. Available at: http://www.journalism.org/node/298 (accessed April 2011).

Kovach, B. and Rosenstiel, T. (2001) *The Elements of Journalism.* London: Atlantic Books.

Law.com (2010) *No Reporter Shield for Mere Blogger, N.J. Appeals Court Says* [Online]. Available at: http://www.law.com/jsp/article.jsp?id=1202451742674 (accessed July 2010).

Leadbeater, C. (2009) *We-think: Mass Innovation, not Mass Production: The Power of Mass Creativity.* London: Profile.

Lechner, F. L. and Boli, J. (2004) *The Globalisation Reader.* Malden, MA: Blackwell.

Lee-Wright, P. (2009) 'Culture shock: New media and organizational change in the BBC', in N. Fenton (ed.), *New Media Old News.* London: Sage.

Lessig, L. (1999) *Code and Other Laws of Cyberspace.* New York: Basic Books.

Lessig, L. (2000) *Open Code and Open Societies,* keynote address at Free Software – a Model for Society? conference, Tutzing, Germany.

Lloyd, C. (2008) *International Symposium on Online Journalism* [Online]. Available at: http://online.journalism.utexas.edu/2008/transcripts/d1p1.pdf (accessed November 2009).

Lloyd, J. (2004) *What the Media are Doing to Our Politics.* London: Constable.

Lloyd, J. (2009) 'Digital Licence', *Prospect Magazine,* July 2009 p. 58.

Lloyd, J. and Hobsbawm, J. (2008) *The Power of the Commentariat* [Online]. Available at: http://reutersinstitute.politics.ox.ac.uk/about/news/news_item/article/power_of_the_commentariat_launched_today.html. (accessed August 2010)

Luft, O. (2010) *National ABCs: Year-on-year Circulation Drops for All* [Online]. Available at: http://www.pressgazette.co.uk/story.asp?sectioncode=1&storycode=45856 (accessed 13 August 2010).

Lyons, M. (2009) 'Chairman's open letter to licence fee payers', 09 September[Online]. Available at: http://www.bbc.co.uk/bbctrust/news/press_releases/2009/september/strategic_review.shtml (accessed November 2009).

Mackey, R. (2009) June 22nd: Updates on Iran's disputed election [Online]. Available at: http://thelede.blogs.nytimes.com/2009/06/22/latest-updates-on-irans-disputed-election-3/ (accessed December 2010).

Mangani, A. (2007) 'The optimal ratio between advertising and sales income', *International Journal of Revenue Management,* 1(1): 65–78.

Manning, P. (2008) *The Press Association and the End of Journalism? How National News Agencies Embrace Convergence in the Twenty-first Century*, paper presented at The End of Journalism? conference, University of Bedfordshire, UK, October.

Marbridge Consulting (2007) *SARFT, MII Co-Issue Online Video Regulation* [Online]. Available at: http://www.marbridgeconsulting.com/marbridgedaily/2007-12-29/article/7063/sarft_mii_co_issue_online_video_regulation (accessed January 2009).

Marcuse, H. (1969) 'Repressive tolerance' in R. Wolff, B. Moore and H. A. Marcuse, *A Critique of Pure Tolerance*. London: Cape.

Marr, A. (2004) *My Trade: A Short History of British Journalism*. London: Macmillan.

Marsh, K. (2010) 'An essential service in the life of a nation', in S. Tunney and G. Monaghan (eds), *Web Journalism*. Sussex: Sussex Academic Press. pp. 107–25.

Marshall, T. (2008) 'The Changing Newsroom', Pew Research Centre's Project for Excellence in Journalism. [Online]. Available at: http://www.journalism.org/node/11961

Mastrini, G. and de Charras, D. (2005) 'Twenty years mean nothing', *Global Media and Communication*, 1(3): 273–88.

Matheson, D. (2004) 'Weblogs and the epistemology of the news: Some trends in online journalism', *New Media and Society*, 6(4): 443–68.

Mawer, J. (2010) *The Future's Local – Ultra Local*, Local Heroes Conference, Kingston University, May.

McCabe, E. (2005) *Looking Back* [Online]. Available at: http://www.photographers.ie/2006/01/looking-back/ (accessed November 2010).

McChesney, R. (2002) 'The Titanic sails on: Why the internet won't sink the media giants', in G. Dines and J. Humez, *Gender, Race and Class in Media*. London: Sage.

McIntyre, T. J. (2010) *Irish Blogger Agrees €100,000 Settlement for Libel* [Online]. Available at: http://www.tjmcintyre.com/2010/01/irish-blogger-agrees-100000-settlement.html (accessed February 2010).

McLellan, M. (2009) *ProPublica Joins the Pro-am Journalism Movement Online* [Online]. Available at: http://www.knightdigitalmediacenter.org/leadership_blog/propublica_joins_the_pro-am_journalism_movement/#When:16:10:10Z (accessed June 2010).

McLuhan, M. (1994) *Understanding Media: The Extensions of Man*. Cambridge, MA: MIT Press.

McManus, J. (1994) *Market Driven Journalism: Let the Citizen Beware?* London: Sage.

McNair, B. (1998) *The Sociology of Journalism*. Oxford: Oxford University Press.

McNair, B. (1999) *Journalism and Democracy*. London: Routledge.

McNair, B. (2006) 'Cultural chaos: Journalism news and power in a globalised world', in S. Allan (ed.), *Journalism Critical Issues*. Maidenhead: Open University Press.

McNair, B. (2009) 'Journalism in the 21st century', *Journalism*, 10(3): 347–9.

Media Standards Trust (2010) *About Us* [Online]. Available at: http://www.mediastandardstrust.org/aboutus.aspx (accessed August 2010).

Medialens (2010) *Faq* [Online]. Available at: http://www.medialens.org/faq/ (accessed August 2010).

Melville-Brown, A. (2008) 'In practice: Media law', *Law Society Gazette*, 19.

Mill, J. S. (1996) *On Liberty/The Subjection of Women*. Hertfordshire: Wordsworth Classics.

Morgan Stanley (2010) *The Mobile Internet Report* [Online]. Available at: http://www.morganstanley.com/institutional/techresearch/pdfs/mobile_internet_report.pdf (accessed August 2010).

Mori (2005) *Opinion of Professions* [Online]. Available at: http://www.ipsos-mori.com/polls/trends/truth.shtml (accessed September 2005).

Moynihan, R. and Henry, D. (2006) 'The Fight against Disease Mongering: Generating Knowledge for Action', *PLoS Med* 3(4): e191.

Muller, A. (2000) 'Screening out the lies', *The Sunday Times*, 23 January.

Murdoch, J. (2009) *The Absence of Trust: James Murdoch's MacTaggart Lecture at the Edinburgh TV Festival 2009* [Online]. Available at: http://www.newscorp.com/news/news_426.html#top (accessed September 2009).

Murdoch, R. (2009) *Rupert Murdoch Before the Federal Trade Commission's Workshop: From Town Crier to Bloggers: How Will Journalism Survive the Internet Age?* [Online]. Available at: http://www.newscorp.com/news/news_435.html (accessed May 2009).

Murdoch, R. (2010) 'Rupert Murdoch: Paywall is going to be a success', *Press Gazette* 4 August. [Online] Available at: http://blogs.pressgazette.co.uk/wire/6848 (accessed August 2010).

Murray, J. (1997) *Hamlet on the Holodeck: The Future of Narrative in Cyberspace*. New York: Free Press.

National Hispanic Media Coalition (2010) *Comments of the National Hispanic Media Coalition in the Matter of Future of Media and Information Needs of Communities in a Digital Age* [Online]. Available at: http://centerformediajustice.org/wp-content/files/NHMC_et_al._Future_of_Media_Comment.pdf (accessed August 2010). Negroponte, N. (1995) *Being Digital*. London: Hodder and Stoughton.

NewsTrust (2010) *About Us* [Online]. Available at: http://newstrust.net/about (accessed August 2010).

Nichols, J. and McChesney, R.W. (2009) 'The death and life of Great American newspapers', *The Nation*. [Online]. Available at: http://www.thenation.com/doc/20090406/nichols_mcchesney (accessed December 2009).

Nordenson, B. (2007) 'The Uncle Sam solution: Should the government help the press?', *Columbia Journalism Review*, Sept/Oct.

NUJ (2007) *Journalism Matters*, Campaign Briefing Paper. London: NUJ.

Ofcom (2009) *Local and Regional Media in the UK* [Online]. Available at: http://www.ofcom.org.uk/research/tv/reports/lrmuk/ (accessed September 2009).

Ofcom (2010) *Ofcom Communications Market Report*, 19 August [Online]. Available at: http://stakeholders.ofcom.org.uk/market-data-research/ (accessed August 2010).

Ohmae, K. (1995) *The End of the Nation State: The Rise of Regional Economies*. Boston: Free Press.

Ohmae, K. (1999) *The Borderless World: Power and Strategy in the Interlinked Economy*. New York: Harper Paperbacks.

Ojebode, A. (2008) *Elendu's Arrest and the Safety of Online Journalism* [Online]. Available at: http://ojebode.blogspot.com/2008/10/elendus-arrest-and-safety-of-online.html (accessed November 2010).

O'Malley, T. and Jones, J. (eds) (2009) *The Peacock Committee and UK Broadcasting Policy*. London: Palgrave.

O'Neill, D. and O'Connor, C. (2008) 'The passive journalist', *Journalism Practice*, 2(3): 487–500.

Örnebring, H. (2009) *The Two Professionalisms of Journalism: Journalism and the Changing Context of Work*. Oxford: Reuters Institute for the Study of Journalism.

Osnos, P. (2009) 'What's a fair share in the age of Google?', *Columbia Journalism Review*, August. [Online]. Available at: http://www.cjr.org/feature/whats_a_share_in_the_age. php? (accessed August 2009).

Parsa, T (2009) 'June 22nd: Updates on Iran's disputed election', in R. Mackey's New York Times Blog [Online]. Available at: http://thelede.blogs.nytimes.com/2009/06/22/ latest-updates-on-irans-disputed-election-3/ (accessed December 2010).

Paterson, C. and Domingo, D. (2008) *Making Online News*. New York: Peter Lang.

Patterson, T.E. (2007) 'Young People and News', Joan Shorenstein Center on the Press, Politics and Public Policy [Online]. Available at: http://www.hks.harvard.edu/presspol/ research/carnegie-knight/young_people_and_news_2007.pdf (accessed July 2009).

Paton, J. (2010) *Press Release*, Journal Register Company, July [Online]. Available at: http:// www.journalregister.com/index.php?option=com_content&task=view&id=345&Ite mid=1 (accessed August 2010).

Peacock, A. (ed.) (2005) *Public Service Broadcasting Without the BBC?* London: Institute of Economic Affairs.

Penn, M. and Zalesne, E.K. (2009) 'America's newest profession: Bloggers for hire', *The Wall Street Journal*, 21 April. [Online]. Available at: http://online.wsj.com/article/ SB124026415808636575.html.

Perez, S. (2008) *The Stats Are In: You're Just Skimming This Article* [Online]. Available at: http://www.readwriteweb.com/archives/the_stats_are_in_youre_just_skimming_this_ article.php (accessed September 2010).

Perez-Pena, R. (2009) 'AP seeks to rein in sites using its content', *New York Times*, 6 April. [Online]. Available at: http://www.nytimes.com/2009/04/07/business/media/07paper. html?_r=2&ref=business (accessed November 2010).

Perrin, W. (2010a) *William Perrin Discusses his Hyper Local Site* [Online]. Available at: http://www.guardian.co.uk/media/video/2010/jan/25/william-perrin-hyperlocal-web-site (accessed August 2010).

Perrin W. (2010b) *Down Your Way: The Future for Local News*, University of Westminster Conference, June.

Peston, R. (2009) 'Richard Dunn Memorial Lecture – What Future for Media and Journalism' [Online]. Available at: http://www.guardian.co.uk/media/2009/aug/30/ edinburgh-tv-festival-robert-peston (accessed August 2009).

Pew Research Centre (2007) *Views of Press Values and Performance: 1985–2007* [Online]. Available at: http://people-press.org/report/348/internet-news-audience-highly-criti-cal-of-news-organizations (accessed June 2008).

Pew Research Centre (2009) *Public Evaluations of the News Media: 1985–2009* [Online]. Available at: http://people-press.org/report/543/ (accessed January 2010).

Pew Research Centre (2010a) *Project for Excellence in Journalism – The State of the News Media 2010* [Online]. Available at: http://www.stateofthemedia.org/2010/ (accessed July 2010).

Pew Research Centre (2010b) *Understanding the Participatory News Consumer: Local News Enthusiasts* [Online]. Available at: http://www.pewinternet.org/Presentations/2010/Aug/Local-news.aspx (accessed July 2010).

Pfetsch, B., Silke, A. and Eschner, B. (2008) 'The contribution of the press to Europeanization of public debates: A comparative study of issue salience and conflict lines of European integration', *Journalism*, 9(4): 465–92.

Picard, R. (2010) 'The Media Business', Journalism's Next Top Model, University of Westminster Conference, 8 June.

Picone, I. (2007) 'Conceptualising online news use', *Observatorio Journal*, 3: 93–114.

Pilger, J. (2004) *Tell Me No Lies*. London: Vintage

Pilger, J. (2006) 'Address to the Heyman Centre for the Humanities, Colombia University'. [Online]. Available at: http://pilgerjohn.blogspot.com/2007_11_01_archive.html (accessed November 2010).

Pilling, R. (1998) 'The changing role of the local journalist: From faithful chronicler of the parish pump to multi skilled complier of an electronic data base', in B. Franklin and D. Murphy (eds), *Making the Local News: Local Journalism in Context*. London: Routledge. pp. 183–95.

Platon, S. and Deuze, M. (2003) 'Indymedia Journalism: A Radical Way of Making, Selecting and Sharing News?', *Journalism*, 4(3): 336–355.

Ponsford, D. (2010) *BBC Moves into mobile market with news app. 17.02.10. Press Gazette* [Online.]. Available at: http://www.pressgazette.co.uk/story.asp?storyCode=45065&sectioncode=1 (accessed February 2010).

Postman, N. (2007) *Amusing ourselves to death: public discourse in the age of show business*. London: Methuen.

Press Gazette (2010) *Warnings Issued Over Unofficial 'Press Card'* [Online]. Available at: http://www.pressgazette.co.uk/story.asp?sectioncode=1&storycode=45824&c=1 (accessed August 2010).

Project for Excellence in Journalism (2005) *The State of the News Media*. [Online]. Available at: http://stateofthemedia.org/2005/ (accessed March 2011)

Project for Excellence in Journalism (2006) *The State of the News Media*. [Online]. Available at: http://stateofthemedia.org/2006/ (accessed March 2011)

Project for Excellence in Journalism (2009) *The State of the News Media*. [Online]. Available at: http://stateofthemedia.org/2009/ (accessed March 2011)

Prophet, S. (2010) *The Future's Local – Ultra Local*, paper presented at the Local Heroes Conference, Kingston University, May.

Purvis, S. (2010) *Ofcom Press Release* [Online]. Available at: http://media.ofcom.org.uk/2010/06/30/halt-in-decline-of-flagship-tv-news-programmes/ (accessed June 2010).

Randall, D. (2000) *The Universal Journalist*, 2nd edn. London: Pluto Press.

Riepl, W. (1913) 'Das Nachrichtenwesen des Altertums mit besonderer Rücksicht auf die Römer'. Leipzig/ Berlin 1913, pp. 4–7.

Robertson, G. and Nicol, A. (1992) *Media Law*. London: Penguin.

Rodriguez, J. (2004) *Embedding Success into the Military–Media Relationship*, United States Army War College Research Project, Carlisle, USA.

Rosen, J. (1999) *What Are Journalists For?* New Haven: Yale University Press.

Rosen, J (2006) 'Web Users Open the Gates' *Washington Post* June 19. [Online]. Available at: http://www.washingtonpost.com/wp-dyn/content/article/2006/06/18/AR2006061800618.html (accessed March 2009).

Rusbridger, A. (2010) 'The Hugh Cudlipp Lecture' [Online]. Available at: http://www.guardian.co.uk/media/2010/jan/25/cudlipp-lecture-alan-rusbridger. (accessed September 2010).

Salter, L. (2004) 'Structure and forms of use: A contribution to understanding the role of the Internet in deliberative democracy', *Information Communication & Society*, 7 (2): 185–206.

Salter, L. (2005) 'Juridification and Colonisation Processes in the Development of the World Wide Web', *New Media and Society*, 7(3): 291–309.

Salter, L. (2008) 'The Goods of Community? The Potential of Journalism as a Social Practice', *Philosophy of Management*, 7(1): 33–44.

Salter, L. (2011) *Conflicting Forms of Use: The Potential of and Limits to the Use of the Internet as a Public Sphere.* Saarbrücken: VDM.

San Francisco Chronicle (2007) *Imprisoned freelance journalist released* [Online]. Available at: http://www.sfgate.com/cgi-bin/article.cgi?f=/c/a/2007/04/03/BAGLRP0PAP4.DTL (accessed June 2008).

Sanders, K. (2003) *Ethics and Journalism.* London: Sage.

Sassen, S. (1996) *Losing Control? Sovereignty in an Age of Globalization.* University Seminars/Leonard Hastings Schoff Memorial Lectures. New York: Columbia University Press.

Scannell, P. (2005) 'The meaning of broadcasting in the digital era', in G.F. Lowe and P. Jauert (eds), *Cultural dilemmas in public service broadcasting – RIPE@2005.* Göteborg: Nordicom, pp. 129–43.

Schiller, D. (1981) *Objectivity in the News: The Public and the Rise of Commercial News.* Philadelphia: University of Philadelphia Press.

Schiller, D. (2007) *How to Think About Information.* Chicago: University of Chicago Press.

Schofield, J. (2010) *Dead-tree Magazine Claims The Web Is Dead, Again* [Online]. Available at: http://www.zdnet.co.uk/blogs/jacks-blog-10017212/dead-tree-magazine-claims-the-web-is-dead-again-10018282/ (accessed September 2010).

Schudson, M. (2001) 'The objectivity norm in American journalism', *Journalism: Theory, Practice and Criticism*, 2(2): 149–70.

Schudson, M. (2009) 'Ten years backwards and forwards', *Journalism*, 10(3): 368–70.

Seward, Z. (2009) *An Extremely Expensive Cover Story — With a New Way of Footing the Bill*, Nieman Journalism Labs [Online]. Available at: http://www.niemanlab.org/2009/08/an-extremely-expensive-cover-story-with-a-new-way-of-footing-the-bill/ (accessed September 2009).

Shirky, C. (2005) *The Ongoing Revolution in Social Infrastructure* [Online]. Available at: http://vodpod.com/watch/4086720-clay-shirkey-on-the-ongoing-revolution-in-social-infrastructure (accessed July 2010).

Simon, D. (2009) 'Build the wall', *Columbia Journalism Review*, July/August. [Online]. Available at: http:///www.cjr.org/feature/build_the_wall (accessed May 2010).

Singer, J. (2003) 'Who are these guys? The online challenge to the notion of journalistic professionalism', *Journalism: Theory, Practice, Criticism*, 4(2): 139–63.

Solomon, N. (2006) *'Corporate Media and Advocacy Journalism' Fairness and Accuracy in Reporting* [Online]. Available at: http://www.fair.org/index.php?page=2885 (accessed September 2006).

Sparks, S. (2010) *An International Perspective*, paper presented to Journalism's Top Model conference, University of Westminster, 8 June.

Starr, P (2009) 'Are we on track for a golden age of serious journalism?', *Prospect Magazine Issue*, 158: 28.

Stelzner, B. (2010) *The Future Shape of News*, Westminster Media Forum Keynote Seminar, 20 May.

Stevens, P. (2004) *Diseases of poverty and the 10/90 Gap*. London: International Policy Network.

Sunstein, C. (2001) *The Daily We – Is the Internet Really a Blessing for Democracy?* [Online]. Available at: http://bostonreview.net/BR26.3/sunstein.php (accessed August 2010).

Szabo, N. (1996) *The Mental Accounting Barrier to Micropayments* [Online]. Available at: http://szabo.best.vwh.net/micropayments.html (accessed May 2009).

Taipei Times (2010) *NCC monitoring Next TV online content* [Online]. Available at: http://www.taipeitimes.com/News/taiwan/archives/2010/08/05/2003479648 (accessed August 2010).

The Arizona Republic (2007) *Sheriff's Deputies Arrest New Times Owners* [Online]. Available at: http://www.azcentral.com/arizonarepublic/news/articles/1019newtimes1019.html (accessed January 2008).

The Australian (2006) *Gagging Justice* [Online]. Available at: http://blogs.theaustralian.news.com.au/garyhughes/index.php/theaustralian/comments/gagging_justice/ (accessed June 2010).

The Daily Telegraph (2008) *Matt Drudge: World's Most Powerful Journalist* [Online]. Available at: http://www.telegraph.co.uk/news/worldnews/1580164/Matt-Drudge-worlds-most-powerful-journalist.html (accessed May 2009).

The Digital Journalist (2009) *Let's Abolish the Term 'Citizen Journalists'* [Online]. Available at: http://digitaljournalist.org/issue0912/lets-abolish-citizen-journalists.html (accessed March 2010).

The Guardian (2009) *Rupert Murdoch: 'There's No Such Thing as a Free News Story'* [Online]. Available at: http://www.guardian.co.uk/media/2009/dec/01/rupert-murdoch-no-free-news (accessed January 2010).

The Guardian (2010) *Rupert Murdoch Defiant: 'I'll Stop Google Taking our News for Nothing'* [Online]. Available at: http://www.guardian.co.uk/media/2010/apr/07/rupert-murdoch-google-paywalls-ipad (accessed April 2010).

The New York Times (2009a) *A.P. Seeks to Rein in Sites Using Its Content* [Online]. Available at: http://www.nytimes.com/2009/04/07/business/media/07paper.html (accessed January 2010).

The New York Times (2009b) *After Police Relent, Bloggers Get Press Credentials* [Online]. Available at: http://cityroom.blogs.nytimes.com/2009/01/09/bloggers-get-press-credentials-after-police-relent/ (accessed September 2009).

The Observer (2010) *Julian Assange, Monk of the Online Age who Thrives on Intellectual Battle* [Online]. Available at: http://www.guardian.co.uk/media/2010/aug/01/julian-assange-wikileaks-afghanistan (accessed August 2010).

Thompson, M. (2006) *Creative Future Press Briefing*, BBC [Online]. Available at: http://www.bbc.co.uk/pressoffice/pressreleases/stories/2006/04_april/25/creative_datail.shtml (accessed 14 March 2008).

Thompson, M. quoted in J. Lloyd (2009), 'Digital Licence', *Prospect Magazine*, July 2009 p. 58.

Thorsen, E. (2008) 'Journalistic objectivity redefined? Wikinews and the neutral point of view', *New Media and Society* (10): 935–54.

Thorsen, E. (2009) *News, Citizenship and the Internet: BBC News Online's Reporting of the 2005 UK General Election*, PhD Thesis, Bournemouth University.

Thurman, N. (2007) 'The globalization of journalism online: A transatlantic study of news websites and their international readers', *Journalism: Theory, Practice & Criticism*, 8(3): 285–307.

Thurman, N. (2008) 'Forums for citizen journalists? Adoption of user generated content initiatives by online news media', *New Media and Society*, 10(1): 139–57.

Thurman, N. (2011) 'Making "The Daily Me"', *Journalism: Theory, Practice & Criticism*, 12(4).

Thwaites, D. (2010) *Local News Visionaries*, Local Heroes Conference, Kingston University, May.

Time Magazine (1952) 'Radio: The Trouble with News' Jan 28. [Online]. Available at: http://www.time.com/time/magazine/article/0,9171,806299,00.html (accessed November 2010).

Tindle, R. (2010) *Keynote Address*, Local Heroes Conference, Kingston University, May.

Ursell, G. (2003) 'Creating value and valuing creation in contemporary UK television: or "dumbing down" the workforce', *Journalism Studies*, 4(1): 31–46.

VAN (2010) *Background* [Online]. Available at: http://valueaddednews.org/about/background (accessed August 2010).

Vujnovic, M. et al. (2010) 'Exploring the political–economic factors of participatory journalism', *Journalism Practice*, 4(3): 285–96.

Wallace, S. (2009) 'Watchdog or witness? The emerging forms and practices of videojournalism', *Journalism*, 10(5): 684–701.

Weaver, D.H. (2009) 'US Journalism in the 21st Century – what future?', *Journalism*, 10(3): 396–7.

Williams, R. (1974) *Television: Technology and Cultural Form*. London: Fontana.

Winston, B. (1996) *Misunderstanding Media*. Cambridge, MA: Harvard University Press.

Wired (2002a) *Deep Links Return to Surface* [Online]. Available at: http://www.wired.com/news/politics/0,1283,51887,00.html (accessed September 2010).

Wired (2002b) *Deep Links Taking Another Blow* [Online]. Available at: http://www.wired.com/news/politics/0,1283,54083,00.html (accessed September 2010).

WSIS (2003) *Contribution from Palestine*, World Summit on the Information Society, Geneva, December, ITU.

Xin, X. (2010) 'The Current State of News Media in China and Emerging Trends'. Paper presented at the Journalism's Next Top Model Conference, Westminster University, London, June.

Index